MIDDLE ENGLISH MARVELS

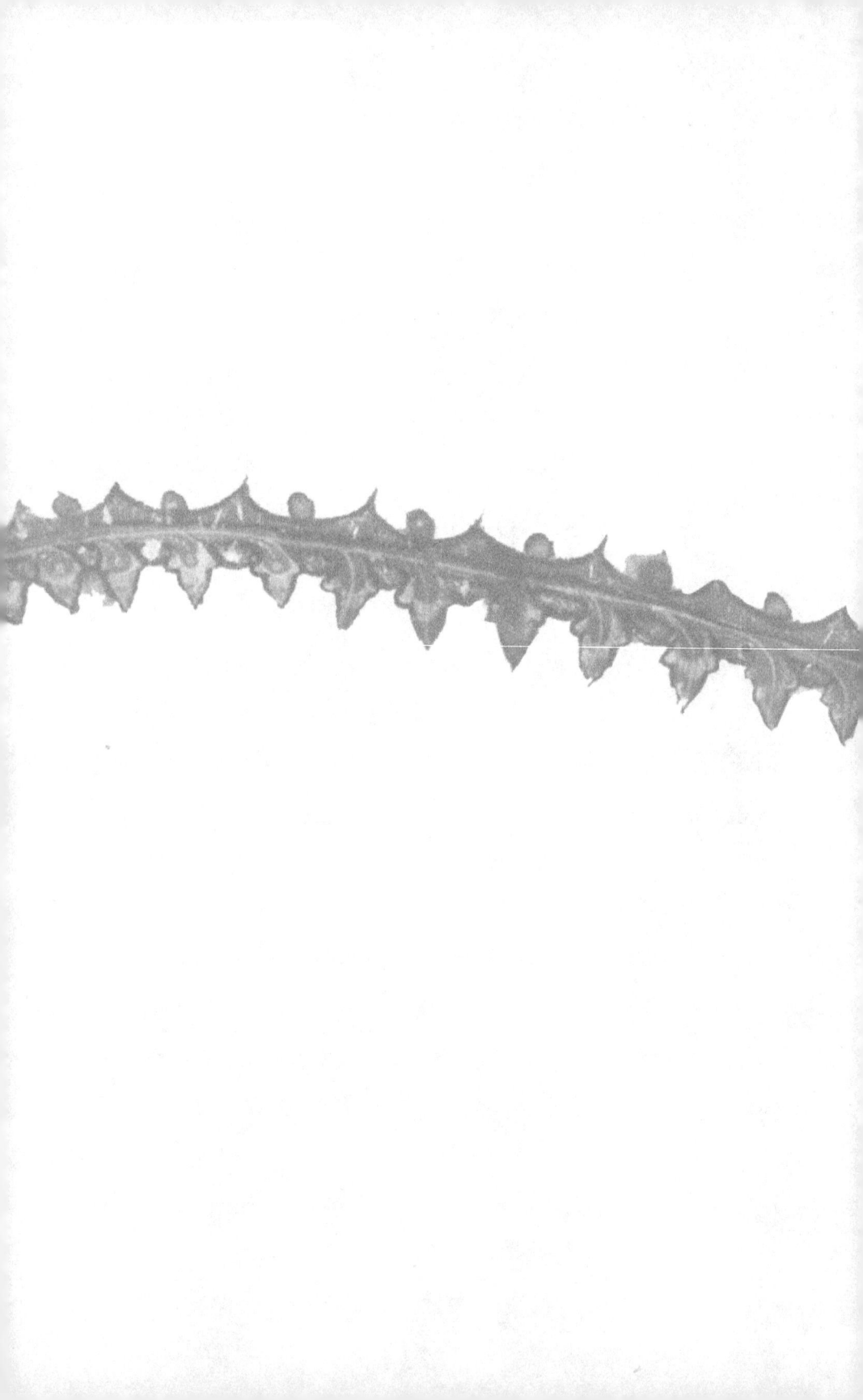

MIDDLE ENGLISH MARVELS

MAGIC, SPECTACLE, AND
MORALITY IN THE FOURTEENTH CENTURY

TARA WILLIAMS

The Pennsylvania State University Press | University Park, Pennsylvania

Library of Congress Cataloging-in-Publication Data

Names: Williams, Tara, 1975– author.
Title: Middle English marvels : magic, spectacle, and morality in the fourteenth century / Tara Williams.
Description: University Park, Pennsylvania : The Pennsylvania State University Press, [2018] | Includes bibliographical references and index.
Summary: "A multidisciplinary interpretation of representations of magic in fourteenth-century romances, and how these texts link magic, spectacle, and morality in distinctive ways. By representing supernatural marvels in vivid visual detail, these texts encourage reactions of wonder that have moral effects within and beyond the narrative"
—Provided by publisher.
Identifiers: LCCN 2017037190 | ISBN 9780271079639 (cloth : alk. paper)
Subjects: LCSH: Romances, English—History and criticism. | Magic in literature. | Marvelous, The, in literature. | Literature and morals.
Classification: LCC PR321 .W49 2018 | DDC 821/.109—dc23
LC record available at https://lccn.loc.gov/2017037190

Copyright © 2018 Tara Williams
All rights reserved
Printed in the United States of America
Published by The Pennsylvania State University Press,
University Park, PA 16802–1003

The Pennsylvania State University Press is a member of the Association of American University Presses.

It is the policy of The Pennsylvania State University Press to use acid-free paper. Publications on uncoated stock satisfy the minimum requirements of American National Standard for Information Sciences—Permanence of Paper for Printed Library Material, ANSI Z39.48–1992.

Titlepage: Detail from *Canterbury Tales* manuscript, ca. 1400–1410, England. EL 26 C 9, Egerton Family Papers, The Huntington Library, San Marino, California.

Contents

ACKNOWLEDGMENTS
vii

INTRODUCTION
Why Marvels Matter
1

1
MIRRORING OTHERWORLDS
Fairy Magic, Wonder, and Morality
11

2
REVEALING SPECTACLES
Virtue and Identity in Fair Unknowns
37

3
MOVING MARVELS
Action and Agency in Courtly Spectacles
63

4
TALKING MAGIC
Chaucer's Spectacles of Language
97

CONCLUSION
How Marvels Matter
127

NOTES
133

BIBLIOGRAPHY
153

INDEX
169

Acknowledgments

This book began to take shape while Betty Campbell and I were collaboratively teaching a course on medieval and Victorian representations of magic. From that point, and in countless conversations since, my thinking about these issues has benefited from her deep knowledge and generous perspective. The project has—and I have—also been sustained by the friendship of Rebecca Olson and Peter Betjemann, who are ideal readers and superb colleagues.

One of the great pleasures of academic life is having an intellectual community beyond as well as within one's institution. Much of the work on this project happened in coffee shops around Portland with Karen Gross, whose warmth and expertise made those sessions both pleasant and productive. Helen Cooper, Susan Crane, Holly Crocker, Alex Mueller, Susie Nakley, Myra Seaman, and Nicole Nolan Sidhu provided vital feedback on early chapter drafts. After a serendipitous dinner conversation, Lynn Shutters became a regular and insightful reader, helping me navigate several tricky parts of the argument. She was also the driving force behind a writing group including Jessica Barr, Suzanne Edwards, and Barbara Zimbalist, which has become an invaluable source of input and support for this project and others.

Writing about marvels gives deeper resonance to a subset of words that are particularly appropriate in this context. Larry Scanlon imparted a sense of enchantment with the Middles Ages that I still carry with me. At a critical juncture in this work, the Morton W. Bloomfield fellowship allowed me to spend a wonderful month at Harvard; I benefited from taking part in the Medieval Colloquium and from discussions with James Simpson, Nicholas Watson, and Daniel Donoghue. At Penn State University Press, Ellie Goodman's attention to and advocacy for this book were nothing short of marvelous.

The British Library kindly allowed me to use images from the Cotton Nero A.x manuscript. I also gratefully acknowledge permission to include revised versions of essays that first appeared in *Philological Quarterly* and *New Medieval Literatures* (published at the time by Brepols): "Fairy Magic,

Wonder, and Morality in *Sir Orfeo*," *Philological Quarterly* 91, no. 4 (2012), and "Magic, Spectacle, and Morality in the Fourteenth Century," *New Medieval Literatures* 12 (2010). The editors and readers at those journals provided helpful comments on those arguments, and the Penn State University Press readers responded thoughtfully to the project as a whole. In the final stages, the copyeditor and production staff attended to every detail with care.

Thanks to all of those who have provided encouragement for this project along the way. Toni Doolen and my colleagues at the Honors College helped me make time for my scholarship and saw it as complementing rather than competing with my administrative responsibilities. My carpool followed the development of these ideas over many miles of commuting and hours of energizing cross-disciplinary conversations. Billie Williams, Rod Williams, and Ryan Williams always believed in the book and enthusiastically celebrated its acceptance. Finally, thank you to Hugo, whose patience and support are now measured not merely in years but in decades.

INTRODUCTION
Why Marvels Matter

Richard II's 1377 coronation procession included many possible sources of wonder. The chronicles record glorious decorations, enchanting music, overwhelming crowds, and wine rather than water flowing through the conduits of the city. But perhaps the most impressive spectacle was the automaton angel that anticipated the coronation itself by extending a golden crown to the king-to-be.[1] This marvel, like many in the Middle Ages, is difficult to classify: It appears to be both spiritual and secular, both mechanical and magical. It also simultaneously entertains and encodes a larger significance, emphasizing Richard's special status. Although the dual potential of marvels aroused anxiety, as we can see in writers like Augustine, Thomas Aquinas, and Isidore of Seville, it also presented productive possibilities that literary texts could manipulate. Marvelous spectacles command attention and require responses that combine the immediate with the reflective, the affective with the cognitive.

Not all literary marvels take advantage of those possibilities, but a group from the fourteenth century does. I argue that these texts represent a coherent and previously unrecognized theory of the marvelous, one focused on the intersection of the magical, the spectacular, and the moral. This theory posits that magical spectacles can provoke forms of wonder that lead to moral actions by characters and open up moral reflection for the audience, particularly on the limits and limitations of ethical systems. The chapters that follow will explore a range of examples, each of which a narrator or character directly identifies as a magical marvel and each of which represents a key moment in this developing theory of the marvelous. Because the phrase "fourteenth-century magical, spectacular, and moral marvels" quickly becomes unwieldy, I will refer to this subset as "Middle English marvels."² As that phrase indicates, this configuration of features appears to be characteristically Middle English. The marvels appear in English texts that distinguish themselves from their sources and analogues in French, German, and Latin by adding magical and moral elements or enhancing those already present. Those texts belong to a Middle English tradition in which the two dominant genres—romance and hagiography—depend on marvelous objects and events.

Magic and *marvel* overlap significantly in the Middle Ages; I have chosen the latter as my central term because of its connotations and its more inclusive denotations.³ In his influential treatment, Jacques Le Goff defines the marvelous broadly in the Middle Ages, distinguishing it from the magical on one hand and from the miraculous on the other;⁴ a number of other writers restrict the definition to natural or mechanical wonders, especially in the form of objects. Middle English usage ranges more widely: in life and in texts, *merveilles* may be mechanical or natural, demonic or divine; they may be intended to inspire devotion, cure a medical condition, or amaze and amuse. Imagination often played a crucial role, as Michelle Karnes has demonstrated; it could "give invented images the status of perceptions and generate the same affective, intellectual, and physical effects as perceived objects," and intervene "in the world by exercising influence, albeit mediated, over bodies."⁵ The term *marvel* encompasses the technological, natural, and supernatural wonders that were important contexts for understanding the Middle English marvels at the center of this study,⁶ and suggests a relationship between secular marvels and their religious complements. That relationship is partly predicated on similar ties to the visual, which *marvel* also implies. Le Goff points out that the etymology highlights this connection: "*marvel* (from the Latin *mirare*, to look at) suggests a visual apparition."⁷

Magic has nonetheless been the more popular critical term, and magic studies has been a growing area of interest for scholars—and especially medievalists—across disciplines. Richard Kieckhefer and other historians have developed and adapted an influential model for classifying medieval magical practices as either natural—more closely related to medicine and science—or demonic—more closely related to religion and ceremony. Applying bat's blood to one's eyes to improve night vision falls under natural magic, while a ritual to obtain a cap of invisibility by drawing a circle, sprinkling it with holy water, reciting a psalm, and then conjuring and bargaining with spirits would be demonic magic.⁸ Careful examinations by Kieckhefer, Claire Fanger, Frank Klaassen, and Sophie Page of texts associated with learned magic have enriched our understanding of that complex category and shown how closely licit and illicit forms might coexist.[9]

In literary texts, modes of magic are even more difficult to discern. Such typing depends on the identification of agency and intent, which literary depictions often obscure, and on some level of access to the practice involved, which literary depictions habitually omit. Readers are not privy to how Morgan le Fay transforms Bertilak into the Green Knight or which processes or figures forged the magical ring in the *Squire's Tale*, for example. Nonetheless, because the magic is exercised in these texts, we learn more about it than in the many romances that, as Helen Cooper has pointed out, introduce magic that later fails to work or goes unused.[10] Corinne Saunders's *Magic and the Supernatural in Medieval English Romance* does the critical work of delineating and contextualizing the various and mysterious forms of literary magic while also demonstrating that it is, and should be, crucial to our interpretations. Saunders's comprehensive treatment establishes the large-scale categories in English romance, such as the distinctions between white and black magic and between the secular and religious forms of the supernatural, and allows us to see where they do and do not overlap with the historical categories.

Saunders's work makes it possible to uncover when texts both draw on and depart from precedent; with that foundation, the current study explores how the marvelous functions in the fourteenth century. This moment in late medieval culture comes at a conjunction of literary, social, scientific, and religious developments that endow marvels with new potential significance. Earlier romances reveal a strengthening correlation between courtly love and magic as a means of discovering or testing that love, as in Marie de France's lays (in which magic brings together the lovers in *Guigemar* and *Yonec*) or *Floris and Blancheflour* (in which the couple proves their love by refusing to use a magic ring). The expanding connection between marvels and morality in romances from the 1300s builds on that correlation. A subgroup of fourteenth-century texts experiment in particular detail with how magic of any type might have moral implications, not only within the narrative but also for the audience, and with how visual description might intensify or attenuate those internal and external effects.

The marvels that test courtly love and chivalric virtues are often significantly visual, a feature that the Middle English marvels amplify—as when the hero of *Lybeaus Desconus* encounters a dragon with gleaming wings, a massive tail, and, in a twist on other extant versions, a woman's face. Such marvels are spectacles in the sense that they include unusual or surprising aspects that contribute to their visual impact, and their representations correlate with a rising interest in spectacles of all types during the same period. Middle English usage reinforces that a spectacle could function as a medium for pointing to or revealing something else, a definition that the loathly lady employs in the *Wife of Bath's Tale* when she explains poverty as a "spectacle" through which a man "may his verray freendes see."[11] Courtly displays were often designed to impress; when they generated wonder—as did the technological marvels that were becoming increasingly popular in thirteenth- and fourteenth-century European courts, like Richard's coronation angel—it took the form of a curiosity about methodology.[12] Within the framework of affective piety, intensely visual miracles and visions, such as those that Julian of Norwich describes, were also intensely moving; didactic potential and visual nature were intertwined in religious culture, as scholars have convincingly demonstrated.

Although secular manifestations of that connection have not yet received much attention, magical spectacles during this same period produced a type of wonder that might be harnessed for similarly moral or ethical purposes. When the Green Knight enters Arthur's court, the courtiers' first reaction is one of "wonder."[13] As the dragon with a woman's face approaches Lybeaus Desconus, "grete wondyr with-all / Jn his herte ganne falle."[14] These spectacles test the moral character of Gawain and Lybeaus while also raising questions about the moral codes that the knights (and, to some extent, their audiences) espoused. How should one respond to figures outside one's community or experience? What constitutes true virtue, and what prompts its failure? Transformations, which could be arresting spectacles while remaining anchored at some level in the human, were especially effective for raising such questions.[15] In exploiting this potential, Middle English marvels eschew the type of detailed and stage-by-stage descriptions that characterize what is otherwise the most influential treatment of transformation in the Middle Ages, Ovid's *Metamorphoses*; they focus less on the process than its effects.

An emphasis on the response elicited is characteristic of marvels, and another reason that I have chosen that term. It can describe a reaction as well as an object or occurrence, and the latter usages retain a focus on the impact: a marvel is something that inspires one to wonder.[16] In the Middle Ages, wonder often has a moral valence. Caroline Walker Bynum's excellent work on medieval wonder (*admiratio*) identifies it as "cognitive, perspectival, non-appropriative, and deeply respectful of the specificity of the world."[17] This wonder reaction avoids appropriating or generalizing; in other words, it takes a moral approach to the marvelous. Jane Bennett discusses the postmodern experience of wonder in similar terms, describing its ability to encourage an "ethical" engagement with the world. Marvels exercise what she calls an "affective force," and an examination of that force reveals that they can influence as well as charm readers. In fact, their influence is greater precisely because they also entertain—an effect that will sound familiar to scholars of medieval literary theory, which understood entertaining texts as better able to inculcate a moral lesson. "One must be enamored with existence and occasionally even enchanted in the face of it," Bennett contends, "in order to be capable of donating some of one's scarce mortal resources to the service of others."[18]

These accounts of medieval and postmodern wonder do construct a slightly different relationship to morality: Bynum's *admiratio* is already a moral approach to the world, whereas Bennett's enchantment is an intermediate response that may lead to moral action. In other words, morality is a precondition for the medieval form of wonder and a potential outcome of the postmodern form. However, not all reactions to marvels in the Middle Ages took the form of *admiratio*. For the Middle English texts under consideration here, the interest lies in the gap between the spectacle and the reaction, in the uncertainty over whether, how, and to what degree that reaction will be moral. The reactions may involve emotions, actions, or both, and they may come from the readers as well as the characters. I suggest that Middle English marvels encourage a moral engagement that is in keeping with Bynum's *admiratio*, and do so by leveraging "the ethical potential of the mood of enchantment" in a way that aligns with Bennett's argument.[19]

Prefiguring her later work on "vital materiality," this argument by Bennett stresses the responsibility and responsiveness of the viewing subject more heavily.[20] The subject must recognize something as marvelous, becoming open to its "affective force" and determining whether and how to respond. Implicitly, the possibility exists that a subject might be enchanted by something or react in some way that would not accord with the sense of ethics that Bennett establishes. Although the formulation of wonder in *The Enchantment of Modern Life* is largely atemporal, the ethics are postmodern; as a result, when we extend Bennett's claims to the fourteenth century, we must follow Bynum's model in querying the texts themselves to see which moral codes are operative. When we also consider the historical context in which these texts were being written, circulated, and interpreted, we can see that Bennett's approach dovetails with the increasing emphasis during the Middle Ages on the responsibility and responsiveness of the viewing subject, a trend that I will locate in optical theory (chapter 3) as well as philosophical and religious discourse (chapter 4).

By invoking wonder in relation to moral issues or questions, these fourteenth-century marvels go beyond the typical use of magic that Michelle Sweeney has highlighted in French and English romances: "the establishment of a marvellous or magical test which reveals to the audience certain aspects of the personality of a given character."[21] Middle English marvels are also more than containers for moral messages; in this sense, they pick up on the ambiguous wonder stories that Carl Watkins identifies in late twelfth- and early thirteenth-century historical texts. By the later thirteenth and fourteenth centuries, Watkins argues, historical writers largely "exclude[d] ambiguous and subversive wonders from their writing," although they could reappear in didactic contexts without the same ambiguous and subversive undertones.[22] In fourteenth-century literary texts, marvels show up with those undertones and thereby facilitate moral contemplation rather than being straightforwardly didactic. The emphasis on reading as a moral activity and the debate about the moral significance of literary texts, especially romances, in the Middles Ages (explored in the first and second chapters) helped to encourage readers' moral engagement at various levels without indicating that edification would be an automatic result.[23]

Like the marvelous, the moral encompasses many possible meanings. Although the term may postdate some of the texts under consideration, I will use *moral* in the late medieval sense of "associated with or characterized by right behavior, virtuous, moral; also, associated with or concerning conduct or moral principles"—in other words, much as we often use the term now to describe behaviors or reactions grounded in beliefs about right and wrong. *Moral code* indicates a set of such beliefs but one less formal, systematized, and value-based than *ethics* would suggest in Middle English usage, which defines the latter as "the science or principles of human conduct, ethics" and "a particular system of ethics, a discussion of moral principles."[24] These terms do not exist in isolation; the marvels in this study operate within the ethical framework of chivalry while invoking moral concerns about how one should treat others outside one's own culture, community, or species.[25] Because morality deals with personal and immediate reactions, however, it is the primary mode for supernatural spectacles that present urgent questions about what constitutes virtuous behavior or which reaction constitutes the right choice.

Although this construction of morality remains consistent, the ways in which the narratives engage with morality and the specific moral questions that they take up do differ. These questions tie into broad concerns, including chivalry (in *Sir Orfeo*), identity (*Lybeaus Desconus*), agency (*Sir Gawain and the Green Knight*), and language (*Canterbury Tales*). Each marvel also invokes other discourses circulating at the same historical moment that overlap in crucial ways with this developing theory of the marvelous. Chapter 1 studies the links between image, memory, and morality in late medieval culture, examining how strange and unfamiliar images were understood to be particularly memorable and therefore particularly useful for instilling moral lessons or modeling moral behavior. I suggest that fairy magic was well positioned to exploit those relationships because it was fundamentally mysterious, had preexisting associations with concerns about moral and amoral behavior, and involved a world that both reflected and opposed the human one. I take the otherworld of *Sir Orfeo* as my central example, exploring how the gallery of suffering and mangled figures kidnapped by the fairies works as a moral and magical spectacle, revealing the fairy moral code while also encouraging reflection on human ethics as expressed through chivalry. From this angle, we can read the poem as thinking through the problem of moral relationships with other cultures.

The second chapter shifts from cross-cultural to intimate encounters to consider the power of marvels to illuminate one's true character. I examine the fair unknown tradition against the backdrop of the emerging correlation between magic and morality in Middle English romance, with *Lybeaus Desconus*—which was as popular in the Middle Ages as it is overlooked today—as the representative case study. Questions about the hero's identity drive fair unknown plots, and this chapter outlines how magical marvels definitively establish both the moral and familial aspects of that identity. Because they are supernatural, these spectacles can reveal a knight's parentage when that knowledge might be unavailable or unreliable from another source. And because they pose such extreme challenges, these marvels allow other characters—and readers—to be sure that the fair unknown has true virtue and not simply its semblance. The more individual nature of the moral issue in these texts (which interrogate one knight's chivalrous identity) requires more individualized marvels, like the woman-dragon in *Lybeaus*, who will return to her human form only with a kiss from Gawain or his kin. Lybeaus's ability to approach that hybrid figure with courtliness as well as courage certifies his knightly lineage and virtue as none of his numerous other feats could. At the same time, this marvel encourages the audience to puzzle over the troublingly inconsistent relationship between appearance and virtue throughout the romance.

As literary texts continue to experiment with marvels and morality, the single scenes or figures give way to series of animated spectacles and, finally, to spectacles that are language-based, emphasizing what is spoken over what is seen. The ways in which such representations might interact with concurrent developments in visual theory are taken up in the third chapter. The spectacles in both Richard II's coronation procession and Cotton Nero A.x resonate with such developments, surveying how different types of visual marvels can do moral work. The cinematic, mobile, and recurring spectacle of the Green Knight (represented in complementary but not identical ways by the *Sir Gawain and the Green Knight* text and the Cotton Nero A.x illustrations) creates an unusually comprehensive test of Gawain's character. It investigates the nature and limits of virtue itself while also raising questions about the compatibility of magical and moral agency, hinting that Morgan le Fay embodies the former while the shape-shifting figure she creates enacts the latter.

More complicated spectacles are more difficult to classify, and the fourth chapter considers how writers like Augustine, Isidore of Seville, Gervase of Tilbury, and Geoffrey Chaucer approached the challenges of defining the marvelous and distinguishing it from the miraculous. Because the *Canterbury Tales* assembles a range of marvels within its pages—resembling medieval collections of marvels in that regard—it offers an especially rich text for examining such classifications in a literary context.[26] I argue that the marvels in Chaucer's *Canterbury Tales* invoke but then flout the expectations—firmly established by that time—of visuality; although his miracles are visual spectacles, magic is often represented minimally. As a result, miracles seem to anticipate an awestruck reaction that may be chased by subtle doubts, and marvels tend to encourage more direct and intense moral contemplation. Focusing on the Squire's and Wife of Bath's narratives, chapter 4 examines how the two most clearly magical tales create spectacles that work through language rather than sight and how those spectacles encourage moral reflection on our communication with and relationships to those outside our community and even species (reviving and extending the concerns identified in the first chapter).

Over the course of the fourteenth century, mostly supernatural—and static—marvels in *Sir Orfeo* give way to interactive marvels that mix the magical with the technological in the *Canterbury Tales*. The major concern moves from moral systems (whether an individual's or a community's), which the marvels reveal, to personal moral character (albeit often still as an embodiment of a code of values), which the marvels test. But the motivating interest in how marvels might be represented through spectacle and how those representations can influence the marvel's moral impact—both within and beyond the text—persists. Recognizing the significant pattern in these Middle English texts may also result in drawing attention to other uses of the marvelous and the moral in other medieval romances, adding new layers to literary understandings of representations of magic and to historical understandings of the development of magic. The concluding chapter explores the range of ways in which marvels and morality are connected in fourteenth- and fifteenth-century English texts, indicating the significance of those concerns and urging a reevaluation of whether and how magic might be "working" in romance, while also highlighting the distinctive nature of the approach shared by the marvels highlighted here.

By focusing on marvels and wonder, I do not want to suggest that only that which is unusual or extraordinary merits scholarly attention, nor do I mean to imply that marvels were the main stuff of medieval lives. As Sarah McNamer has demonstrated, "historical realities are not always joined to what is arresting."[27] By the expansive definition that Middle English itself employed, however, marvels were at the heart of late medieval culture. At the same time, the very singularity of any given marvel, whether secular or religious, gave it the potential to produce the intellectual, emotional, and moral effects that motivate this project.

CHAPTER ONE

MIRRORING OTHERWORLDS
Fairy Magic, Wonder, and Morality

Fairyland is an ideal setting for examining the nexus between the moral and the magical. Although there are many possible sources of wonder in the Middle Ages,[1] fairies induce a form that is particularly intense (because of their connection to magic) and that balances fear with fascination (because of their own status as simultaneously anthropomorphic and otherworldly). The wonder they inspire is readily connected to moral issues and concerns; especially when fairies' appearances and social structures reflect courtly ideals, the moral questions they raise can be relevant to human behaviors and beliefs associated with chivalry.[2] Several Middle English marvels leverage these linkages between fairies and humans, but none capitalizes on the potential moral implications to the degree that *Sir Orfeo* does.

The poem's fairies have often been read in the context of its Celtic aspects or as part of its reimagining of the classical legend. The critical history of the poem has taken shape largely around the investigation of such contexts; because this retelling of the Orpheus legend incorporates elements from multiple medieval discourses, critics have examined several frameworks—Celtic, Christian, classical, and historical[3]—to determine which is primary and how the text exploits the layering of these multiple possibilities.[4] Scholars have also placed the romance in a rarefied literary context, admiring it as an aesthetic object (perhaps more than any other non-Chaucerian Middle English text) and focusing on the ways in which *Sir Orfeo,* like the classical version, thematizes music and the arts.[5] Whether seeking to identify the best sources and contexts or exploring the poem's artistry and representation of artistic pursuits, critics have emphasized the two primary departures from the Orpheus legend—the refiguring of the underworld as a fairy otherworld and the apparently happy ending—as significant but perplexing.[6] These same concerns carry over into more recent studies of the poem, which show increasing interest in issues of kingship[7] and gender[8] and thereby complicate rather than resolve the central puzzles.

The very persistence of those puzzles suggests another possible framework: theories of wonder. Wonder can be an emotion, a way of seeing, or a mode of engagement; it can be a reaction to objects or events that are aesthetic, natural, or supernatural. In every case, however, wonder is an active and productive response that can operate on readers, listeners, or viewers as well as characters. If we consider *Sir Orfeo* within the context of wonder theory, we can draw together not only the poem's aesthetic and cultural influences, but also medieval and modern experiences of it, despite the intervening aesthetic and ethical shifts.

This perspective opens up new ways of seeing the poem as an aesthetic object and new ways of understanding both the gallery and the ending. The gallery of human figures apparently kidnapped by the fairies becomes a spectacle that is moral as well as magical, and thereby tied to similar spectacles like the Green Knight's beheading in *Sir Gawain and the Green Knight* and the loathly lady's transformation in the *Wife of Bath's Tale*. The moral code of the gallery is supernatural rather than human, however, and the lingering effects that Heurodis exhibits from her tenure there trouble the romantic convention that magic may try human and chivalric virtues but cannot overcome them. Rather than testing those qualities in order to reaffirm them, fairy magic in *Sir Orfeo* casts doubt on the nature of those ideals, and, consequently, the resolution of the romance takes on a different and unsettling significance. It leaves its audiences in a state of wonder.

Fairies and Wonder

Richard Firth Green points to the ubiquity and significance of belief in fairies during the Middle Ages, arguing that such beliefs have meaningful "consequences for literary analysis." One such consequence is the recognition that, "far from being a convenient, if picturesque, plot device, magic constitutes the narrative mainspring of many romances."[9] Middle English representations of fairy magic and the reactions it provokes—which generally fall within the category of wonder—bear out this claim. Caroline

Walker Bynum notes that "the wonder-reaction ranges from terror and disgust to solemn astonishment and playful delight,"[10] and fairies arouse responses at both ends of that spectrum in the various medieval texts in which they appear. Although they might be seen as outcast or fallen angels or as secular supernatural spirits, they were usually attractive and often threatening as they exercised power within the narrative.

In John Gower's "Tale of Constance," the accusation that the heroine is "of faierie" explains how she could be beautiful and desirable to the king while still purportedly producing an unnatural child.[11] Although false in this case, that accusation draws on the representations of "true" fairies in other narratives. In *Sir Launfal,* the fairy mistress appears to be unbelievably beautiful and wealthy; her powers are correspondingly impressive, and she uses them to reward the worthy Launfal and to punish the dishonorable queen by blinding her with a breath (a moral component added by the poet, as we will explore in the next chapter). The fairy of *Thomas of Erceldoune* has a more vulnerable beauty, which she temporarily loses when she reluctantly sleeps with Thomas, yet she retains the power to bring him to fairyland and bestow the gift of prophecy. The fairy knight of *Sir Degaré* initially follows a romantic script—he is handsome, skilled in battle, and declares his love—but he then rapes the maiden. Heurodis's description of the fairies in *Sir Orfeo* highlights their fairness ("Y no seiȝe neuer ȝete bifore / So fair creatours y-core") and wealth (the Fairy King's crown is made "of a precious ston," and he shows her "castels & tours" and "his riche stedes ichon"); however, their violent threats also drive her to the brink of madness.[12] These depictions of and reactions to fairies give us a sense of the expectations that they might call up for a medieval audience.

In Middle English, the word *fairy* could indicate enchantment generally, as it did in texts by Chaucer, the *Gawain*-poet, and others. *Sir Orfeo* has the earliest recorded usage of *fairy* in that sense, in the passage describing the kidnapping of Heurodis: "Þe quen was oway y-tviȝt, / Wiþ fairi forþ y-nome" (192–93).[13] This fact is not simply an interesting bit of philology; it signals an interest in magic as a narrative element. By using fairy magic rather than some other form, the poem sets itself up to affect the audience in crucial ways. It distances the magic from the human, raises the expectation that morality will be an important issue, and establishes the magic in use as more mysterious than other forms. These effects draw on the cultural as well as the literary contexts of the fairy.

Fairies are magical, but the specific type of magic has proven resistant to classification. The classic studies of premodern fairy origins and types remain those by Minor White Latham and C. S. Lewis,[14] and more recent work continues to treat fairies as a singular phenomenon in the Middle Ages. Corinne Saunders classifies most examples of medieval literary magic via the black-versus-white distinction, whereas fairies, like miracles, require their own category as another form of the supernatural.[15] James Wade treats as notably distinct not only fairies as a group, but also each specific depiction of them. His 2011 *Fairies in Medieval Romance* focuses on what he terms "internal folklore"—namely, the idea "that in each romance containing the ambiguous supernatural there is a unique imagining of fairies and of the Otherworld at large."[16]

The singularity of fairy magic results in part from the fact that, unlike most other types, it involves no human practitioner. Magic practiced by humans may be powerful or not, evil or not, but—even when it involves commanding a magical agent rather than practicing enchantment directly—it remains connected to the human at some level. Fairy magic is completely other. In most texts, including *Sir Orfeo*, such magic is never directly witnessed; we see its effects while its nature and limits remain fundamentally mysterious. This view accords with the emphasis on alterity in general treatments of fairies in medieval romance.[17] As Helen Cooper notes, "fairies occupy that dangerous borderland that cannot be controlled by human will and is not susceptible to the normal operations of prayer"; in other words, fairies are not human, but neither are they undoubtedly divine or demonic.[18] The resulting distance between the fairy and the human paradoxically enables the mirroring effect between the two worlds in *Sir Orfeo* upon which critics have remarked.

The appearance of fairies signals the presence of magic and also sets up the expectation that morality will be a significant issue. Jack Zipes, in his study of the history of literary fairy tales—a generic designation that originally described stories about fairies—argues that their moral aspect is key to defining the genre and helps to explain why it has persisted: fairy tales "incorporate a moral code that reflects upon the basic instincts of the human being as a moral animal and suggest ways to channel these instincts for personal and communal happiness."[19] In the Middle Ages, this generic characteristic takes the shape of two opposing traditions on fairies' morality. In one, they are amoral, which is another marker of their difference from humanity and a warning for those who might encounter them. In the other, they dispense justice (often compensating for human failures, as in various versions of *Lanval*) or facilitate a moral education (as in the *Wife of Bath's Tale*).[20] The divergence of these two traditions hints at what a central issue morality is in depictions of fairies. Because they wield considerable power over the humans with whom they interact, it is critical to know into which category any given fairy falls.

Since it lacks a connection to the human, and since its practitioners have such variable natures, fairy magic seems more mysterious than other types. It also has no clear source beyond the fairies' own unexplained magical natures, and the methods by which it is practiced or through which it works are unknown. Fairy magic does not conform to other historical models—most notably, the categories of natural and demonic magic[21]—precisely because it lacks defining characteristics other than being used by fairies. In its broader definition, the term *fairy* seems to have connoted a sense of mystery; patterns of usage suggest that more foreign or less comprehensible magic is likely to be named in this way. In *Sir Gawain and the Green Knight*, for instance, Arthur's court identifies the Green Knight as "fantoum and fayry3e" before the nature of the enchantment becomes known.[22]

The portrayal of fairies and their magic as mysterious in *Sir Orfeo* is consistent with the literary tradition of fairies as figures whose motives and natures were unknowable, and therefore sources of wonder.[23] It is only when they create a spectacle that we catch a glimpse of their magic and the moral code by which it operates. This pressure on the visual helps to explain *Sir Orfeo*'s focus on the external rather than the internal, a feature that scholars have noted;[24] in particular, the poem underscores the ways in which bodies can signify to those who behold them. In her discussion of fairies' prophetic powers, Cooper observes that "those of supernatural origin know of hidden things directly, by a privileged form of consciousness unlike ordinary forms of thought. It follows that they are almost never portrayed from the inside: we are not shown what kind of thought-process produces such knowledge."[25] This second point holds true outside the context of prophecy as well and suggests why both Orfeo and the audience need an external spectacle like the gallery to provide insight into the workings of the Fairy King's mind. The unpredictable nature of fairies makes this insight all the more valuable.

The Gallery as a Moral Spectacle for Orfeo

The gallery has captivated readers of *Sir Orfeo,* but no consensus has been reached about its nature or significance. Some critics have seen it as a version of either the Celtic otherworld or a classical underworld, and others have argued for the significance of its resistance to a single interpretation; Bruce Mitchell found the scene so anomalous that he contended that it must be a later interpolation.[26] Especially since Seth Lerer's influential reading of artistry in *Sir Orfeo*, critics have discussed the gallery as a set piece demonstrating the poet's aesthetic skill.[27] Some have gone a step further by suggesting that the aesthetic dimension of the gallery excepts it from moral connections or importance; this approach can be seen as part of a tradition that identifies the romance as a whole as lacking a moral undertone.[28] In his study of the gallery, Alan J. Fletcher argues that it creates "a morally vacant space."[29] Interpreting the poem within the context of fourteenth-century interests in magic, morality, and spectacle, however, reveals that the aesthetic and the moral are deeply intertwined in the gallery. An awareness of this dual motivation, in turn, gives us insight into the otherwise mysterious nature of the Fairy King. The gallery is a moral spectacle in two senses: it reveals the moral code of the fairies, and it encourages a moral reaction from readers. Its revelatory function plays an integral role in the narrative, and an examination of the spectacle in that light offers possible answers to many of the troubling aspects of the poem, including why the Fairy King abducts Heurodis, why he releases her, and why the poem glosses over Orfeo's reunion with Heurodis in favor of his reunion with the steward.

As the first detailed magical spectacle, the gallery is presented to have maximum impact on the audience. The scene stands out because so many other instances of magic in the narrative are not portrayed as visual spectacles, including Heurodis's kidnapping and Orfeo's entrance into the fairy world. When the fairies snatch Heurodis from within the ranks of armed knights, the absence of any visible display is remarkable:

> Ac ʒete amiddes hem ful riʒt
> Þe quen was oway y-tviʒt,
> Wiþ fairi forþ y-nome
> —Men wist neuer wher sche was bicome.
> (191–94)

Despite the overwhelming show of force and the knights' vows that they will die to protect the queen, human efforts prove completely ineffective against the fairies. The fairy magic is all the more mysterious and threatening because not only do those present not understand it, but they do not even see it. Heurodis is there and then gone.

Similarly, when Orfeo enters fairyland after his long sojourn in the wilderness, he does so in an understated moment. After catching sight of Heurodis among a group of ladies out hunting, he follows them: "in at a roche þe leuedis rideþ, / & he after, & nou3t abideþ" (347–48). This entrance may have supernatural implications for readers familiar with Celtic folklore, but the narrative presents it matter-of-factly rather than as a cause for wonder. The description immediately shifts to what Orfeo saw "when he was in þe roche y-go" (349). Although this view of fairyland is spectacular and implies the marvelous nature of the scene, it is not until we see the gallery of human captives inside the castle wall that we know for certain that he has come into a magical space.

The gallery brings together the elements of magic and visual spectacle. The text underscores this convergence by describing the figures in a meticulous and horrifying inventory:

> Þan he gan bihold about al,
> & sei3e liggeand wiþ-in þe wal
> Of folk þat were þider y-brou3t,
> & þou3t dede, & nare nou3t.
> Sum stode wiþ-outen hade,
> & sum non armes nade,
> & sum þurth þe bodi hadde wounde,
> & sum lay wode, y-bounde,
> & sum armed on hors sete,
> & sum astrangled as þai ete;
> & sum were in water adreynt,
> & sum wiþ fire al for-schreynt.
> Wiues þer lay on child-bedde,
> Sum ded & sum awedde,
> & wonder fele þer lay bisides:
> Ri3t as þai slepe her vnder-tides
> Eche was þus in þis warld y-nome,
> Wiþ fairi þider y-come.
> (387–404)

This spectacle is both aesthetic and narrative (much like Heurodis's self-mutilated body, which I will discuss in more detail below). Those qualities are underscored by the ways in which this catalog of different types of suffering echoes the opening lines' survey of the different types of lays ("Sum beþe of wer & sum of wo, / & sum of ioie & mirþe al-so, / & sum of trecherie & of gile" and "sum of bourdes & ribaudy," 5–7, 9). One element—fairy magic—unites the suffering figures. A related element unites the lays: they deal with "ferli [marvelous] þing" (4). In fact, the narrator suggests, such a "þing" is the prerequisite and inspiration for a lay:

> When kinges miȝt our y-here
> Of ani meruailes þat þer were,
> Þai token an harp in gle & game
> & maked a lay & ȝaf it name.
> (17–20)

Several hundred lines later, this scene fulfills those generic expectations by presenting the central marvel of the story. The fact that it includes a "wonder" number of figures identified as "meruails" cements the marvelous status of this gallery (401, 409).[30]

Although the descriptions of the groups are brief, the number described and the parallel structure that the text uses to present them create an accretive effect. Felicity Riddy notes that "the 'taken' in their various postures are described with a studied rhetoric that gives the scene the frozen and formal qualities of a tableau: they are images of grotesquerie rather than suffering and their total effect is macabre."[31] That "total effect" also depends on the number of figures and, correspondingly, the number of tortures or types of suffering on display. The scene is detailed because of the quantity of figures that it includes, not because of the amount of information about each figure, and that focus inspires more horror than would a more intense focus on fewer figures and their suffering. Dramatic spectacle, Bernard Beckerman has argued, is characterized "by marked increases in scale or number or both. . . . [It] depends on infinite redundancy."[32] *Sir Orfeo* adopts this approach rather than the intense focus on individuals that most of the other spectacles in this study demonstrate; here, the number of figures and the number of ways in which they suffer make the gallery spectacular and impress the reader. The text directly connects such effects of scale to wonder; in addition to the "wonder fele" figures in the gallery, the fairy castle's towers are "wonder heiȝe" (356).

Even as the most obvious and detailed magical spectacle, however, the gallery includes ambiguities that heighten the threatening and mysterious nature of the marvel. We do not see the fairies actively practicing magic in this scene any more than we did in Heurodis's disappearance. Instead of showing us magic at work or in progress—which might demystify the fairies as well as the gallery itself—the text reveals the terrible and terrifying effects of the fairies' power. We know that the fairies are responsible for the gallery, but we do not know exactly what they have done to the figures or whether that magic represents the limit of their abilities or merely a facet or fraction of them. The passage indicates that in the human world, these people are believed to be dead, although they are not, and states twice that the fairies brought the figures here. But did the fairies seize people who were near death and preserve them in that liminal state (an interpretation that connects this gallery to the underworld of the Orpheus legend)? Or were these people violently punished for resisting, as the Fairy King threatened Heurodis she would be? In other words, did the violence attract the fairies, or are they responsible for it?

Most critics follow Dorena Allen's emphasis on the gallery victims as "taken"—a view that downplays the fairies' potential power by casting them as collectors rather than creators, opportunists rather than artists.[33] However, Allen's argument is more nuanced: she also suggests that the spectacle includes some who "may have suffered the bloody violence with which, earlier in the poem, Heurodis herself is threatened."[34] In other words, the gallery can be read as a hybrid spectacle that contains figures brought to fairyland under a variety of circumstances. Indeed, a reading of every figure as "taken" would not account for the fact that we have two categories of victims: some who are suffering (391–400) and some who are sleeping peacefully (401–4). Although the poet offers a more detailed catalog of the former group (which is less homogenous than the latter), both seem sizeable. If we see the fairies as creating a subset of the figures according to how they responded to the fairies' "invitation," then we can resolve this inconsistency.

Here, I am also drawing on John Block Friedman's argument that "the fairy king's threats to Heurodis provide a completely adequate explanation for the mysteriously torn men and women within the walls of his castle. . . . [He] may have used violence on other captives and what he threatened could actually have transpired in the case of the people Orfeo finds within the castle walls."[35] This interpretation tallies with the contemporary belief that fairies could "change both men and women into other beings and carry them with them to *elvenland*."[36] Although the victims in *Sir Orfeo* remain recognizably human, they exhibit the same combination of transformation and relocation; they are recreated as fixtures in the gallery. Nonetheless, the poem does not offer proof of whether or in what terms any figures other than Heurodis might have been threatened, or how their reactions might have led to their addition to the gallery. Furthermore, the suffering of some of the figures (especially those in lines 396–99) looks more likely to be the result of human misfortune than supernatural intervention. I therefore see this explanation as filling out Allen's argument rather than adequate on its own. Taken together, these readings suggest that the fairies both are drawn to suffering and produce it. The hybridity and ambiguity of the spectacle preserve the mystery of the fairies' potentially limitless magic and intensify the horror of the scene.

Orfeo and the reader encounter the tableau without warning or explanation; the poet never explicitly reveals how the fairies acquired or created the figures (or which figures entered the gallery by these methods or others). However, the representation of Heurodis in the gallery indicates that her case falls into the category of those shaped by the fairies: "Þer he [Orfeo] seiȝe his owhen wiif, / Dame Heurodis, his lef liif, / Slepe vnder an ympe-tre" (405–7). She appears asleep under the tree, as she was when the Fairy King first approached her, rather than in the more active and defensive position she assumed before being kidnapped. Because Heurodis is not frozen in the position in which she was taken, we can conclude that the fairies determined her state and that they did so partly as an aesthetic display and partly as a reward for obedience. The inclusion of Heurodis provides the strongest evidence that the fairies selected these victims and are responsible for at least some of the conditions, painful as well as peaceful, in which the figures appear.

The assertion in line 403 that "eche was þus in þis warld y-nome" may therefore contain a dual meaning. The key word is "þus," which seems to refer, in some cases, to the *forms* in which the figures appear and, in other cases, to the *ways* in which they were taken. On one hand, this line suggests that the gallery figures were taken from the human "warld" while in the midst of such suffering. That interpretation appears to hold true for the women who "lay on child-bedde," for example, or the people who were "astrangled as þai ete"; both of these descriptions contain realistic details that tie them to common human experiences. On the other hand, some figures may not appear in exactly the condition or position they exhibited when the fairies kidnapped them (as Heurodis does not). For those victims, "þus" could refer to the manner in which they were taken: peacefully, for those who obeyed, and violently, for those who did not.

Although Heurodis's obedience might seem debatable, the active opposition to her abduction came not from her but from Orfeo and his knights. By showing up at the same spot, she has conformed to the Fairy King's instructions that she should reappear "to-morwe . . . / Riȝt here vnder þis ympe-tre" (165–66). In fact, the narrative echoes that phrase when Heurodis returns the next day "riȝt vnto þat ympe-tre" (186). She returns with a group of armed knights, but there is no actual confrontation, and the knights do not hinder the fairies at all. What Orfeo imagined to be resistance instead works as compliance. When warning against opposition, the Fairy King tied his threat specifically to questions of place: "& ȝif þou makest ous y-let, / Whar þou be, þou worst y-fet, / & to-tore þine limes al" (169–71). His primary concern is "whar" Heurodis will be, and the chief way in which she might defy him, he suggests, is by being elsewhere. In this reading, it is because she is in the appointed spot that her body remains whole and she joins the sleepers rather than the sufferers in the gallery.[37]

By introducing the spectacle at this moment and by delaying the mention of Heurodis's presence, the narrative positions the gallery to have the maximum effect on Orfeo. However, the text does not record any overt response on his part: "& when he hadde bihold þis meruails alle / He went in-to þe kinges halle" (409–10).[38] We might expect a reaction to the sight of his wife, if not to the many other figures trapped in the gallery, but however much it may affect readers, the scene has no visible impact on Orfeo. I would argue that its effects are revealed as the narrative unfolds: his behavior and speech during the rest of his time in fairyland must be interpreted in light of this spectacle. Furthermore, I suggest that the gallery, far from intimidating or horrifying Orfeo, is a heartening sight. It is—as unlikely as this initially seems—a moral spectacle.

The gallery works as a moral spectacle because it hints that the Fairy King keeps his word. He promises Heurodis that he will take her and that she will be dismembered if she tries to resist; he does take her and, because she obeys, she remains whole. Her subsequent appearance in the gallery suggests that similar encounters also led to the inclusion of some of the others there—especially the two significant groups that bookend the poet's description. The catalog begins with those who seem to be missing body parts, echoing the Fairy King's threat to Heurodis that her "limes" would be torn off, and ends with those who are sleeping intact. These groups suggest that the Fairy King's threats as well as his promises were truthful. Although the suffering figures might appear to confirm his lack of ethics (because he caused the suffering and/or found it appealing), the spectacle ironically reinforces that he adheres to at least one moral standard: keeping his word.[39] We can read the gallery of grotesques as a physical manifestation of that attitude, revealing the Fairy King's integrity in addition to his propensity for violence and interest in human suffering. The latter pair of characteristics might horrify Orfeo and the reader, but the former may be a hopeful sign. If Orfeo can get the Fairy King to make a commitment about Heurodis, then he can expect the king to keep that promise, and that is precisely how the plot plays out. We have no direct access to the fairies' thoughts or reasoning, or to their traditions or mores; the only way to ascertain their values is by interpreting this external spectacle. The poem demonstrates that recognizing morality within another culture involves processes of enactment and inference and that any understanding that emerges must necessarily be partial and tentative. We can identify certain elements of the fairies' moral code, but we cannot claim to have a grasp of their moral natures or to know whether that code forms the basis of an ethical system.

In addition to providing limited but vital insight into the Fairy King's moral code, the gallery reveals his aesthetics and the value that he places on visual appearance. Because the gallery contains human figures in states that the fairies appear to have determined as well as other human figures whom the fairies appear to have kidnapped and preserved in the midst of painful experiences, it functions as an artistic collection; the fairies have not simply assembled but actively created a museum of human suffering. They are artists as well as curators, and although the aesthetic displayed may be antithetical to human morals, the gallery reflects how the fairies value humans and why humans interest them. This set of interests illuminates the Fairy King's aesthetic rather than erotic (or simply unfathomable) motivations for kidnapping Heurodis and establishes the foundation for his otherwise peculiar objection to reuniting the spouses.

After Orfeo plays his harp, the Fairy King vows to grant him any request. When Orfeo asks for "Þat ich leuedi, briȝt on ble, / Þat slepeþ vnder þe ympe-tre" (455–56), however, the king balks:

> "Nay!" quaþ þe king, "Þat nouȝt nere!
> A sori couple of ȝou it were,
> For þou art lene, rowe & blac,
> & sche is louesum, wiþ-outen lac:
> A loþlich þing it were, forþi,
> To sen hir in þi compayni."
> (457–62)

This objection is an aesthetic one: imagining the spectacle that their union would create, the Fairy King finds Heurodis and Orfeo a mismatched pair. Orfeo's suffering has transformed his body, bringing him closer to the macabre sufferers in the gallery than to Heurodis, whose beauty has been restored and preserved. The fairies' moral code—which dictates that they must keep their promises, however repugnant—clashes with their aesthetic interests in this exchange. Although the aesthetic reaction initially dominates, Orfeo persuades the king to keep his word by uniting the two values and explaining the moral in terms of the aesthetic. "ȝete were it a wele fouler þing," he chides the king, "to here a lesing of þi mouþe" (464–65). A moral failing, Orfeo suggests, is uglier than an unharmonious pairing. This idea concretizes the figurative concept of a blemish on one's character. He reminds the king that "þou most þi word hold" (468)—a conviction supported by the courtly atmosphere, but also by the victims in the gallery—and the king immediately acquiesces. Although the speed of his capitulation has led some critics to see this moment as an "impulse" or a "lapse,"[40] the gallery spectacle establishes a foundation for both the refusal and the acquiescence, rendering them predictable and reflective of the Fairy King's nature, rather than as departures from it. The gallery indicates that, however frightening and supernatural the Fairy King might be, he can be reasoned with on this point.

The Gallery as a Moral Spectacle for the Audience

The first moral function of the gallery operates within the text: it signifies critical components of the fairies' moral code to Orfeo and to the audience. The gallery offers a window onto the Fairy King's rationale and reveals that fairy magic practices are not random or uncontrolled. A second moral function extends beyond the text: the gallery inspires wonder that in turn encourages moral reflection by the audience on the values of human courtly society.[41] In exposing the fairies' moral code, the magic spectacle also exposes that code's similarities to and departures from human ethics, particularly those associated with courtly behavior and chivalry. This comparison may prompt deeper reflection. *Sir Orfeo* hints that there are parallels not only between the two courts, but also between practicing magic and practicing chivalry. Both involve exercising power guided by certain values; we could draw an even tighter analogy by seeing both as including, though certainly not limited to, a form of aggression or violence balanced by a commitment to a form of honor.[42] In each case, visual spectacles—like the gallery, or the gathering of Orfeo's troops, or a tournament or battle more generally—allow us to see the impact of those practices and make inferences about some of the values behind them. Over the course of the poem, the visual spectacle of the gallery generates larger and more complex effects.

The importance of the gallery as a visual and aesthetic spectacle indicates that we might treat it as not simply a vivid description but a type of image within the text, and this status allows it to function as a spectacle that encourages a moral reaction. Both image theory and medieval culture offer justifications for approaching the gallery as an image; in combination, they suggest how it might work in roughly similar ways for fourteenth- and twenty-first-century audiences. W. J. T. Mitchell has argued that the distinction between the visual and the verbal is artificial and unsustainable because "all media are mixed media, and all representations are heterogeneous; there are no 'purely' visual or verbal arts."[43] Although Mitchell is primarily interested in modern "imagetexts" and attitudes toward them, the very term *image* evolves to reflect this heterogeneity during the 1300s. Its use to denote a physical object or material representation dates to at least 1225, but during the fourteenth century it also takes on the sense of a mental picture.[44] Scholars have noted a related overlap between ideas of reading and seeing or visualizing in the Middle Ages; texts were understood to inspire mental images, and particularly in the fourteenth century, both reading and seeing "were part of the same bodily operation, involving perception and cognition in the search for knowledge."[45]

The gallery's status as an image is important because that allows us to understand its function within the narrative in different terms and offers a historically valid basis for interpreting it as a spectacle that could have moral overtones and effects on medieval as well as modern audiences. Mary Carruthers, who has demonstrated the close associations between image and memory in the Middle Ages, shows that images could act as structures to aid memory, and that images themselves were considered to be more memorable—a characteristic that twenty-first-century mental athletes continue to exploit.[46] Memory was "an integral part of the virtue of prudence, that which makes moral judgment possible," Carruthers explains, and "it was in trained memory that one built character, judgment, citizenship, and piety." In short, "a person without a memory ... would be a person without moral character."[47] This connection depended on the creation of mental images because the ability to call up such pictures from memory enabled virtue and helped "in moving the will to initiate courses of action."[48] These mental images could be derived from reading as well as past experience. Poetry, for instance, had the potential to affect readers' morality, and that potential was heightened if the poem used "marvels" or "strange and wonderful images," because those "move the memory better than the ordinary."[49]

Other critics have examined the didactic power of devotional images in religious as well as literary contexts.[50] This power was changing shape in the fourteenth century, as Shannon Gayk notes: "although the primary justifications for images throughout the earlier Middle Ages emphasized their didactic uses and thus their relation to texts, by the fourteenth century apologetics increasingly focused on the image's superior ability to stir emotions."[51] During the fourteenth century, then, many writers and readers not only would have understood images to be connected to memory and—especially in the case of religious images—didacticism, but also would likely have begun to recognize their emotional power. If we bring these strands of thought together, we can see the potential for secular, marvelous images like the gallery and the other spectacles in this study to hold tremendous significance for a medieval audience. Although most of the scholarship on images and didacticism has focused on religious icons and images, the critical work on memory confirms that secular images would also have held the power to communicate ideas or lessons, particularly if those images were "strange and wonderful" and if the message they conveyed concerned morality. Such marvelous secular images would be closely related to the miraculous ones that operated so powerfully in the contexts of hagiography and affective piety.

Caroline Walker Bynum finds that wonder in the Middle Ages "is induced by the beautiful, the horrible, and the skillfully made, by the bizarre and rare, by that which challenges or suddenly illuminates our expectations, by the range of difference, even the order and regularity, found in the world," and especially by "events or phenomena in which ontological and moral boundaries are crossed, confused, or erased."[52] Fairies are beautiful and horrible as well as rare, and their fraught connections to humanity and morality (as explored above) made them likely to elicit this kind of wonder reaction from a medieval audience. The fairies' gallery in *Sir Orfeo,* as a striking and singular manifestation of an alien morality and terrifying aestheticism, fits Bynum's definition even more precisely. Modern theories of wonder and enchantment note a comparable effect and allow us to parse in more detail the affective response that links the apprehension of a marvel like the gallery to moral analysis.

The sources and nature of wonder have shifted over time,[53] but modern scholars' and readers' interest in the gallery might still best be categorized as "wonder" (a common term in medieval romance) or "enchantment" (which indicated a literal subjection to magic in Middle English but is now used figuratively, and often as a near-synonym of "wonder"). Rita Felski, who advocates enchantment as a productive mode of engagement for literary scholars, sees it as "characterized by a state of intense involvement, a sense of being so entirely caught up in an aesthetic object that nothing else seems to matter."[54] The political theorist Jane Bennett describes enchantment as "a state of wonder" or a "state of interactive fascination" that, like Bynum's medieval wonder, may be tinged with fear.[55]

Although they can have slightly different valences in current usage, both "wonder" and "enchantment" describe a reaction to secular marvels, and, in both cases, that reaction involves a cognitive as well as an affective component.[56] "Medieval philosophers and theologians emphasized wonder as a first step toward knowledge," concludes Bynum.[57] Historians of science Lorraine Daston and Katharine Park similarly identify wonder as a "cognitive passion" in the medieval and early modern periods.[58] Centuries later, that characterization still holds true. In his study of wonder in more recent scientific and aesthetic contexts, Philip Fisher returns to that productive duality: "the details of thought, of problem solving, of the analysis of works of art where a slow unfolding of attention and questioning takes place within the presence of the work are all questions within the domain of wonder."[59] Although wonder and enchantment may begin as passive reactions, they lead to active engagement: marvels make us think.

This cognitive effect is especially pronounced when the marvel that we observe has a visual dimension. Wonder and enchantment are often described as types of gazes or as responses to visual stimuli. In the twelfth century, Richard of St. Victor explained the experience of divine contemplation in terms of wonder: "Whence comes wonder except from an unexpected and incredible manifestation? . . . The more greatly we marvel at the novelty of a thing, the more carefully we pay attention to it. The more attentively we look, the more fully we come to know."[60] Stephen Greenblatt, examining wonder in the later context of museum exhibits, defines it similarly as "the power of the displayed object to stop the viewer in his or her tracks, to convey an arresting sense of uniqueness, to evoke an exalted attention."[61] Fisher agrees that "wonder is a relation to the visible world" and notes that this visual aspect "opens up the connection between aesthetics and thought."[62] The uses of "wonder" (104, 356, and 401) and "meruail[es]" (18, 409, and 598) by the *Orfeo* poet—and the popularity of the word "gallery" among scholars to describe the human victims of fairy kidnapping—hint at the analogous ways in which the narrative's spectacles operate in the medieval and modern eras, arresting the listeners/readers/viewers and engaging their attention in particular and intense ways.

What interests me here, in addition to the claim that marvels make us think, is the possibility that they encourage specifically moral reactions. This possibility returns us to medieval philosophers' ideas about the moral potential of strange and wonderful images. Among the current theorists mentioned, Bennett explores this possibility most fully, contending that "the mood of enchantment may be valuable for ethical life."[63] Although she focuses on "everyday marvels" in the postmodern world, her conclusions can be adapted to our consideration of medieval marvels. She identifies "metamorphing creatures" or "crossings" as one possible source of enchantment, suggesting that they "enact the very possibility of change; their presence carries with it the trace of dangerous but also exciting and exhilarating migrations."[64] This point recalls Bynum's observation that boundary-crossing medieval phenomena inspire intense wonder, and we can imagine the gallery figures in this category, arrested in the process of transforming from living to dead, or migrating from the human to the fairy domain. We might see the fairies themselves as a parallel case: they are neither entirely human nor entirely other, literally and figuratively moving between worlds. If such crossings provoke enchantment or wonder, then those reactions can in turn foster moral reflection and even action. Might meditating on these crossings, Bennett muses, "render one more open to novelty, less defensive in the face of challenges to norms that one already embodies, and thus more responsive to the injustices that haunt both cross-cultural and cross-species relations?"[65] *Sir Orfeo* seems to encourage similar responses in its depiction of the cross-cultural encounter between Orfeo and the fairies, which challenges the "norms" of courtly conduct; in other words, the poem elicits an affective and moral reaction that is driven more by the immediate circumstances than by the larger ethical system in place. Here again, the diction is key: Orfeo "behold[s]" the gallery (387), and that verb may call up for the medieval audience what Sarah McNamer describes as "a historically specific way of seeing: a compassionate gaze ... presented as if it ought to generate a somatic impulse to hold the sufferer in a protective, ameliorative embrace."[66]

I have already suggested that the gallery reveals aspects of the fairies' moral code to Orfeo, who then exploits that knowledge in his negotiations with the king. When we think of the gallery as a spectacular image that might have didactic and enchanting effects based on its ability to engage the audience's memory and emotions, however, we can see a bigger picture, metaphorically speaking. In exposing the fairies' moral code, even incompletely, the gallery shows the audience both that the fairies are other and that they are not as other as we might expect. In fact, the partial nature of that revelation may encourage more curiosity about the fairies' morality and its potential connections to human ethics. The fairies' interests in aesthetics over virtue and in visual displays of violence are initially horrifying but, upon consideration, uncomfortably close to some of the values of chivalry itself, especially as it was often represented in romances (a point that might be apparent not only to a medieval audience in western Europe, but also to a modern one whose attitudes have been shaped, implicitly or explicitly, by that tradition). The parallel grows stronger if we see the fairies as having committed violence to enact a punishment that their moral code justifies. The gallery functions like a mirror, reflecting a few aspects of chivalric ethics that have not been distorted so much as pressed to the extreme. The scene does not signal that the audience should reject chivalry, but encourages them to ponder its limits and pitfalls; in other words, the gallery may induce readers to wonder whether all of the ethics of chivalry are moral.

The gallery also warns of the limits and pitfalls of enchantment itself. Mirroring can be bidirectional, and in the same exaggerated way that the fairy court mirrors the human one, the fairies' enchantment with the human mirrors the human characters' and readers' enchantment with the fairies. The fairies' response lacks the edge of wariness that Bynum and Bennett describe as a component of wonder or enchantment, and it may be that missing piece that allows the fairies' fascination with humanity to become damaging to both worlds. From this perspective, the gallery represents a cautionary tale, a case study in what might happen if one becomes enchanted by the wrong thing or in the wrong way, applying moral values that privilege the self over the other. If we define "moral" in Bennett's terms, as openness to difference and change and resistance to injustice, then enchantment may result in moral reflection and action—it may even be most likely to do so—but that is not the only possible outcome.[67] Both chivalry, as a code of values, and enchantment, as a mode of engagement, must be paired with self-reflection.

"Vision, in the medieval world," writes Suzannah Biernoff, "did not leave the viewer untouched or unchanged."[68] This observation holds true not only for representations of biblical events or saints' miracles, but also for other kinds of sights, including textual magical spectacles like the gallery. Critics have made much of the parallels between the fairy court and its human counterpart, and the gallery image exposes the complex nature of the relationship between the two worlds: Both value beauty, but define it differently. Both embrace violence, but for different purposes. Both have a high regard for keeping one's word, but otherwise have different moral standards. Both have the capacity for enchantment, but may act on it differently. The poem suggests that some of the similarities are positive. The turning point in each court, for example, involves a person's keeping his word to Orfeo—the Fairy King's delivery on his promise is soon followed by the steward's delivery on his. Other similarities, such as the emphases on aesthetics and violence, are subtler and more disquieting, and Heurodis comes to embody those. In both courts, she functions primarily as a physical signifier, and this condition intensifies rather than abates as the poem progresses, troubling what scholars have traditionally viewed as the happy ending.

Heurodis as Signifying Spectacle

Scholars have seen the reunion between Orfeo and Heurodis as the most salient difference between the Middle English poem and its classical source. Although not unique in this respect, the romance does differ from the most widely circulated versions of the classical legend in the Middle Ages. Orpheus loses Eurydice when he cannot resist looking back at her as they exit the underworld, but Orfeo and Heurodis successfully reunite and return to the human world and their own court. In both versions, readers have seen the outcomes as determining the overall tone of the narrative, classifying the classical legend as tragic and the medieval romance as happy.[69] A happy ending appears in some other adaptations of the Orpheus story, and it is possible that these texts and/or an undiscovered French source with a similar resolution would have provided a more immediate context for the poet or some medieval readers of *Sir Orfeo*.[70] Nonetheless, the classical legend was well known in the Middle Ages, and that reference point encourages readers to scrutinize Orfeo and Heurodis's departure from the underworld/otherworld, since that is when Orpheus lost Eurydice. The denial of any description of Orfeo's reunion with Heurodis hints that it may not be an entirely happy outcome, and the continuation of the story after their reunion suggests that it does not resolve the narrative. Although Heurodis has drawn less critical attention than the ending,[71] a focus on her character highlights the reunion's problematic nature. Even before the fairies install her in their gallery, Heurodis functions primarily as a signifying spectacle. After her return from the fairy world, this status is exacerbated: she never speaks or seems to return to being a fully human character.[72] Her silence, combined with the displacement of the emotional reconnection onto Orfeo's steward, undermines the reading of the conclusion as joyous.

The representation of Heurodis's body conforms to late medieval devotional and artistic practice. Christ offers the most obvious medieval example of a body that functioned symbolically and demanded diligent interpretation, but Caroline Walker Bynum has examined how women's bodies might also become devotional symbols.[73] Beginning in the thirteenth century, Walter Simons observes, "it was increasingly argued that the female body, in particular, could be an instrument to communicate religious concepts and feelings."[74] Although the representation of Heurodis's body as a signifying spectacle draws on this foundation, her spectacle operates in a primarily secular context. The idea that the human body could signify in secular as well as religious ways predates the fourteenth century, but that period saw increased attention to the visual aspect of such signification—a trend to which Heurodis's representation seems to contribute.[75] This trend is roughly contemporaneous with a rising interest in spectacle that affected depictions of the human body; as Michael Camille argues, "the human body came into its own as a site of spectacle and metaphorical projection in the fourteenth century."[76] The phrase "site of spectacle" is an apt description of Heurodis's body, which appears and disappears at critical narrative moments and signals dramatically to both Orfeo and the reader throughout the poem. Although the attention to a single body over time differentiates this spectacle from the gallery, which was a collection of bodies frozen in time, we might read the text's later visual interest in Heurodis's body as focusing in on the one element of the gallery image that escapes its textual frame.

We learn early that Heurodis is as beautiful as we would expect a romance heroine to be; she is "a quen of priis" and "Þe fairest leuedi, for þe nones, / Þat miȝt gon on bodi & bones" (51 and 53–54). Her beauty suggests her nobility and virtue while also signaling that she is qualified to be queen. When she awakens from her initial meeting with the fairies, her reaction is disturbing both because it is such a frenzied physical response and because it damages that beauty: "sche froted hir honden & hir fet, / & cracched hir visage—it bled wete; / Hir riche robe hye al to-rett" (79–81). Orfeo remarks on these same details when he sees his wife:

> Þy bodi, þat was so white y-core,
> Wiþ þine nailes is all to-tore.
> Allas! þi rode, þat was so red,
> Is al wan, as þou were ded;
> & al-so þine fingres smale
> Beþ al blodi & al pale.
> (105–10)

Although she inflicts the damage on herself, Heurodis has been turned into a spectacle of suffering by this first encounter with the fairies, and so this moment prefigures what we see on a much larger scale in the gallery.[77] The pathos depends heavily on the beauty that the narrative established earlier as appropriate to the courtly and romantic context and that Orfeo—as well as, implicitly, his court—admired and valued. In other words, the destruction of her beauty as a signifying spectacle relies on the narrative's prior construction of that beauty as a particular value. The language in Orfeo's description reminds us that Heurodis embodied those conventions of beauty while also placing her claim to them firmly in the past ("Þy bodi, þat was so white y-core . . . þi rode, þat was so red"). Her beauty has been reversed, turned inside out—what should be white has been bloodied, and what should be red has become pale.

I argued above that Heurodis's disappearance does not qualify as a magical spectacle because it happens invisibly. However, Orfeo's knights do present a visual spectacle in that scene. In an attempt to protect Heurodis from abduction, Orfeo brings to the tree "wele ten hundred kniȝtes wiþ him, / Ich y-armed, stout & grim" (183–84). The knights take up a formation around the queen, swearing that they will die to protect her, "ac ȝete amiddes hem ful riȝt / Þe quen was oway y-tviȝt" (191–92). Heurodis is literally at the center of the spectacle, and her disappearance reveals the human show of force as inadequate, underscoring how overmatched Orfeo and his knights are. He musters an impressive show of force, but the fairies unmask that as an impotent display. Although their magic is less spectacular in this scene than Orfeo's army, it is more effective.

The first time that Orfeo sees Heurodis after her abduction, she is in the midst of a fairy hunting party rather than a human army. She remains silent—as she has been since relating her dream earlier in the text—but presents another embodied spectacle that conveys her feelings to Orfeo. "For messais þat sche on him seiȝe, / Þat had ben so riche & so heiȝe," the narrator explains, "Þe teres fel out of her eiȝe" (325–27). This response dramatizes Heurodis's reaction to Orfeo's changed appearance and, in the process, hints at her love for him and sorrow over their separation. Additionally, her tears insinuate to Orfeo that the situation causes her to suffer. Her companions hurry her away, and he reacts with a speech expressing the effect "þis siȝt" has had on him (334). He suggests that neither he nor Heurodis "dar[ed]" to speak (336), but this scene also establishes important parallels with the earlier post-dream reaction when Heurodis used her body to demonstrate her suffering and Orfeo read it accordingly. By this time, Orfeo's body has become a spectacle in its own right—a point that the Fairy King, a character closely attuned to spectacle, will make soon thereafter, when he disparages Orfeo as "lene, rowe & blac" (459). Although the changes to his body may be less violent and immediate than those that Heurodis inflicted on herself, they are no less dramatic, visible, or significant. Orfeo's appearance reveals his radically altered lifestyle and his suffering to Heurodis, engaging the two of them in a true exchange despite the fact that no words are spoken.

In the gallery scene, Heurodis's body signifies more passively to Orfeo as it reveals the critical information about the Fairy King's moral nature. The fact that Orfeo recognizes his wife "bi her cloþes" (408) indicates that he is again responding to physical signs, and also suggests how her agency has declined: she has moved from speaking and acting emphatically, to silent and constrained action, and finally to total passivity. Orfeo does not recognize her facial expression, bodily characteristics, or position, but the way in which her body is clothed.[78] When the Fairy King voices his aesthetic objection to the reunion and describes Heurodis as "louesum, wiþ-outen lac" (460), he, too, is reading her body as a signifier. Despite the different intents and contexts, the initial description of her beauty in Orfeo's court seems to be the closest parallel. That parallel suggests that Heurodis's primary value is aesthetic in both worlds and that her defining characteristic may be the status of her body as a signifying spectacle. The treatment of Heurodis's beauty alludes to the importance of Eurydice's appearance (and Orpheus's inability to resist looking at her) in the classical legend, but it also implicitly critiques romantic convention and portrayals of women in courtly love.[79]

After the king responds to Orfeo's chiding by allowing him to take Heurodis, we might expect a moving reunion. If this is the happy ending—and the key departure the poem makes from the famous classical version—then it would seem to merit substantial representation. Instead, the text moves quickly past the reunion and return to the human world, dwelling more on the length of the journey than the successful reunion of the couple:

> His wiif he tok bi þe hond
> & dede him swiþe out of þat lond,
> & went him out of þat þede;
> Riȝt as he come þe way he ȝede.
> So long he haþ þe way y-nome
> To Winchester he is y-come,
> Þat was his owhen cité.
> (473–79)

Heurodis still does not speak and, once again, she disappears from the narrative. As the repetition of singular masculine pronouns underscores, the description focuses on Orfeo and his actions and travels, with Heurodis as an assumed but obviously secondary companion. It may be that the fact of the reunion is the vital element here, and the poet eschews a sentimental scene that would not advance the narrative. Nonetheless, because the deviation from the classical legend puts particular pressure on this moment, and because the narrative does contain a sentimental reunion between Orfeo and his steward, I suggest that this minimalist description feeds doubts about how the exposure to fairy magic has affected Heurodis and encourages readers to reconsider her role in the human court. This reconsideration extends the moral reflection on courtly and chivalric ethics that began with the gallery.

Heurodis never recovers after the fairies abduct her—never returns to being fully human or to having the more (if not completely) developed character she once had. The poem emphasized her physical aspect early, but the corporeal progressively becomes her sole mode of being and communicating. After her kidnapping, Heurodis neither speaks nor acts significantly, beyond the tears she cries in the forest. When she is reunited with Orfeo and returned to the human world, the situation becomes more rather than less pronounced; she vanishes again instead of returning to the narrative in a meaningful way. To the extent that Heurodis's presence remains a signifier, it speaks primarily to Orfeo's claim to the kingship. As a number of scholars have suggested, his recovery of her acts as an important predicate for the larger recovery of his kingdom.[80] Susan Nakley has argued that women's bodies suffer the cost of national sovereignty in Chaucer's romances,[81] but *Sir Orfeo* offers an inverse example: Heurodis's body must be saved as her voice is sacrificed in order to confirm Orfeo's right to reclaim his position as sovereign.

As Orfeo prepares to return to court, he arranges for his wife to stay with a poor beggar. His solitary return affords readers the reunion scene we might have expected earlier, with the substitution of the steward for Heurodis. In this scene, the disguised Orfeo figuratively conjures his own mutilated body: "y founde in a dale / . . . a man to-torn smale" (537–38). The use of "to-torn" here echoes his description of Heurodis's mutilation of her own body (106) and her recounting of the Fairy King's threat (171, 173). Both of those spectacles proved illuminating for Orfeo, so perhaps it is not surprising that he projects a similar one in order to probe the steward's moral character. Lacking the extreme distress that drove Heurodis to injure herself or the magical agency behind the suffering figures in the gallery, Orfeo works to create a similar effect through narrative—a specter rather than a spectacle that will nonetheless be vivid enough to function as a moral test. By evoking the striking scenes that prefaced the spouses' separation (Heurodis's self-mutilation) and then reunion (the gallery), this move prepares the ground for a similar resolution.

Spurred by the apparent evidence of King Orfeo's death, the steward speaks movingly of the loss he feels—"allas! wreche, what schal y do / Þat haue swiche a lord y-lore? / A, way! þat ich was y-bore!" (544–46)—and swoons. This swoon serves as another bodily spectacle that signifies. Convinced by the demonstration that the steward "was a trewe man / & loued him as he auȝt to do" (554–55), Orfeo happily reunites with him. The steward's reaction is suitably impressive: "ouer & ouer þe bord he þrewe, / & fel adoun to his fet" (578–79). The court responds similarly, identifying Orfeo with one voice as "our lord, Sir, & our king" (582). They then immediately "baþed him, & shaued his berd, / & tired him as a king apert" (585–86); after these ministrations, he embodies his kingly identity and restoration appropriately. Heurodis is brought to join him, and with both of their bodies now apparently in their proper conditions and locations, the action of the poem can conclude.

This lengthy scene, with tender speeches and actions on both sides, contrasts sharply with the abbreviated depiction of the reunion with Heurodis. It is true that Orfeo does not need to test Heurodis as he tests the steward; the narrative gives no hint that she has been unfaithful or untrue, and her absence is not of her own volition. However, if the spousal reunion is the crux that differentiates the romance from its classical source and the most significant reason why it ends happily, we must be troubled by the contrast. Just as the poem displaces the reunion scene onto the steward, it delays the joyous ending until Orfeo discovers that his kingdom endures and awaits his return. These features suggest that the most prominent difference between the two versions of the story is Orfeo's role as king rather than the recovery of his wife. Their reunion is an effect of that change instead of being the central alteration.

Heurodis's role as a silent signifier does not simply relegate her to a symbolic function in the narrative; her silence has further profound ramifications. The Fairy King's aesthetic objection draws attention to the more elemental divide that has arisen between the spouses as a result of Heurodis's time in the fairy kingdom (and particularly the gallery). She has been fundamentally altered and cannot return completely to her previous self. Orfeo's time in the wilderness may have changed him, too, but the transition back to court remains more possible in his case because he has been permitted a more active role than Heurodis throughout the narrative. Orfeo recovers his wife's physical form, but the human powers of his love and music—both of which we might see as aspects of his chivalry—finally fail to counteract the effects of the fairy magic.[82] The poem does not celebrate the depth of marital love or the triumph of human artistry; it warns of the danger of magic and its revelatory potential. One of the ironies in *Sir Orfeo* is that Heurodis's condition is not so much a transformation of her earlier self as an exaggeration of it. The poem hints that she was always, to some extent, a physical spectacle. In recognizing that the ending may not be as happy as it initially seems, we must realize that the same is true of the beginning: the beautiful Heurodis in her happy marriage has the same disturbing parallels with the later Heurodis that the human court has with its fairy counterpart. Far from providing an escape from human realities, the fairy world has returned those to us in a magnified form.

Replacing the underworld of the classical legend with fairyland is not an arbitrary reimagining of the source; it is an update of the legend that brings it in line with contemporary aesthetic interests in the connections between marvelous spectacles and morality. Where there was no magic, the poet added it. Where there was a minor spectacle, the poet enhanced it. Where there was a potential moral resonance, the poet amplified it. The ending describes the narrative as "þis meruaile" (598), echoing the opening observation that lays are defined by marvels (17–20) and suggesting a synecdochical relationship between the central marvel, the gallery, and the poem itself. When we view it in this context, and with an awareness of medieval and modern theories of wonder, the gallery scene becomes not an anomaly or a site of conflicting evidence and interpretations but a signal of the nature of the fairies' magic as well as their moral code, which proves essential to the resolution of the poem. Even after being removed from the gallery, however, Heurodis's body functions as another uncanny signal, indicating how her kidnapping continues to reverberate through the narrative despite the spouses' reunion and return to the human world. The poem also silently encourages its audience to wonder whether the human world parallels the fairy world in other equally unsettling ways. Ultimately, the magical spectacle not only reveals the fairies' morality, but also provokes questions about human virtues and the value and power we assign to them. The next chapter focuses squarely on human virtue, taking up texts from the fair unknown tradition that raise questions about distinguishing true virtue from its semblance. Supernatural figures turn out to be particularly well equipped to resolve those questions through spectacles that involve private encounters rather than a static public tableau.

CHAPTER TWO

REVEALING SPECTACLES

Virtue and Identity in Fair Unknowns

The fairies' gallery in *Sir Orfeo* provokes questions about the nature of human moral codes, but other marvels resolve doubts about an individual's moral character. Romances often embed such revelatory marvels in the discourse of virtue: a hero confronts a marvelous obstacle or challenge in order to prove that he possesses the requisite chivalric virtue(s). In *Sir Gawain and the Green Knight*, Gawain must demonstrate courage and courtesy through his marvelous trials; in the *Wife of Bath's Tale*, the knight must respond to his shape-shifting spouse by applying his new moral perspective on women's desire. Marvels can be especially vital to fair unknown narratives, which must reveal not only the hero's character, but also his name or lineage.

In what may have been the most popular Middle English Arthurian romance, the resolution to the comprehensive mystery of the fair unknown's identity takes the shape of a dragon with a woman's face.[1] Until very recently, *Lybeaus Desconus* was as unpopular with modern critics as it was popular with medieval readers; foundational assessments of the poem focused on its possible authorship by Thomas Chestre and its ostensible aesthetic shortcomings. M. Mills, who sought to establish Chestre's canon in the 1960s, set the tone for subsequent evaluations of his work, characterizing him as "a literary hack who made uncritical use of any material that presented itself to him, obsessed with his rhyme-patterns beyond all other things and quite prepared to leave any number of contradictions and loose ends in his narratives."[2] Later critics rehabilitated *Lybeaus* and Chestre on aesthetic grounds, attending especially to the manipulation of the fair unknown genre.[3] The poem is now enjoying a resurgence of interest, in which the dragon lady figures significantly;[4] this chapter investigates the moral dimension of that enchanted figure, examining how the marvel addresses questions of identity that include chivalric virtue as a key component and thereby furthers the characteristic fourteenth-century interest in magic, spectacle, and morality. *Lybeaus* continued to be popular well into the 1400s, when its inclusion in the Ashmole manuscript alongside more overtly moral texts implied an interest in its representation of virtue over its representation of marvels.[5] As I will argue in the conclusion of this chapter, that shift tracks with the evolving values of romance in the fifteenth century.

Lybeaus was not only a popular romance, but also, in many ways, a prototypical fair unknown narrative. Its plot, which closely resembles the French *Le Bel Inconnu*, follows a knight's attempts to demonstrate his worthiness and discover his lineage while on a quest. In the last third of the poem, he finally accomplishes both ends by battling two sorcerers and rescuing a maiden who has been transformed into a dragon but retains her own face. This feature seems to be Chestre's innovation, since the creature is simply a "worm" in other versions.[6] She kisses the knight, and immediately loses the wings and tail to become a beautiful lady. Her transformation reveals the knight's identity since, as she explains, only the kiss of Gawain or his kin could undo the magic. That kiss therefore engenders two discoveries: of the lady's beautiful (and naked) true shape, and of Lybeaus's kinship with one of the most famous knights of King Arthur's court.

In the poem's marvelous episodes, we see magic functioning as a test of individual virtue—something that occurs in several other late fourteenth-century romances. What is most interesting about fair unknown narratives in the context of this study, however, is the connection to a third concern: identity. In these narratives, identity is twofold, involving both name/lineage and character/virtue. *Lybeaus* shows a particular investment in this issue, treating "Lybeaus Desconus" (or "the fair unknown") as the character's first and last names rather than referring to him as "the Unknown" or "the knight" as other versions did.[7] Like other fair unknown romances, *Lybeaus* is also deeply concerned with virtue as an aspect of the hero's identity. Later texts pick up on that emphasis; in *The Squire of Low Degree*, the eponymous character wishes that he were "a kynges sonne, / . . . / Or els so bolde in eche fyght / As was Syr Lybius, that gentell knight," and the lady later rehearses the *Lybeaus* plot in a speech exhorting the squire to perform chivalric feats.[8] Although virtue seems to be largely a condition of being rather than a specific quality in Chestre's portrayal (i.e., the question is whether Lybeaus is virtuous, instead of which virtues he might have), "doughtiness" turns out to be the crucial element that signifies a general state of virtue within the chivalric moral code *Lybeaus* espouses. Both a fair appearance and noble deeds are insufficient to prove Lybeaus's character—only through the marvelous spectacles, I argue, can he definitively prove his worth and verify his identity to the audiences within and outside of the text, allowing the narrative to end.

Marvels and Morality in Romance

Fair unknown narratives' interest in knightly virtue draws on the larger correlation between morality and romance, which can be facilitated or complicated by the presence of magical marvels. Although it is difficult to characterize the romance genre definitively because it spans multiple continents and centuries, magic has long been considered one of its key components.[9] Some studies have called that assumption into question for English romance, arguing that, when magic does appear there, it is of only minor importance. John Finlayson has demonstrated that magic is rarely integral to Middle English romances,[10] and Helen Cooper's examination of ineffective magic in English romances indicates that its decorative or nominal purposes are predominant. She remarks that "magic and the supernatural often appear oddly supplementary: decoration rather than substance"; this "narrative uselessness is matched by [a] lack of any obvious ethical or emotional function."[11] However, as we have already seen in the previous chapter, magic can serve important moral functions, especially when it takes the form of a visual marvel.

In medieval romance, morality commonly enters the narrative in the form of chivalrous codes of behavior tied to courtly love. Magical marvels provide an effective way of testing characters' virtue in that context, and, as a result, magic usually appears in texts in which courtly love is also a central concern.[12] This is one reason, I propose, that some early English romances contain little or no magic, including *Havelok the Dane* and *King Horn* (both of which date to the 1200s). In *Horn*, the earliest known English romance, Rymenhild gives the hero a ring before he leaves to earn his knightly reputation; the ring is meant to protect him, but it is not obviously effective or even clearly magical. In *Havelok*, a marvelous light issuing from the hero's mouth signifies his noble birth and destiny, but this sign (which occurs three times, once accompanied by an angel's explanation) seems more miraculous than magical. Another thirteenth-century romance, *Floris and Blancheflour*, includes a fair amount of magic, although it seems primarily to serve the decorative function that Cooper identified; the narrative describes both a magic well that turns blood-red if a lady who is not a virgin washes her hands there and a magic ring that will save the wearer's life, but neither element is used during the narrative and so neither becomes a fully realized marvel. Because courtly love is at the heart of *Floris and Blancheflour*—which includes magic—but is subordinate to national or political concerns in *King Horn* and *Havelok the Dane*—which do not—these romances hint at a nascent correlation between magic and courtly love in early English romance.

This correlation holds true beyond English romances and, in many cases, magic plays a much more prominent role. Magic tends to fulfill two functions that sometimes overlap: bringing lovers together (after which their love may be vetted by nonmagical means) and testing their love. In Marie de France's twelfth-century *Guigemar*, for instance, the hero boards a magic ship that takes him to the lady who becomes his beloved, but the rest of their adventure turns on the physical tokens of love that they exchange—a knot that only she can untie and a belt that only he can unfasten, both of which seem to require individual skill or knowledge rather than sorcery. In another of Marie's lays, *Yonec*, the lovers can meet only because the knight is able to transform into a hawk and fly to the window of the room where the jealous husband has imprisoned the lady. In some romances, magic operates as a temptation, and characters' repudiation of it signifies the strength of their love. This type of test appears in *Floris and Blancheflour*, in which both of the lovers refuse to use the magic ring to save themselves, and Marie's *Les Deux Amanz*, in which the hero refuses to take a magical potion to help him win his love.

Later romances follow a similar pattern by using magic to facilitate or examine courtly love, with English poets often choosing to translate romances that foreground magic and/or raising the profile of magic relative to their sources. In *Partonope of Blois*, which is based on a twelfth-century French text but appears in English in fifteenth-century manuscripts, "a Shyppe of ffayre" brings Partonope to his eventual lover, Melior.[13] She turns out to be a magical figure in her own right, and the condition that he must not see her for the first year and a half tests their love in a Cupid-and-Psyche-like twist. Although the French poet prefaces the poem with a discussion of love, the English version opens by calling attention to the "meruellys and wonders many and ffele" that appear in "olde storyes" like this one.[14] In *William of Palerne*, which likely dates to the mid-1300s, a nobleman is transformed into a werewolf by obviously magical means: his stepmother uses "nigramauncy" and "coninge of wicchecraft" to make an ointment "bi enchaunmens of charmes."[15] This enchanted figure brings William and a different Melior together, and a friend's magic makes William love her, but subsequent nonmagical events test their love. The part that magic plays in that love is more prominent here than in the French source, in which the friend uses an herb to bring out William's feelings.[16] Similarly, *Lybeaus Desconus* includes more magical figures, in number as well as in degree, than the earlier French version.[17]

The presence of courtly love does not always ensure that a romance connects magic and morality, but these examples hint at the ways in which courtly love can provide a foundation for that connection. A set of chivalric rules and expectations govern courtly love, and when magic enables or certifies that love, it draws on the same ethic. Lovers who are brought together by magic must then demonstrate that their relationship has qualities that satisfy the criteria of courtly love, such as an enduring devotion to each other; lovers whose relationship is tested by magic are able to show that their love can overcome extreme trials. However, the link between magic and morality is most direct in those texts in which magic takes the form of a marvel that explicitly tests chivalric virtue, allowing the hero to prove his worthiness. A hero who triumphs with the help of magic creates doubts about his own heroism;[18] overcoming a marvelous opponent or obstacle, however, provides an extreme testament in that regard.

In many cases, the test concerns the protagonist's interactions with an enchanted or transformed figure (whether as a possible lover, potential foe, or some combination of the two). The *Wife of Bath's Tale*, *Partonope of Blois*, *William of Palerne*, *Sir Gawain and the Green Knight*, and *Lybeaus Desconus* all portray marvelous figures who cannot be easily defined or categorized, and those difficulties create a moral dilemma regarding how the figures should be treated. Caroline Walker Bynum has examined the fascination with figures of hybridity and metamorphosis, suggesting that "thinkers such as Ovid or Marie de France, for whom metamorphosis provides the fundamental metaphor, tend to employ and find meaning in narrative and to plumb the possibilities and horrors of replacement-change—apotheosis, disappearance, or loss. Identity is explored via threats to it."[19]

I would add that the marvelous aspect intensifies such threats, and so the hero's response functions as an important test of his own moral identity: his ability to negotiate the dilemma of how to treat those figures within the chivalric code certifies his character. One might argue that—in an unusual reversal of gender roles—this is the test that the werewolf's wife fails in Marie de France's *Bisclavret*. The association between the marvelous and the moral, then, often plays out in the context of an intimate relationship between characters—frequently, but not always, lovers—governed by the larger ethical system of chivalry.

The Semblance and Reality of Virtue

Audiences for medieval romances would be primed to expect virtuous figures and to anticipate that their virtue would be tested in the course of the narrative.[20] Within the romance tradition, the fair unknown trope heightens those concerns because the hero's fate depends so heavily on demonstrations of his virtue—demonstrations that must be repeated and increasingly impressive before the final resolution can be reached and his identity can be revealed. Medieval discourse often follows the vector from class or occupational identity to virtue: who people are (nobles or peasants, clergymen or laymen, etc.) determines how virtuous they will or should be and which virtues they should exhibit. Observers can judge whether a person's virtue correlates appropriately with his or her identity. In the fair unknown tradition, however, the protagonist's lineage as well as his character must be confirmed in order to settle his identity. The virtues he exhibits point back to that identity, reversing the traditional vector, but it remains incomplete until the discovery of his name and/or parentage. *Lybeaus Desconus* is a particularly interesting example of how a marvel can resolve both aspects of the fair unknown identity dilemma. I will focus first on virtue: what virtues must Lybeaus demonstrate, and how can he demonstrate them convincingly? In other words, what test or obstacle is sufficient to establish his reputation?

A number of medieval romances exhibit a concern with what we might describe as the semblance of virtue. Lee H. Yearley offers a helpful definition: "a semblance of virtue exists if an agent chooses a virtuous action for consequences, such as material gain or enhanced reputation, that a nonvirtuous person would desire."[21] This definition resonates with the explanation of hypocrisy in *The Book of Vices and Virtues*: "þat is a synne þat makeþ schewe þe good wiþ-out þat is not so wiþ-ynne."[22] The concern over the connection between exterior action and interior motivation is not confined to religion; it is also central to chivalry. In *A Knight's Own Book of Chivalry*, Geoffroi de Charny outlines various types of men who are worthy when measured by their actions, but explains that the most worthy men also have worthy motives. For example, there are those who do not consider the benefit or advantage for their friends or the harm done to their enemies, but, without giving or taking advice, they ... perform personally many feats of arms.... [They] take part in many good battles without attempting to contribute in any other way, but they cannot be reproached in relation to the honor earned through bravery; and these men, who have seen so many great days of combat and made such a fine contribution by their physical exploits, should indeed be called worthy, although as for being worthy in the truest sense, it would be possible to do better.[23]

In other words, feats of bravery are admirable in their own right; when knights undertake these feats for virtuous reasons (here, for the communal rather than the individual good), they become truly worthy. The question of whether a knight has true virtue or only its semblance becomes pressing in the case of a fair unknown like Lybeaus, whose deeds are the only evidence for his character. Although medieval texts often connect appearance and virtue, fairness alone is insufficient proof of virtue; similarly, a string of triumphs over human foes or tests cannot completely resolve doubts about a knight's worthiness.

Indeed, individual agency, for Lybeaus as for other fair unknowns, is inadequate; he cannot prove his identity or his knighthood solely through his own effort, although seeking out increasingly dangerous situations does increase the chances that the necessary external validation will occur. This view may be a secular twist on Augustine's critique of pagan virtue as self-directed: pagans (and hypocrites) fail "to direct their actions to their true final end and instead [set] up themselves and their own self-image as that for the sake of which they act."[24] In Lybeaus's case, his actions are not entirely selfish, but they do work to define his "self-image" in both public and private ways. Although the text raises questions about whether his virtue is true, it does not critique his efforts to demonstrate that virtue so much as it suggests that those efforts are doomed to fall short.

The ultimate source of virtue is divine. No one can have the qualifications of high merit, Charny explains, "except purely by the grace of God and of His gentle Mother and of His heavenly court."[25] In *Lybeaus*, only another kind of supernatural intervention—magic—can confirm that virtue. Magic does not exercise the same level of power as God because it does not instill virtue; instead, it creates marvels that function as important—indeed, as the best—tests of virtue, allowing readers to distinguish the semblance from the reality. We cannot tell whether Lybeaus is truly courageous or merely behaving that way in an attempt to build his reputation until he faces something so overwhelming that any semblance of courage would fail, and so he must meet it with true virtue. Only supernatural means can create such an imposing opponent, one whose defeat so persuasively demonstrates the hero's character. Ultimately, this proof of his virtue leads to a proof of his identity, also by means of a magical marvel, and so addresses both of the audience's questions about Lybeaus.

The issue of virtue in *Lybeaus Desconus* has not yet attracted much sustained critical attention beyond the observation that it, like many other Middle English romances, tends to be more interested in morality than French sources or analogues. Stephen Knight's work is an exception; he notes that Middle English romances "show variety in form, source and topic, but they share the figure of the knight and the ethic of chivalry: all definitions of the genre, however hesitant, recognize that point of convergence." Knight suggests that although some "simply promulgate an ideology . . . naively," *Lybeaus Desconus* does so "with some complexity."[26] Chestre is more overtly moral than his sources—he makes the sorceress Dame d'Amore more clearly evil, for example.[27] The morality in the text is not reductive, however; it connects to the interest in magic, and that set of interests connects to the general fourteenth-century trend that we have been examining. Within this context, the morality lends a new dimension to the narrative and suggests resonances with other Middle English romances that approach morality in similarly complex ways.

The moral aspect is also heightened and connected to magic in *Sir Launfal*, the poem for which Chestre directly claimed authorship. Even if we do not accept the attribution of *Lybeaus* to Chestre, these two poems—along with Southern *Octavian*, discussed below—appear together in Cotton Caligula A.ii, and this shared manuscript context encourages us to examine thematic as well as stylistic connections among the texts. Chestre positions Guenevere prominently at the outset of *Sir Launfal* and establishes her immoral reputation immediately: "the lady bar los of swych word / That sche hadde lemmannys under her lord, / So fele ther nas noon ende."[28] This setup pays off in the end, when Dame Tryamour blinds the queen as a punishment for her lies: "wyth that Dame Tryamour to the quene geth, / And blew on her swych a breth / That never eft myght sche se" (1006–8). Ironically, taking away the queen's sight becomes a visual spectacle. The blinding does not appear in other versions, and its addition underscores the moral issues in the narrative.[29] Chestre also adds a more overtly moral element to the promise that Dame Tryamour exacts from Launfal, whom she directs not simply not to speak of her but to "make no bost of me" (362)—a word choice with connotations of pride and vanity. In Chestre's texts, or this subset of Cotton Caligula A.ii, moral issues are often bound up with magical practices; Dame Tryamour, for instance, is able to enact the blinding through her fairy magic. She metes out punishment as appropriately as she doled out gifts to Launfal based on his status not only as her beloved, but also as a "gentyl and hende" knight (313). Such fair restitution is exactly what Guenevere failed to accomplish earlier in the poem (67–72). In *Sir Launfal*, magic enables a reward for moral virtue and, more spectacularly, the punishment of immoral behavior via the blinding of the queen; in *Lybeaus Desconus*, spectacular magic is associated with moral virtue and identity.

The differences between the two poems are partly because of the nature of *Lybeaus Desconus* as a fair unknown narrative. Although some fair unknowns conceal their identity rather than being unaware of it, Lybeaus's true name and paternity are mysteries to him. However, the poet shares that information with readers at the outset:

> Wise of witt and a wight wereour
> A[nd] doughty man of dede.
> His name was Sir Gyngelayne,
> Gotten he was of Sir Gaweyne,
> Vnder a forest syde.[30]

The portrait is soon fleshed out with details about the protagonist's appearance—"Gyngelayne was fayre of sight, / Gentyll of body and of face bryght" (13–14)—and the reassurance that he was a "dughty childe" (24). I will discuss later the effects of this early, if not premature, revelation; here, I want to focus on the characteristics that are most closely associated with the hero: his fairness and his doughtiness.

The knight's most crucial quality is his fairness, and the poem invokes that visual quality in close proximity to the revelation of his name, suggesting that both elements are integral to his identity. Referring to him as "Lybeaus" (which could be translated as "the fair") or "Sir Lybeaus" rather than by "Lybeaus Desconus" or simply "Desconus" (which could be translated as "unknown") throughout the narrative underscores his fairness rather than his status as an unknown knight and thereby preserves this connection. Virtue and fairness were often conflated in the Middle Ages, with the latter visually signaling the former or serving as a kind of manifestation of it; fair unknown stories put this conflation to the test before reaffirming it.

Reputation, which can also be figured as one's name, is valued so significantly within romance that its delayed certification creates poignant suspense. Readers may assume that the fair unknown's identity will be proven or his character revealed, but the exact degree of testing that will allow that to occur is an open question in most narratives, including *Lybeaus Desconus*.[31]

The other characteristic similarly underscored in this initial description is Lybeaus's "doughtiness." Although it is initially presented as a single virtue, it comes to stand in for virtue more broadly and for whether Lybeaus can be understood to be a moral knight. Some romances present virtues as integrated into a cohesive whole; critics have traditionally read the pentangle in *Sir Gawain and the Green Knight*, for example, as signifying the unity of courtly and Christian virtues. For Lybeaus, however, doughtiness is not one virtue among equals but one with an emblematic value. In *The Book of Vices and Virtues*, a roughly contemporary text, "doughtiness" is one of "sixe þinges" that are considered "wel honourable," and it is specifically connected to "Goddes knyȝtes."[32] In fact, it seems to be the essential knightly virtue: "prowesse in knyȝthode is cleped douȝtynesse," and young knights must "suffre moche woo to schewen douȝtynesse."[33] In modern terms, we might refer to this as "bravery," "courage," or "boldness." The text describes a metonymic relationship between virtue and doughtiness: "vertue makeþ a man hardy as þe lioun, strong as þe olifaunt, stedefast and lestynge as þe sonne, þat euere-more renneþ and neuere is wery; þan is þer no douȝtynesse but in vertue."[34] In other words, it is not a simple matter of doughtiness being a virtue, or even being the signal virtue; virtue also makes a person brave. By extension, tests of courage might function as valid tests of virtue overall—and that is what happens with Lybeaus.

His doughtiness continues to be tested with each episode in the narrative. With each victory, his reputation builds. When Lybeaus is first awarded the quest for Lady Sinadoun by Arthur, Elene bewails that "thou wilt send a childe / That is witles and wylde / To dele eny doughty dent" (184–86), but Lybeaus's first triumph changes her mind (459–61). By the second fight, he has a reputation ("rennoun," 473) to maintain. As Lybeaus sends back his conquered opponents to Arthur's court, his reputation increases; by the time he defeats the giants, he possesses "gentill fame" (717). This cumulative process is not only about his feats, but also about the reporting of them to Arthur's court. The maiden and the dwarf who accompany the knight are the impetus for his ultimate trial but come to fulfill an important function as witnesses to, and narrators of, his triumphs along the way (1236–41 and 1725–33). The victims/defeated knights serve a similar purpose, disseminating the reputation more widely, if with less continuity (1263–65); the narrative focuses on how the knight's feats build his renown, and on the agency he exercises in creating his own fame. Although fighting other skilled opponents allows Lybeaus to demonstrate a certain level of doughtiness, only supernatural contests can create the extreme tests necessary to establish beyond all doubt that he has that virtue, not just its semblance.

Marvels in *Lybeaus Desconus*: Dame d'Amore and the Palace

Like virtue, the marvelous is a common element in romance. It is especially vital, Nicola McDonald argues, to popular romance: "what so distinguishes popular romance as a genre is the way in which it forges its meanings out of the clash between the marvellous and the mundane."[35] In fair unknown narratives, marvelous elements can serve several functions related to the knight's identity. First, they reinforce the hero's knightly status.[36] Magic protects the protagonist during all or nearly all of his exploits in *Le Bel Inconnu* and *Wigalois*, and in Thomas Malory's portrayal of Gareth, magic also keeps him disguised and facilitates his healing. Second, encountering marvelous opponents like giants and dragons allows a fair unknown to prove his worth more directly and demonstrates that the marvelous may carry negative as well as positive valences. Finally, a marvel can uncover or prompt the revelation of the knight's parentage. In *Sir Degaré*, the eponymous hero possesses a pair of gloves that were a gift from his fairy father to his mother and that will only fit her hands. When Degaré remembers—just in time—to have the beautiful princess whom he is about to marry try on the gloves, she recognizes them. She reveals herself as his mother and shares what she knows about his paternity. Later, he clashes with a fairy knight who recognizes his own lance in Degaré's hand and identifies himself as Degaré's father.

A number of scholars have seen the deployment of the marvelous in *Lybeaus Desconus* as simplistic. M. Mills suggests that Chestre has a tendency to make the "marvellous ... become matter-of-fact," and John Finlayson describes the romance as having "the air of being dependent on the marvellous, of being a fantasy, rather than any imaginative exploitation of marvels or literary sophistication."[37] In addition to employing the marvelous in ways typical of fair unknown narratives (to prove worth and uncover lineage), however, the romance uses magical characters to interrogate the relationship between exterior appearance and interior virtue. This section will examine how the hero negotiates encounters with the sorceress Dame d'Amore and a pair of clerk magicians, demonstrating his worth in increasingly challenging tests. The following section will consider how the visual marvels of the dragon lady and her transformation finally resolve Lybeaus's identity by establishing his character and his paternity, respectively.

In *Lybeaus Desconus*, the marvelous includes various types of magic, as Corinne Saunders has demonstrated.[38] The three texts often attributed to Chestre all employ marvels, but not all in supernatural forms: *Octavian* identifies several "marvels" but none is obviously magical, while the other two romances make important and varied use of magic. In *Sir Launfal*, Chestre incorporates scenes from the sources, especially *Graelent*, that add more magic to the story. Although all of the magic seems to come from the fairy Dame Tryamour, it takes different forms throughout the narrative: her appearances and disappearances over the course of seven years, a servant who becomes invisible, a purse that refills itself, and protection in battle. The significance of magic in *Lybeaus Desconus*, in contrast, becomes apparent well into the narrative, when Lybeaus falls in love with the Dame d'Amore on the Ile d'Or. This episode marks the beginning of a new phase in the tests of his virtue, one that uses magic to raise the stakes. Because he has demonstrated his virtue as much as he can in a natural context, the romance now harnesses the supernatural to enable a new level of testing. Lybeaus initially falters at this fresh challenge, falling under the Dame's spell and suspending his quest, but later reacts virtuously when encountering more threatening magic from the clerks and a more impressive marvel in the shape of the dragon lady.

At first, the Dame seems to be a typical courtly lady, if a little more forward. It is only after we have heard how Lybeaus is drawn to her for the usual reasons—beauty, status, etc.—that we learn that she knows "sorcerye" (1486). Chestre associates that magic first with music and then with her face:

> Whan he [Lybeaus] sawe hir face
> Hym thought that he was
> Jn paradice on lyve;
> With false lies and fayre
> Th[u]s she blered his eye.
> (1491–95)

This passage suggests that her beauty is an illusion, tying into the overarching interest in the relationship between appearance and virtue. The Dame's deception on this front is roundly condemned: "evill mote she thryue!" (1496).

The romance consistently demonstrates that Lybeaus has interior virtue as well as exterior beauty, and episodes along the way raise this issue in relation to other characters. In some early cases, as in the contest between the two ladies for the prize of the falcon, external appearance is a virtue in and of itself. Dame d'Amore, however, establishes why you cannot trust what you see, especially when magic is involved, and thus why Lybeaus cannot be judged a noble knight simply on the basis of his fairness. She is beautiful yet proves not to be virtuous; later, the dragon lady, who is the subject of sorcery rather than its perpetrator and whose beauty survives enchantment rather than being created by it, will show that beastliness is no more reliable an indicator of character than is fairness. *Sir Launfal* is similarly preoccupied with exterior appearances, but it skews closer to the earlier episodes in *Lybeaus* than the later ones by presenting those appearances primarily as proofs rather than as possible deceptions. Its key binary is appearance versus disappearance (or the classic presence versus absence) rather than false appearance versus true. *Lybeaus Desconus*, however, extends its concern with how characters look to examine the untrustworthiness of the information communicated by physical appearance—a moral concern that will be most vividly communicated to the readers through the marvel of the dragon lady. That approach helps the audience trust the final conclusion that Lybeaus's virtue has been sufficiently tested, and we can rest assured that, in his case, exterior and interior match.

The first magical episode derails the knight's quest and leads to "dissehonour" (1505), making it all the more appropriate that he must finally confront magical marvels to prove his honor. Elene identifies the dishonor, but her reproach suggests that the problem lies in loving a woman who knows sorcery rather than in the sorcery itself: "for the love of o woman / That mekyll of sorcery canne / Thow doste the grete dissehonour" (1503–5). This knowledge of sorcery translates into active coercion as the Dame keeps Lybeaus from his original commitment. In one version of the text, she "made" Lybeaus stay with her;[39] in another, she distracted him so completely that he "for-gate" his other companions and responsibilities (1481). Nonetheless, in this case—perhaps because of the gender of the magician, or perhaps because the visual marvel is less unusual—the effects are easily overcome; Elene's rebuke makes Lybeaus's heart "breke / For sorowe and for shame," and he immediately resumes his quest (1510–11). Despite Chestre's condemnation of the Dame, he leaves sorcery itself open to rehabilitation. It is a tool that has been employed for dishonorable ends in this case, but might have other uses.[40]

Lybeaus proceeds directly from the Ile d'Or to Sinadoun, closely linking these two magical episodes. Before we see the dragon lady, however, we witness another magical encounter. Lambard, the steward at Sinadoun, sets up the scene by revealing that the men holding the Lady are not knights, as Lybeaus expects, but "clyrkys of nigermansye" (1756), and that they have made a palace "queynte of gynne" by "nygrymauncye" and "ffayreye" (1763, 1767, and 1768). That palace lives up to Lambard's billing; when Lybeaus enters it, "off men more nor lasse / Ne sawe he body nor fface / Butt mynstralis cladde in palle" (1848–50). The music is vaguely otherworldly—"suche maner mynstralsye / Was neuer with-in wall" (1855–56)—and so is the hall itself, which is "wrought with jmagerye" so wondrous that "nowher none fayrer nas / That he hade seyne withe eye" (1871 and 1873–74). The setting becomes overtly and threateningly magical when the torches go out, the minstrels disappear, and the hall begins to "shake" and "quake" (1887 and 1888). The heavy invocation of magic and the multisensory description of the marvelous palace signal the importance of the episode that is about to unfold.

In this strange space, however, a familiar kind of knightly encounter plays out. Lybeaus enters the castle "egir" to know "who shulde with hym fight" (1861 and 1862)—a question that, especially in this romance that is preoccupied with identity and character, hints at a curiosity about the natures as well as the names of his opponents. But the magicians appear as typical "men in armes twayne" (1901), and one verbally challenges Lybeaus. Similarly, the hall—which the poem has firmly established as otherworldly—becomes a standard "felde" on which they battle (1899). The narrator provides details about the armor and horses as well as the hard-fought blows as an entirely traditional, if somewhat lopsided, joust unfolds between the knight and two necromancers inside their magical castle. One version of the poem highlights the resemblance of the fight to those in other narratives, saying that "thei fyght, / As gestours tellys at bord."[41]

When Mabon confesses to having "venymed" the swords (2022), Lybeaus simply resolves to fight harder:

> "J will nought of thi yefte,
> For all this worlde to wynne;
> But lay on strokys swyfte:
> One of vs shall other lefte
> The hede by the chynne!"
> (2026–30)

Fighting with renewed vigor, he kills Mabon and turns his attention to Yrayne—who has disappeared. It is only now, when combat has effectively ended, that sorcery clearly enters into it. This disappearance causes Lybeaus to worry that "he will with sorcerye / Do me tormentrye: / That is my moste care" (2055–57). This concern reappears after the lady has been disenchanted; as Lybeaus mounts his horse to leave the castle, he is "glad and blythe," but "sore [he] dradded Jrayne / For he was noght j-slayne, / With speche lyste he do him spylle" (2115 and 2118–20).

The resolution to this persistent concern is anticlimactic; when Lybeaus tells the story to a wider audience, he describes the lady's praise for his feats. "My fone thou haste slayne, / Mabon and Yrayne," he reports her as saying (2139–40). Critics have noted this inconsistency and seen it as evidence of Chestre's shortcomings as a poet, although they have also acknowledged that "an uncertainty about the fate of the second enchanter ... was of very long standing in the story of Lybeaus."[42] I wonder if we might read this element differently. The absence of magic in the fight paradoxically underscores the importance of the magic: the primary difference between this fight and all of Lybeaus's previous ones is that the possibility of magic is vividly invoked.[43] By bookending an otherwise apparently traditional fight with reminders of the magical settings and characters that make it different, the poem highlights the clerks' magic as a significant threat. The confusion over Yrayne's fate allows this impression to linger, deepening our sense of magical potential and involvement.

Because the marvelous setting gives way to a more familiar one, and because the threat of magical combat never fully materializes, this confrontation does not provide the final confirmation of Lybeaus's virtue. However, this episode does begin to resolve doubt over his doughtiness. His eagerness to fight the clerks after learning their nature is one sign of his courage, and his redoubled vigor after learning of the poisoned swords is another. In describing that final head-to-head with Mabon, the narrator tells us definitively, "Lybeous was more of myght" (2034). After slaying Mabon, Lybeaus's fervor is unabated: "J tell you for certayne, / To fight more hym lyste!" (2041–42). Chestre's version heightens the stakes in terms of traditional combat by making Lybeaus fight the clerks simultaneously rather than sequentially, as he does in other versions, but avoids the obviously magical elements—including a fire-breathing horse and a knight whose body emits smoke and slime after being beheaded—that mark *Le Bel Inconnu*'s portrayal of the fight.

The fact that Lybeaus's doughtiness and skill hold up under the constant, if ultimately unrealized, threat of magic marks them as impressive. A different kind of magic—one that involves more spectacular visual marvels and more complex moral issues—will be required to prove absolutely both his virtue and his identity. At the same time, the fact that the clerks do not use magic in the fight continues to preserve magic's status as a neutral force. This depiction of magic allows the dragon lady to transition from being a fearsome creature that Lybeaus must confront to an enchanted lady whose transformation credibly demonstrates his lineage.

The Marvel of the Dragon Lady

Because of her critical role in the narrative and because Chestre's portrayal of her differs from those in the analogues, the dragon lady features prominently in the relatively scanty critical history of *Lybeaus Desconus*. James Weldon examines "the serpent-woman enchantment and the naked disenchantment" as "Chestre's original contributions to the fair unknown story" and reads these elements as commenting on "the legal issue of female marital consent."[44] Susan Crane connects the character to the same shape-shifting tradition that included the loathly lady narratives, and Eve Salisbury sees her as representing the monstrous-feminine.[45] Stephen Knight focuses on the social ramifications of her transformation: "Released by the hero's courage, the lady turns from an enchanted serpent into a submissive wife. From a sexually hideous and threatening Lamia she becomes the ideal and property-bearing wife."[46] What interests me most about the transformation scene is its position at the crux of the narrative: why does the marvel of the dragon lady's transformation resolve the questions about the knight's nobility and identity that his many earlier exploits could not?

The dragon lady's appearance—which follows close on the heels of Yrayne's disappearance—is the foundation for that spectacle:

> As he [Lybeaus] sate thus in halle,
> Oute at a stone walle
> A wyndowe fayre vnfelde;
> Grete wondyr with-all
> Jn his herte ganne falle
> And he sate and be-helde.
> A worme ther ganne oute-pas
> With a womanes face:
> "Yonge Y am and nothinge olde."
> Hir body and hir wyngis
> Shone in all [þ]ynchis,
> As amell gaye and gilte.

Hir tayle was mekyll vnnethe,
Hir peynis gryme and grete,
As ye may listen and lere.
(2061–75)

All eyes—Lybeaus's as well as the readers'—are drawn to the creature, her physical presence, and her behavior in this scene. The dragon lady invokes the poem's interest in appearance as tied to character, but her figure also reveals the poem's investment in visual marvel. The climax of the narrative—and the resolution of the knight's twofold quest to rescue the Lady of Sinadoun and establish his own reputation—rests on the representation of the creature's spectacular appearance.[47] Dame Tryamour's spectacular appearance at the climax of *Sir Launfal* fulfills a similar purpose by certifying Launfal's claims about the nature of his beloved, although it is her beauty rather than her beastliness that impresses.

By representing the "worme" with a "womanes face" when other known versions simply have a worm, Chestre underscores the creature's enchanted nature: this form could only be the result of supernatural agency. The juxtaposition also highlights the other contradictory elements in the creature's appearance. Her wings are "gaye and gilte," for instance, but also "gryme and grete." She is a hybrid figure rather than one who has fully transformed (in physical appearance, at least) from human to creature; her body mingles the exotic and the familiar, the attractive and the frightening. In the long term, the woman's face makes the coming kiss seem less threatening or shocking, and sets us up for the resolution, in which Lybeaus and the lady will marry. In the short term, however, that face makes the creature more perplexing and therefore a greater test for Lybeaus. Rather than fighting a dragon, he must figure out how to react to a creature that seems to call for violence on the one hand and chivalry on the other. This conundrum may explain his paralysis when confronted with the dragon lady: the ethical system in which he participates offers no clear guidance on the appropriate reaction, and he struggles to make a moral choice in the face of this unusual and immediate situation.

Whereas earlier events in the magical castle left Lybeaus "dismayed" (1893) and full of "care" (2057), this creature inspires "grete wondyr"—partly because of these irreconcilable elements and conflicting signals. As we saw in the previous chapter, a wonder reaction indicates deep engagement and includes cognitive as well as affective components. In addition to feeling wonder, however, Lybeaus is "so sore … agaste / Hym thought his herte to-braste" (2079–80) as the creature approaches. This reaction leaves him curiously passive for the crucial moment in the poem: "and ere that Lybeous wiste, / The worme with mouth him kyste / And clypped aboute the swyre" (2082–84). The detail that the worm kissed him "with mouth" reminds us of the hybrid nature of the creature and hints that we are witnessing a kiss between Lybeaus and the enchanted lady rather than a beast.[48]

Given what I have argued about Lybeaus's virtue, his passivity in this moment seems peculiar. In the French version, the serpent signals to the knight not to kill her, but in Chestre's version Lybeaus seems paralyzed by the sight of her. However much courage and virtue he has shown up to this point, the serpent woman seems to undermine that before paradoxically proclaiming his nobility. As Crane observes, "Lybeaus's passivity and fear before the serpent are startlingly inappropriate to the combat he was engaging... yet his passivity and fear are necessary to the adventure's happy resolution in that they prevent him from killing or driving off the enchanted woman. She, in turn, quickly glosses Lybeaus's incapacity as a heroic action she must reward.... Lybeaus's momentary incapacity thus leads to establishing his identity as Gawain's son and to winning a wife and property."[49]

This passivity is necessary for the narrative to move forward, but we might read it as a moral reaction as well as a narrative expedient; in other words, not resorting to violence may be a further sign of Lybeaus's virtue. The fact that the worm bears a woman's face, which perhaps makes the signal not to kill her unnecessary, strengthens this possibility. We can identify another specific virtue in play here: courtesy. *The Book of Vices and Virtues* suggests that, in addition to doughtiness, courtesy is a fundamental quality of knighthood: a "newe knyȝt... schapeþ to be curteis."[50] Facing the dragon lady requires Lybeaus to display both virtues appropriately. As I explain in the next chapter, the tests he undergoes resemble in some ways the trials in *Sir Gawain and the Green Knight*: Gawain must also confront a magically transformed figure and display courtesy as well as courage.

However, the poem clearly indicates that Lybeaus's reaction—like Gawain's in the Green Chapel—is tinged with fear. In both cases, the knight's ability to remain still is itself a sign of courage; a lesser knight would likely have fled. *The Book of John Mandeville* describes a situation akin to what Lybeaus faces as an explicit test of knightly virtue: a woman whom Diana has transformed into a dragon is destined to "dwelle so into the tyme that a knyght come that is so hardy that der go to hure and kysse here mouth." One "doughti and hardy" knight resolves to kiss her, but when he "say the huge beest he fled away." A second man sees her unenchanted form and gets knighted for the express purpose of rescuing her and thereby obtaining riches and lands, but when "he saw her come out of her cave in shap of a dragon he hadde so greet drede that he fleyghe." Note the emphasis on the visual spectacle in both cases: the sight of the dragon overwhelms the men's courage, despite their knowledge of her true form. These men prove to have the semblance of extraordinary virtue rather than the reality. According to Mandeville, no knight has yet had the necessary courage, and so the challenge remains unmet, but "when a knyght cometh that is so hardy to kysse hure mouth, he shal turne that damysel to hure owen shappe."⁵¹ As we have seen and will return to below, Chestre also draws attention to his dragon lady's "mouth," which appears in her human face.

A similar episode—with a similar emphasis on the fearsome appearance of the dragon—occurs in the twelfth-century German romance *Lanzelet*. Here, kissing the dragon is not merely a test of knightly courage but the ultimate test of the ultimate knight's virtue. Lanzelet performs the "audacious kiss," allowing the lady to return to her human self, and this act of courage marks him as "the best knight now alive." The narrator later underscores this point: "through this it was proven, when the maiden was thus transformed, that there was no knight so excellent as Lanzelet as long as he lived." The key proof is his doughtiness, which is literally inimitable: "the dauntless Lanzelet ... acted so valiantly that he dared undertake that which has never been done again."⁵² The hero, who began the romance as a fair unknown, learns his identity halfway through the romance, but it is not until he passes this definitive magical test of virtue that Lanzelet moves to reclaim his patrimony and thereby initiates the resolution of the story.

As a spectacularly magical figure, the dragon lady in *Lybeaus* presents a greater challenge than did the clerks, whose magic never manifested itself during their fight, and Lybeaus passes this ultimate test of courage by seeking out and facing her rather than fleeing. However, Lybeaus still needs an external authority to provide the necessary information about his identity. He has done all that he can do, and he—like the reader—awaits the final step that is beyond his control. That affirmation comes immediately after the kiss, when the dragon lady regains her human shape and gives a pivotal speech. She reminds us of Lybeaus's actions and the proofs that he has offered before finally offering the information that is necessary for interpreting her transformation as a sign of his identity. The passage is worth quoting at length:

> And aftyr this kyssynge
> Off the worme tayle and wynge
> Swyftly fell hir froo:

> So fayre, of all thinke,
> Woman, with-oute lesynge,
> Sawe he neuer ere thoo;
> But she was moder naked,
> As God had hir maked:
> The[r]for was Lybeous woo.
> She sayde, "Knyght gentyll,
> God yelde the thi wille
> My foon thou woldest sloo!
>
> Thowe haste slayne nowthe
> Two clerkys kowthe,
> That wroughten by the fende.
> Este, west, northe and sowthe,
> With maystres of her mouthe,
> Many man con they shende.
> Thorowe ther chauntement
> To a worme they had me went,
> Jn wo to leven and lende,
> Tyll [J] had kyssed Gaweyne,
> That is doughti knyght, certayne,
> Or some of his kynde."
> (2085–108)

Notice that the necromancers' "mouthe[s]" are the source of their "chauntement," while the dragon lady's and Lybeaus's are the means of undoing the magic. Their kiss causes the marvelous transformation that certifies his identity, but her speech, I contend, provides an important complement.

The kiss leads to a double disclosure of identities. First, the lady's true form is revealed—and revealed in all of its particulars, since she appears "moder naked, / As God had hir maked." As a hybrid creature, her identity may be more in question than Lybeaus's, and the revelation of that identity is correspondingly spectacular, perhaps explaining the relatively detailed description of this transformation compared with many others in Middle English. A serpentine shedding of skin exposes her human form: "off the worme tayle and wynge / Swyftly fell hir froo." This outcome is the instant effect of the kiss. The first revelation sets readers up for the second, when the lady explains the cause behind her transformation: she would be a "worme" until she "kyssed Gaweyne / . . . / Or some of his kynde." Whereas magic prompts the discoveries of the hero's parentage in *Sir Degaré*, here magic proves Lybeaus's identity directly, and he undergoes a metamorphosis as surely as the lady of Sinadoun does, albeit less visibly. By establishing his status as Gawain's son, the unenchanted lady effects the final stage of the transformation that has motivated the entire narrative, moving Lybeaus from fair unknown to known and named knight.

We might have some doubt about the specificity of the revelation; after all, the lady names Lybeaus as Gawain's "kynde" rather than his son. A number of factors support the reading of this moment as the central revelation, however. First, "kynde" could mean "offspring" as well as "kindred." Additionally, it can designate one's "essential" or "inherent character."[53] We can therefore see this usage not as confusing or imprecise but as uniting the twin concerns of the poem: Lybeaus's character and identity. Second, the poem disclosed Lybeaus's specific identity near the outset: "his name was Sir Gyngelayne, / Gotten he was of Sir Gaweyne" (7–8). This information, along with the fact that the knight is the son of Gawain in related narratives, guides our interpretation of "kynde" and alleviates the need to reiterate details that might detract from the action in this critical moment. Third, while some manuscripts reaffirm Lybeaus's identity through a later speech by his mother or Gawain, the two manuscripts generally believed to be the best—Lambeth Palace 306 and Cotton Caligula A.ii—do not, suggesting that the mystery has been sufficiently resolved by the lady's transformation and speech.[54]

If we look closely at the lady's speech, then we will see that it does much more than reveal Lybeaus's paternity. She begins by praising his defeat of the clerks, whom she casts as formidable opponents. This victory helps to establish his virtue as the grounds for his identity, which she then names and associates with the key knightly quality of "doughti[ness]." As she continues, she extends that identity. Now Lybeaus becomes not only Gawain's son, but also a landowner and the future husband of the lady herself:

> Syr, for thou savyst my lyfe,
> Castellys fifty and five
> Take Y will the till,
> And my-sylfe to be thy wyfe.
> (2109–12)

As Salisbury points out, the English version of the narrative demonstrates a "sharpened focus on marriage and Lybeaus' acquisition of legitimacy" compared to the French version.[55] Marriage plays a key role in the resolution of other fair unknowns' identities as well, as in *Sir Perceval of Galles* and

Malory's "Tale of Gareth," in which marriage serves as the final sign that Gareth has proven himself. In this case, it may be that "husband to the former dragon lady of Sinadoun" is a more distinctive identity than "illegitimate son of Gawain"—the former comes with significant property, is a sign of the feats Lybeaus has accomplished, and draws on arguably the most memorable and vividly portrayed character in the narrative. In its privileging of the lady's role, the poem resembles another serpent-woman story, *Melusine*, in which the bride more actively helps her husband establish a dynasty by advising him about how to acquire lands, building fortresses and churches, and producing sons. In both narratives, the husband's noble identity provides a necessary foundation for such expansion. The ways in which the lady reshapes Lybeaus's identity depend on the initial discovery: these outcomes are fitting for a son of Gawain, and that paternal lineage allows him to undo the enchantment and leads to his other roles as landowner, lord, and husband.[56]

Lybeaus himself furthers this process when he reports back to the people of Sinadoun. His speech begins with the same emphasis as the lady's and fuses her words with his. Because the reports of his exploits have been so important to the story, and because this is the first time that Lybeaus offers his own report, this speech signals both that a critical point has been passed in the development of his reputation and that, in its new form, his reputation is deeply intertwined with the lady's. Here we have another reason that the early mention of Lybeaus's name does not render this scene anticlimactic for the reader: because his identity develops so significantly over the course of this speech, any later mention of Lybeaus as Gawain's son Gyngelan would be regressive. He has already moved beyond that role.

The establishment of Lybeaus's identity allows the narrative to end, but critics are divided over precisely how he proves it. Crane points out that the proof is not a single event: "Lybeaus's identity consists in the recognition he wins from the court, from Arthur as much as from his lost father Gawain."[57] Helen Cooper also suggests that there is a kind of aggregate effect: Lybeaus's "innate nobility [is] confirmed by action, by recognition, and by the touchstone of magic."[58] Ilan Mitchell-Smith reads Lybeaus's journey as an education in how to use the appropriate amount of violence against different types of foes.[59] Although it is the set of magical events that seems to lead to the establishment of Lybeaus's courage (by defeating the two sorcerers) and paternity (by reversing the lady's enchantment, which only a man of Gawain's kin could do), scholars are also divided over the role of the magic in the resolution of the romance. Linda Marie Zaerr argues that "sorcery is not the important part of the challenge Lybeaus faces," whereas

James Weldon interprets "Chestre's disenchantment scene" as "push[ing] the story beyond the theme of the hero's identity."⁶⁰

In the reading that I have outlined, however, magic is the critical element in both testing Lybeaus's virtue and uncovering his identity. His physical appearance—since he is, after all, the *fair* unknown—has hinted at his nobility from the outset. Throughout the narrative, all of his actions demonstrate his virtue, but the most conclusive proofs come in his reactions to the magical figures, the magicians, and, especially, the dragon lady. He has true "doughti[ness]," not merely its semblance. These proofs, however, do not help to pin down his specific identity. That question can only be settled through a revelation of knowledge, whether by natural or supernatural means; the poem employs a visual and magical spectacle to that end.

It is hard to imagine that a nonsupernatural or nonspectacular device could serve the same function, given the narrative pressure that has built up to this point, more than two thousand lines into the poem. Indeed, other fair unknown narratives rely on marvelous sources for this type of information: a disembodied voice, later attributed to a fairy, reveals the hero's identity in *Le Bel Inconnu*, and a figure in Purgatory who transforms from beast to man reveals it in *Wigalois*. We can see a similar pattern in one of the other poems generally attributed to Chestre, the Southern *Octavian*. Although not a fair unknown narrative, it does take up the question of whether two brothers will live up to their royal lineage. The brothers are separated from each other and from their father, the emperor; while Octavian grows up with his mother, Florent is raised by Clement the butcher. A marvel affirms the special nature of each brother: Florent defeats an imposing giant, and a lioness accompanies Octavian, nursing him when he is young and fighting alongside him in battle when he is older. Neither of these marvels is overtly supernatural, however. I would suggest that magic is less necessary in these cases because the brothers' identities are well known within the narrative (unlike Lybeaus's, which is revealed only to the reader). Their paternity is established at the outset, in part to make clear that accusations about the infidelity of the emperor's wife are false, and when they are separated from their family, they still carry their names with them. The question, then, is not about their lineage but about their natures, and the natural marvels are sufficient to confirm their special status. Magic becomes crucial when the stakes are higher, when the narrative must discover identity and certify virtue rather than reinforce what is known or expected.

Magic is easily adapted to this role because, in addition to its supernatural and spectacular nature, it was associated with knowledge and often performed by educated practitioners. Although sorcery might also carry negative connotations, the text has depicted magic as a neutral element. The transformation scene downplays any such connotations by using the lady as the intermediary for the magic and by making her disenchantment—the undoing of the magic—the means by which Lybeaus's paternity is certified. The magic involved in the transformation has an almost objective aura that gives it authoritative weight. The lady's "chauntement" and its conditions were established long before Lybeaus arrived, and, although fortuitous in narrative terms, it appears to work as a mechanism set in place with a trigger whose conditions Lybeaus happens to satisfy. The process is a straightforward matter of cause and effect. People might be mistaken, but this marvelous proof seems indisputable.

That ultimate proof is the dragon lady's body. Women's bodies were often mechanisms of temptation or testing in romance, either in beautiful or loathly forms. The dragon lady's body is a focus of this romance, reflecting both the narrative function of the former and the generic conventions of the latter. Her form is the crux of the poem, which makes it all the more interesting that Chestre altered that form by giving the worm a woman's face. I discussed above how this hybridity heightened the spectacle and created a special challenge for Lybeaus, but the specific nature of this change also affects how we view the lady and her role as the agent for the revelation of his identity. The dragon lady's representation prompts readers to set aside any doubts about Lybeaus's identity, in terms of character as well as paternity, and to ponder the relationship between appearance and virtue in a variety of contexts.

Perhaps the most obvious result of Chestre's alteration is the suggestion of a parallel between the dragon lady and Eve or the serpent from Genesis.[61] Portrayals of Adam, Eve, and the serpent in medieval art sometimes gave the serpent a female face—usually one that reflected Eve's. However, the dragon lady embodies redemption rather than temptation, and, as E. Jane Burns points out, woman-headed serpents do not have "the problematic woman's lower body that plagues Eve."[62] Here, the figure ties into the theme that physical appearance, whether attractive or repellent, does not reflect the interior character of either women or men. The allusions to the serpent and to Eve heighten the problem of the lady's appearance. Nonetheless, any resemblance falls away with her wings and tail which prove to be unrelated to her character, which is trustworthy and virtuous within the context of the poem and qualifies her as a fitting partner for Lybeaus. Her situation developed through no fault of her own, distinguishing her both from Eve and from other medieval serpent-women, such as those in *Lanzelet* and

Melusine, whose enchanted forms were punishments for moral failings such as mistreating a would-be lover or a father. After her transformation, however, Melusine quickly becomes the primary moral agent in that narrative and another example of a virtuous serpent-woman.

Melusine assumes her hybrid shape for one day a week and remains a woman from the waist up, but the enchanted lady of Sinadoun keeps only "a womanes face" (2068). The ambiguous phrasing initially leaves open the possibility that the worm has "a" woman's face but not necessarily the face of the lady. However, the process of undoing the enchantment has no apparent effect on her visage, suggesting that what we have seen all along is the lady's human face. We might see the preservation of her face as a reminder of how "the female body is a materialization of monstrosity of which others are iterations: it is the monstrous body from which all bodies—monstrous or not—emerge, and from which all identities must cleave."[63] In this context, however, I argue that retaining her face signals that the lady has maintained her identity throughout the enchantment. Crane persuasively argues that "shape-shifting paradoxically figures constancy rather than mobility, an integrity of the self,"[64] and the constancy of the woman's face within her changing body offers unusual visual evidence of that integrity. The fact that her people have heard and recognized her voice, despite being unable to see her within the castle, further underscores her continuity of self (1773–75).

Because she is both substantially enchanted and fundamentally herself, the lady can mediate between the magical and nonmagical contexts, bringing back information from the former into the latter. This mixed nature also increases her credibility as the one who discloses Lybeaus's identity: she is able to rely on the authority provided by the supernatural knowledge that results from the magic, but she herself is untainted by any negative aspects of the magic. Eve Salisbury has suggested that Lybeaus's rather hasty departure after the lady's disenchantment may indicate that he still sees her as a potential monster.[65] I would note that the abruptness of his exit forms an instructive contrast with his dalliance with the Dame d'Amore: her sorcery prevented him from leaving, but the Lady of Sinadoun exercises no such powers. This detail eases any potential concern that the lady will suffer long-term effects from her enchantment that might prove problematic in the happily-ever-after ending that the poem constructs for her and Lybeaus.[66] She is not, in other words, another Heurodis.

My interpretation of the dragon lady focuses on the marvelous rather than the monstrous, which has been adeptly explored by Salisbury and other scholars, but those two discourses intersect on issues of identity. Because monstrous bodies can destabilize identity, the involvement of a partly or potentially monstrous figure might seem more likely to undermine than verify Lybeaus's identity. Monsters "are disturbing hybrids whose externally incoherent bodies resist attempts to include them in any systematic structuration," writes Jeffrey Jerome Cohen, "and so the monster is dangerous, a form suspended between forms that threatens to smash distinctions."[67] A female monster exacerbates the problem; as Sarah Alison Miller argues, "the most troubling, most secret, and most transformative facet of female monstrosity—that meaning communicated by its dissolving corporeal margins—is that its porous borders *fail* the monster's task of bringing into shape the contours of the clean and proper self, precisely because they are the very porous borders from which the self must clumsily cleave."[68] However, because the dragon lady retains some visual aspect of her own identity, and because the narrative casts her enchanted body as a litmus test for Gawain's kin, her transformation becomes the decisive confirmation of Lybeaus's identity. Although her hybrid body may threaten identity construction more generally, her return to a fully human form restores not only her own singular self, but also Lybeaus's long-lost identity, and those restorations are all the more authoritative because of the earlier mystery about both of their identities. This development encourages readers to wonder about the complex connections between self and other as well as between semblance and reality.

The dragon lady episode also shows the evolving attitude of the poem toward the nature and utility of magic. It functioned as a deceptive illusion that jeopardized the knight's honor in the episode with the Dame d'Amore, an as intimidating threat that required courage in the fight against the magicians, and, finally, as the authoritative source that satisfied the central mysteries of the poem. As practiced by the Dame and the clerks, magic involved secret and powerful knowledge; as embodied by the dragon lady, magic slips from intimidating to wondrous but retains that essential connection to knowledge. That shift serves the purposes of the narrative, which relies on magic to be both the final test of courage and the source of reliable revelations. *Lybeaus Desconus* makes careful use of magic spectacle and deftly connects it not only to personal virtue, but also to the fundamental issue of identity, adding a new element to the fourteenth century's interest in the relationship among magic, spectacle, and morality. The next chapter will demonstrate that marvels that test a knight's virtue can also interrogate the nature of virtue itself, raising questions about how moral and marvelous agency interact. As the concerns increase in scope, the marvels increase in intensity.

CHAPTER THREE

MOVING MARVELS

Action and Agency in Courtly Spectacles

In the fourteenth century, marvels of various types were becoming widespread in European courts as well as in courtly texts like *Sir Orfeo* and *Lybeaus Desconus*.[1] The most famous example of the former is the garden at Hesdin, where various mechanical figures and water-spouting devices delighted guests.[2] In England, courtly marvels in both contexts peaked during the reign of Richard II, which was closely associated with spectacle; as Gordon Kipling notes, "whether we look to the tournament, the royal entry, or the pageant play, . . . Richard's reign witnessed an extraordinary efflorescence of civic pageantry and courtly spectacle."[3] Richard's coronation pageant—the first known of its kind, or at least the first for which we have such detailed descriptions—was one such spectacle.

As he approached the Cheap, Richard encountered a "somercastell,"[4] or pageant tower, with four damsels on top, who were scattering gold coins. The *Chronicon Angliae* describes the marvel that literally and figuratively capped this spectacle: "upon the castle's pinnacle, which had been erected between the four turrets, in the manner of a belfry, had been set a golden angel, bearing a golden crown in its hands, which was constructed with such ingenuity that, upon the king's coming forth, bending down, it reached out the crown towards him. There were discovered that day in the city moreover numerous other devices, in honor of the king, which would take too long to enumerate singly here."[5] Thus, as Scott Lightsey observes, Richard became "England's first monarch to be crowned by a mechanical marvel."[6] Although this moment, and the procession as a whole, surely provided entertainment for the young Richard as well as the witnesses, the automaton also serves significant political purposes. It reinforces the status of the king-to-be in a publicly visible and particularly memorable way—a seal of approval that might loosely be connected to the dragon lady's more intimate certification of Lybeaus's identity and status, discussed in the previous chapter. Lightsey, who examines this automaton at length, teases out its social and theoretical implications as well as its relationship to the similar angel in *Piers Plowman*; here, I focus instead on the nature of the marvel itself and what it suggests about how a Ricardian courtly audience might be prepared to interpret marvels in other media.

The golden angel is clearly a mechanical rather than a magical marvel. Those categories might be closer in the Middle Ages than today,[7] but the reference to the angel's ingenious construction and the allusion to "other devices [alia multa]" that were "adinventa"—"found" or, possibly, "invented"—indicate that the audience understood it to be created by technology rather than sorcery. The materials for the pageant tower appear in the goldsmiths' guild's record books, in which the term "somercastell" connects the structure to siege engines;[8] these records further certify the pageant's nature as crafted in the physical rather than the supernatural sense. The distinction is also apparent in the reactions that the angel provokes: it is the mechanical aspect that so impresses, and more specifically, the fact that the figure moves (it "was constructed with such ingenuity that ... bending down, it reached out the crown towards him [qui tali ingenio factus fuerat, ut ... coronam porrigeret inclinando]").

The angel's actions create the appearance of responsiveness and therefore agency. The description acknowledges that the angel was "set [positus erat]" and "constructed [factus fuerat]" by human hands, which makes it all the more startling that Richard's approach seems to activate the movement ("upon the king's coming forth [adventanti regi]"). This encounter follows the general pattern of events in this section: the king's initial appearance prompted the maidens to scatter golden leaves; as he drew nearer, they threw coins; and when he approached the castle, they offered cups of wine.[9] We might also remember that this angel appears on a moveable tower and to a traveling procession. Although many marvels were apprehended in a single glimpse or consisted of a static sight (like the Fairy King's gallery in *Sir Orfeo*), the marvelous aura in this case depends on motion that creates a narrative effect. In this highly mobile context, a stationary golden angel would not have produced the same reaction or carried the same significance.

The dependence on motion creates a paradox for mechanical marvels: the very fact that they can be experienced—and replicated—on demand contributes to the wonder that they arouse, but the process of repetition must eventually dull that wonder. In this respect, the angel comes closer to the magical marvels that are my focus. Although magical marvels could, in theory, be replicated, they rarely were, and much of their impact derived from their singularity. The angel on the pageant tower is also singular: it has been created for this one moment, this one action, this one king. It will not be crowning anyone else, and its singularity transfers to Richard, who is thereby recognized as the sole legitimate heir and ruler. Unlike the other elements in the description—the leaves, the coins, the maidens, and the other devices—there is only one angel; similarly, although Richard is accompanied by lords and watched by the crowds, he is the only king-in-the-making.

This coronation is not, however, his only one: the angel's gesture will be repeated the next day by the archbishop and the earl of March in Westminster Abbey. This procession will also not be the only spectacular one in Richard's reign. Similar events occur with the arrival of Anne of Bohemia and the reconciliation of London, and in both of those processions, we have echoes of the angel atop the castle. This feature was so well received, in fact, that "the heavenly castle became the single most popular pageant structure in the repertoire of the civic triumph."[10] Later in Richard II's reign, as well as in some other instances, the angels seem to be people in costume rather than automata.[11] In Maidstone's *Concordia*, which describes Richard's royal entry in 1392, the movement of the figures remains marvelous:

> They now descend, the young man and the girl as well;
> There was no ladder, nor could any steps be seen.
> They came enwrapped in clouds, suspended in the air,
> But what device was used, believe me, I don't know![12]

Although it involves mysterious motion, the character of this marvel is fundamentally different. The figures themselves are human and present a dual rather than a singular effect. The emphasis ultimately falls on the objects that they present—especially a pair of crowns that were "finely fashioned out of gleaming brand new gold" and of which "the workmanship surpassed the substance, as was shown / By novel subtlety of artist and of art"—rather than on the marvelous agent and its coronation act, as in the original instance.[13] The ways in which the mechanical marvel is echoed, first by the formal coronation and later by other instances of pageantry, seem to enhance rather than diminish its significance; it prefigures the main event in the first case (or, as Lightsey argues, may have enacted an alternate version of it for this different audience)[14] and becomes the key reference in the second, the source to which the later reenactments implicitly point.

One reason that the motif may have become so popular is that it stretches back beyond the coronation procession to an important set of religious references. The religious overtones of the angel are obvious, but Kipling has argued that the larger pageant invoked both New Jerusalem and advent, and that the king was thereby positioned as the Christ figure.[15] Medieval audiences would have been well practiced in interpreting religious marvels, and the angel automaton mingles the religious and the marvelous in ways that not only highlight but also help to create the youthful Richard's kingly identity and authority. The angel functions as the central marvel of the coronation procession and perhaps, we might argue, of the full slate of coronation events. In the emphasis on its motion, the singularity that persists through reenactment, and the ties to religious iconography, it parallels another courtly marvel that carries similarly complex undertones: the Green Knight in *Sir Gawain and the Green Knight*. And like the angel, the Green Knight is positioned within a contextual framework—here, the Cotton Nero A.x manuscript—featuring marvelous spectacles of various types that its courtly audience would be able and expected to interpret carefully.

Seeing Marvels

Before turning to the text, I want to consider in more detail how marvels might have been seen, literally and figuratively. We explored in the first chapter some of the ways in which visual descriptions of marvels could encourage a response of wonder with affective, cognitive, and moral elements; here, we will examine the philosophical and scientific discourses relevant to the experience of seeing a marvel—an experience becoming more common in late medieval Britain. Two trends related to visuality are particularly significant in this regard: evolving theories about how vision constructed the relationship between subject and object (and, ultimately, about the agency of the viewer) and the increasing presence of spectacle in religious as well as courtly contexts. The fourteenth century lies at the conjunction of those trends. Theories of vision changed over the course of the thirteenth and fourteenth centuries as medieval thinkers began to embrace the intromission over the extramission theory—emphasizing the viewer's interpretive role—and both religious and courtly spectacles became more popular and elaborate from the fourteenth century into the fifteenth. Late medieval romances could take advantage of these developments by portraying magic in strongly visual terms and relying on the audience to interpret such spectacles attentively; in *Sir Gawain and the Green Knight*, we can also see the marvels as they were imagined and interpreted in manuscript illuminations.

Spectacles were central to literature and society in this period; as Sarah Stanbury has observed, late medieval England "was attuned to and even troubled by its 'culture of the spectacle.'"[16] The coronation procession discussed above is one example of how the royal court staged ceremonies and events, often on a vast scale, to serve a number of purposes, from demonstrating power to dispensing justice to providing entertainment. Technological marvels and automata, including clocks, table fountains, optical-illusion-producing mirrors, and mechanical people, animals, and trees, as well as Richard's crowning angel, appeared in European courts during the thirteenth and fourteenth centuries along with more familiar spectacles such as jousts, battles, and feasts.[17] Spectacle—whether performed, as in religious ceremonies or cycle drama, or represented through visual imagery—was also vital to the Church and especially the affective piety movement. That use of spectacle would famously become a point of contention in Lollardy and, later, the Reformation.

Most recent scholarship concerning representations of and reactions to medieval spectacle emphasizes either political and urban ceremonies or religious imagery. Critics treating the former have primarily examined the multivalent forms that ceremonies take and the purposes they serve;[18] critics studying the latter have done so chiefly in the context of the image debates from the late fourteenth and fifteenth centuries, which disputed the didactic dimension of religious imagery.[19] In other words, scholars have focused on either secular spectacle or religious didacticism. These two strands of thought come together in the case of literary marvels that were both spectacular and didactic, a combination of qualities that fit with evolving ideas about how sight worked.

The idea that religious images could be instructive is often traced back to Gregory the Great, who chided Serenus, bishop of Marseilles, for destroying statues of the saints in 600. "For what writing provides for readers," Gregory wrote, "this a picture provides for uneducated people looking at it, for in it the ignorant see what they should follow and the illiterate read the same from it."[20] However, the shift from extramission to intromission reconfigured the relationship between viewer and visual object more broadly. Extramission, which emphasized the determining role of the seeing subject, dominated the early and high Middle Ages, but intromission, which elevated the significance of the object, became the late medieval model of vision, gaining dominance roughly in parallel with the development of poignant devotional images associated with affective piety. This shift in models did not merely reflect a change in ideas about how vision worked, then; it also affected how people designed and produced images. As Michael Camille explains, intromission "took the emphasis away from vision and [put it] onto the power of images themselves," a transfer of agency from subject to object.[21] Rather than the subject's bringing meaning to what she or he sees, the object contains meaning that the subject discerns or extracts. The viewer's primary activity in extramission was projection; in intromission, it was inference. The latter understanding of vision as a way of apprehending the potential meanings of what is seen allows the possibility that spectacles might have didactic effects: they can contain meanings that the viewers would be responsible for identifying and internalizing. This potential is one reason why marvels represent such useful moral tests; they are the sources for some of the most impressive and memorable spectacles.

Optical theory and courtly poetry were not mutually exclusive. When Cambyuskan's people seek to understand the marvelous horse in the *Squire's Tale*, for instance, they mention literary, magical, and scientific precedents, adducing that "Alocen, and Vitulon, / And Aristotle, that writen in hir lyves / Of queynte mirours and of perspectives."[22] Even those poets and other producers or consumers of spectacles who may not have been reading optical theory would have been exposed to some of the same ideas in practice from other sources.[23] For example, treatments of religious marvels assumed that they would have a moral resonance, although, as Caroline Walker Bynum's *Christian Materiality* has shown, such marvels were themselves troubled by questions about matter, transformation, and decay.[24] All of the secular marvels in this study have religious undertones—transformed bodies echo the Eucharist, for instance—and the Green Knight, who survives his beheading, recalls the resurrection of Christ as well as the physical suffering of saints. Although these marvels may or may not invoke intromission theory for the poet and audience, they do allude to religious marvels and thereby mobilize an analogous interpretive response: the moral significance of related religious marvels strengthens these secular marvels' tie to morality.[25] Similarly, courtly and urban spectacles "were designed to impress events on collective memory"[26] and thus demonstrated the impact of visual marvels in a way that literary texts could emulate through vivid description. These spectacles are similar to the strange and therefore memorable poetic images that we saw, in the first chapter, associated with moral judgment. In other words, these effects work in concert: a memorable spectacle or mental image might impress a moral quandary or message more deeply on the audience.

Such connections to morality enhance the narrative utility of spectacle, which was already associated with the practice and representation of magic. Magical practices involved spectacles in the form of images (e.g., diagrams), objects (e.g., charms, amulets, and talismans), and performances (e.g., rituals). Those elements also appeared in literary portrayals of magic. However, I am most interested in the magical spectacles that were unique to romances and other literary portrayals—magical events and effects that could operate as realities within the fictional framework. I have suggested that when a spectacle involved supernatural agency and induced a wonder reaction, it might more precisely be described as a marvel. Today, we often see magical marvels represented through the use of "special effects," whether visually and audibly apparent—as with the neon-green glow and otherworldly sounds that accompany the arrival of the Green Knight at Arthur's court in the 1984 film adaptation *The Sword of the Valiant*—or evocatively described, as with the many exercises of magic in the *Harry Potter* books.

Literary marvels in the Middle Ages can contain a similarly strong visual aspect. The romance *Chevalere Assigne*, which likely dates to the fourteenth century, follows the fates of seven siblings who are born with silver chains around their necks and transform into swans when those chains are removed. The Middle English poet omits many of the nonmagical episodes from the French source, distilling the romance into a story that highlights the enchantment.[27] The abbreviated narrative concludes with six of the children returning to their human forms, while the seventh, unable to transform because his chain has been destroyed, grieves and beats himself with his bill until his feathers are covered with blood. This passage creates a vivid textual image that lingers with readers, and the same could be said of the fairies' gallery in *Sir Orfeo*, the dragon lady in *Lybeaus Desconus*, and the beheading scene in *Sir Gawain and the Green Knight*.[28] The existence of *Chevalere Assigne*, in similarly abbreviated form, as a pictorial narrative on a fourteenth-century ivory casket further indicates the spectacular power of the transformations and the deep visual dimension of the romance itself.[29] By depicting magic in strongly visual terms, these texts exploit "the drive to *see*" that Stanbury identifies as "one of the great passions and great myths structuring medieval representation."[30]

Although all of the literary portrayals of magic in this study play with the connection between the visual and the magical, the intense visualization of the *Sir Gawain and the Green Knight* marvels stands out. We cannot be sure about whether the *Gawain*-poet was aware of the intromission-versus-extramission debate or how much knowledge they might have had of the role of spectacle in magical practice. However, their works demonstrate that they were familiar with courtly spectacles and with the expectations of and associations with religious marvels, which frequently involved transformation and occurred in highly charged moral contexts.

Moral Marvels in Cotton Nero A.x

The poems of Cotton Nero A.x share an operating assumption that poetry is capable of doing moral work. In fact, we might see the poems as a set of experiments with different strategies to that end, and despite the various forms they take, all of these strategies depend on the use of visual marvels, from Gawain's encounters with the Green Knight to Jonah's sojourn in a fish's belly.[31] The manuscript includes four ornamented capital faces that Paul F. Reichardt argues "become images of the manuscript's own readers" and can be understood as a "sequence [that] reflects a growing interest and concern," particularly "with the ideas of purity and perfection."[32] These faces might act as not only readers, but also viewers, underscoring the focus on the visual and registering the affective and moral reaction that the poems encourage from their audience.

Cleanness and *Patience* are sermon-like or homiletic in form, using negative exempla drawn from the Bible to show the consequences of immoral or sinful behavior. The former employs direct address, whereas the latter interpolates the figure of the speaker as the one working through the lesson and thus offering a template for the reader. Near the conclusion of *Cleanness*, the narrator summarizes the poem's didactic work: "Þus vpon þrynne wyses I haf yow þro schewed / Þat vnclannes tocleues in corage dere / Of þat wynnelych Lorde þat wonyes in heuen."[33] Note the orientation to the reader and the suggestion of the visual ("I haf yow ... schewed"). The "þrynne wyses" in which the narrator has shown the consequences of uncleanness might all be classified as miracles or religious marvels: the flood, the destruction of Sodom and Gomorrah, and the prophetic writing on Belshazzar's wall. *Patience* focuses on one particular biblical marvel—the fish swallowing Jonah—and offers a similarly direct promise to instruct at the outset: "wyl ȝe tary a lyttel tyne and tent me a whyle, / I schal wysse yow þerwyth as holy wryt telles" (59–60). This time, however, the narrator models the act of hearing and being changed by the marvelous exemplum; after narrating it, he records his own reaction: "forþy when pouerté me enprecez and paynez innoȝe / Ful softly with suffraunce saȝttel me bihouez" (528–29). This reads like a statement of moral as well as spiritual growth, a journey on which the reader is implicitly invited to follow.

Pearl and *Sir Gawain and the Green Knight* present more courtly narratives, but once again differ in their mode of address: the former draws us into the first-person experiences of the dreamer, and the latter offers a more distanced and primarily third-person view of Gawain's adventures and tests. The *Pearl* dreamer embodies a response to marvelous events: "my goste is gon in Godez grace, / In auenture þer meruaylez meuen," he says upon falling asleep (63–64). Although his role is similar to the *Patience* narrator's in that regard, here the reader must evaluate whether the speaker has absorbed the full import of what he witnesses. *Sir Gawain and the Green Knight* allows similar room for interpretation but without interposing such a strong narrating persona between the reader and the events to be interpreted. The ornamented capital faces appear in these poems—three in *Pearl*, and the fourth, with the most pronounced emotional expression, in *Sir Gawain*—offering a guide for the reader's response in these less overtly didactic contexts. The marvels in these texts are not strictly biblical, as in the other two, but they both center on marvelous transformed figures that others struggle to understand. Morgan le Fay reshapes Bertilak as the Green Knight, and the Pearl Maiden takes on a new form after her death and elevation to Christ's bride.

Although *Sir Gawain and the Green Knight* has the fewest direct biblical ties, it has an additional ethical context that the other poems in the manuscript lack: the established discourse of Arthurian ethics. As discussed in the introduction to this study, Middle English usage distinguished between morality, which was about virtuous behavior and often involved affective and immediate responses, and ethics, which described a code or system of values, but the two frequently intersect.[34] All of the texts examined here work within the chivalric system of ethics to some degree; *Sir Gawain and the Green Knight* also belongs to a more distinct strand of Arthurian ethics. Jane Gilbert acknowledges the variety of ethical concerns among Arthurian texts but suggests that they nonetheless participate in a kind of ongoing discourse:

> Ethically speaking, this means entering into debates whose topics are, largely, the following: love in various forms, both between men and between men and women; tension between emotional and

institutional bonds (as between heterosexual love and marriage, or between homosocial love and feudal ties); masculinity and femininity (primarily, as they mean for men); allegiance and its conflicts; personal loyalty and betrayal; justified and unjustified violence; power and governance, with their rights, obligations, and dangers; the nature of the court and the roles of courtier and overlord; [and] social and moral hierarchies, viewed both positively as order and negatively as inequality.... Arthurian ethics as a field of study relates to and reflects on these moral debates and their constraints.[35]

Although nearly all of these issues feature at some level in *Sir Gawain and the Green Knight*, understanding "allegiance" as including institutional as well as personal ties seems to highlight "allegiance and its conflicts." Gawain's commitments to courtliness, knighthood, and his own reputation, as well as his promises to the Green Knight, Bertilak, and the lady, fall within this ethical framework. The events and conflicts that unfold call for moral actions and reactions, particularly toward the magical figure of the Green Knight, whose unusual and spectacular nature challenges the limits of chivalric virtue. As an Arthurian narrative, the poem is suited to consider both moral and ethical issues, and most scholars agree that it concludes with a message along those lines, even if that message is neither obvious to the readers nor clearly received by the characters.[36]

If Arthurian ethics provides a general context for interpreting the moral significance of the marvels in *Sir Gawain and the Green Knight*, then the Cotton Nero A.x manuscript provides a local context. All four of the poems utilize visual marvels—whether secular, religious, or some combination of the two—as a method for imagining the outcomes of moral choices or inculcating moral lessons.[37] The poet expands on the sources for his exempla, adding emotional and visual detail that increases their impact and renders them more memorable. As Mary Carruthers has shown, many medieval texts contain "verbal pictures which are described as 'paintings' even though no drawing accompanies them."[38] In the sole surviving manuscript, all four poems contain not only "verbal pictures," but also, and unusually, illuminations that correspond to them in complicated ways. Kathleen L. Scott explains that "the owner of the book around 1400 made the exceptional gesture for his time of adding full-page pictures to a vernacular work; no other manuscript with a Middle English text had, so far as is known, been illustrated with pictures in this format, and only a few others ... had been illustrated at all."[39] Although some critics have dismissed these images as crude or careless, Reichardt persuasively argues that, like the ornamented capital faces, "the sequence of illustrations ... can be read as a composite design with a coherent significance" and as a "virtual 'fifth text' of the manuscript."[40] It provides another visual aspect to the reading experience, whether in the manuscript itself or in the many modern editions that reproduce one or more of those illustrations alongside the text, and another implementation of fourteenth-century ideas about visuality and spectacle. In a more literal sense than the "verbal pictures," the illuminations are spectacles on the page.

Four images accompany *Sir Gawain and the Green Knight*.[41] The first, which prefaces the text, depicts the beheading scene in Arthur's court. The second shows Bertilak's lady visiting Sir Gawain in his bedchamber, and the third represents Gawain's arrival at the Green Chapel and confrontation with the Green Knight. The final illustration portrays Gawain's return to Arthur's court. As scholars have noted, the details of these pictures (in terms of dress, for example) do not always follow the textual descriptions.[42] However, the illustrations focus on the marvels and the moral testing that they enable; as Jennifer A. Lee notes, "in choosing the subjects for his pictures, the illustrator appreciated the 'entertainment' of the poems and followed the action and marvelous events recounted. His primary concern, however, was to assess and express the 'instruction' contained in the poems."[43] The emphasis on "issues related to the morality of kings and royal courts" is one of the themes that Reichardt proposes that the Cotton Nero A.x images share.[44] The representations of the Pearl Maiden and the heavenly city, the disembodied hand at Belshazzar's feast, Jonah's entering the fish's mouth, and the images of the Green Knight make up the second, third, sixth, seventh, ninth, and eleventh of the twelve illustrations in the manuscript; taken together, they suggest that visual marvels might be a predominant concern not only of the final poem, but also of the manuscript as a whole. Additionally, the resonances between these images suggest similar ties between the spiritual and secular marvels: the collection privileges their shared visual nature above the different classifications into which they might be divided.

The first and most famous image associated with *Sir Gawain* represents its most spectacular marvel: the decapitated-yet-alive Green Knight (fig. 1). Gawain appears both in the upper portion of the image with the other representatives of the court, including Arthur and Guinevere, and in the lower portion facing the Green Knight, who holds his own head in his hand. Blood flows from the Green Knight's torso and his head, suggesting the violent and recent nature of their separation and underscoring the marvelous nature of the event as well as its "sacramental and sacrificial overtones."[45]

This dual scene gives the image a narrative dynamic, suggesting the active nature of the marvel that will be crucial to its intra- and extratextual effects. It also shows Gawain as integrated into the Arthurian community and separated out as its representative, foreshadowing that both the chivalric ethic and Gawain's individual virtue will be tested by this marvel. In the lower scene, he faces the Green Knight, holding the axe in hand. This position dramatizes Gawain's courage in this confrontation and creates a contrast with the figure of the frightened queen, who appears immediately above him and clutches at Arthur while seeming to gaze at the Green Knight's head, her line of sight crossing the division between the scenes. It is interesting that this decapitation image appears before the narrative begins; the arrangement might suggest that the image is emblematic of or foundational to the narrative itself—certainly it is the mental picture that seems to stay with modern readers, who have been affected no less than Guinevere is by the spectacle of the Green Knight with head in hand. Not surprisingly, this scene is also highlighted in modern adaptations of the poem, like *The Sword of the Valiant*.

The remaining illustrations appear after the text of the poem. The bedroom scene focuses on the lady as the central figure, hinting at the spectacle that her body becomes in the poem (fig. 2). The closed and intimate space—with a curtain drawn around the perimeter to enclose the lady, Gawain, and his bed—contrasts sharply with the open and public space of the first image, and the darker background colors here reinforce that contrast. However, the sight line from the lady to Gawain seems to mimic that from Guinevere to the Green Knight, perhaps suggesting that Gawain himself becomes a source of wonder in the middle of the poem. This wonder might attach to his demonstrations of virtue and resistance to temptation, or to the uncertainty about his ultimate fate.

The third image has parallels to each of the previous two. Like the second, it shows a private encounter between two characters—an encounter that also functions as a moral test—against a darker background, filled in here with features from the landscape rather than the bedroom (fig. 3). It depicts the two figures in postures and positions similar to the lower portion of the first image—one standing and holding an axe to the right, facing one on horseback to the left—but this time the Green Knight is the former and Gawain the latter, showing how their roles are reversed in the second encounter. It is "as if their identities had been exchanged," Maidie Hilmo observes, "or as if the one is a doppelgänger or dark side of the other."[46] We must be reminded of one crucial difference: although Gawain's position

MOVING MARVELS 75

FIGURE 1
The Green Knight and Gawain in Arthur's court. *Sir Gawain and the Green Knight*, MS Cotton Nero A.x (art. 3), fol. 94v. © The British Library Board.

FIGURE 2
Lady Bertilak and Gawain. *Sir Gawain and the Green Knight*, MS Cotton Nero A.x (art. 3), fol. 129. © The British Library Board.

is similar to the Green Knight's in the first image, the hero's head is still attached. The Green Knight's marvelous nature is suggested here by his greater size, towering over Gawain, and the fact that his body has returned to its intact form in this repeat appearance. These images represent two decisive moments in the moral testing of Gawain and, as I will argue in more detail below, two primary agents in that testing: the Green Knight and the lady. The third agent, Morgan le Fay, is present only implicitly as the one responsible for the Green Knight's enchanted appearance and performance at Arthur's court; this representation fits with her largely behind-the-scenes role in the poem.[47]

The last image is again a communal one, and again Gawain appears to be both part of and separate from the community—integrated by his connection to the king via the sword that they are both touching, but separated by his kneeling position, which places Gawain below and makes him smaller than the other three courtly figures, who stand together (fig. 4). The green girdle, which might recall Gawain's failings, his encounters with magic, and/or his separation from the court, is absent. Whereas Hilmo reads this final miniature as an allegory of New Jerusalem that concludes the manuscript as a whole,[48] I see it as a more ambiguous scene that leaves the audience with unanswered questions.

Taken together, these images present an interpretation highlighting the marvelous and moral aspects of the poem. The illustrator may not have been faithful to the details of the description, but the illustrations do accurately feature the most significant scenes and key into the most important issues within that interpretive framework. At the same time, they preserve the mystery around a number of elements, including Morgan le Fay, Bertilak in his human form, the pentangle, and the girdle. In short, these illuminations represent some of the mental images that medieval readers might have associated with this text (and that at least one did)—the type of images that, I have been arguing, would have been kept in their memory and might have influenced their moral sensibilities. In that figurative sense, these are moving images even though they are fixed on the page. We see emblems of knightly behavior, emphasizing the virtues that Gawain exhibits when he takes up the Green Knight's challenge, evades the lady's seduction, faces the Green Knight a second time, and returns to Arthur's court. But the images, especially the third and fourth, also hint at the limits of Gawain's courage—the extreme contexts, created by marvels, in which it falls short of the chivalric ideal. The illustrations, like the poem itself, feature visual marvels that encourage the audience to wonder about whether there might

FIGURE 3
The Green Knight and Gawain at the Green Chapel. *Sir Gawain and the Green Knight*, MS Cotton Nero A.x (art. 3), fol. 129v. © The British Library Board.

FIGURE 4
Gawain's return to court. *Sir Gawain and the Green Knight*, MS Cotton Nero A.x (art. 3), fol. 130. © The British Library Board.

be reasonable limits to virtue and how we might respond to those whose virtue has faltered.

All three elements under consideration in this project—magic, spectacle, and morality—may be more prominent in *Sir Gawain and the Green Knight* than in any other fourteenth-century text, but here ethical concerns are nearly as prominent as moral ones.[49] Although chivalry was certainly important in earlier texts and also subtly critiqued in *Sir Orfeo*, it was usually accepted as a framing discourse; *Sir Gawain and the Green Knight* instead interrogates chivalry, bringing those ethical concerns into the foreground. The narrative is interested in the ethical system itself as well as Gawain's individual embodiment of it, and the Green Knight is the crux for both. As a marvel, the Green Knight possesses several unusual qualities—including not only his visual impact, but also his extraordinary animation and ability to reappear—that make him a challenging opponent for Gawain as well as a memorable object lesson for the audience. But he also becomes a moral agent, leveraging the marvel that Morgan shaped and collaborating with his wife to carry out a more subtle and definitive test of Gawain's virtue. All of these effects rely on the audience's ability to apprehend and interpret visual marvels—skills that fourteenth-century courtiers, in particular, would have had ample opportunity to hone. In the rest of this chapter, I will suggest that the poem's visual marvels signal the presence of ethical and moral concerns for the characters as well as moral ramifications for the audience, even as those marvels foreclose a full understanding of either the magic or the morality at work.

Moving Spectacles

From the first stanza, the poet signals that *Sir Gawain and the Green Knight* will be deeply concerned with "wonder" (15). The next stanza suggests one reason why, characterizing Britain as a land singularly rich in marvels: "mo ferlyes on þis folde han fallen here oft / Þen in any oþer þat I wot, syn þat ilk tyme" (23–24). These early hints suggest not only that we will see magic, but also that it will be unusually spectacular and integral to the narrative. Magic, however, has been less important to critical interpretations of the poem than one might expect (or than the titles of scholarly articles and books might lead one to believe), and critics have generally seen questions about whether the girdle is magical or how Morgan creates the Green Knight as unanswerable given the existing evidence.[50] They have been more interested in the use of visual description in the poem. Alain

Renoir influentially described *Sir Gawain and the Green Knight* as "cinematographic," and later scholars such as Sarah Stanbury have explored its arresting visual dimension in detail.[51] The representation of marvels is integral to that impression; the scenes of the Green Knight's entrance and beheading, in particular, are vividly realized for the audience—in the text as well as, as we have seen, the manuscript illustrations—and the courtiers within the poem register the impact of those sights.

The efficacy of the marvelous, for Gawain and Arthur's court as well as for the audience, depends on the specific ways in which the poet deploys it. Before Gawain beheads him, the Green Knight's supernatural qualities already make him an opponent whom only the bravest knight could face. Two factors further enhance that marvelous nature: his post-decapitation animation and his later remanifestation. These abilities, along with his appearance, make him a marvel suited to inspire wonder in a public context rather than in the intimate encounter that was the more typical mode for literary magical marvels in this period, and thus to test an ethical system—in this case, Arthurian chivalry—rather than an individual moral belief or code. However, the recurrence of the marvel also enables a more intense and comprehensive test of Gawain's chivalric virtue; such recurrences were uncommon, whether measured against the variety of marvels that appear elsewhere in Cotton Nero A.x or against the magical marvels in other fourteenth-century texts. Ultimately, the marvel reveals that Gawain has courage, but—rather than stopping there, as most similar tests, even supernatural ones, do—it also tracks where that courage begins to fail. In other words, this marvel creates a test that is distinct in both degree (because it is more frightening than a nonsupernatural opponent or obstacle) and kind (because it can not only uncover whether a knight possesses a virtue, but also map its limits). All of the marvel's qualities—visuality, animation, recurrence—also make it a more memorable vector for the audience's moral attention.

Suspense heightens the impact of the first glimpse of the Green Knight. His appearance is preceded by a sound—"anoþer noyse ful newe neȝed biliue" (132)—that creates wonder about the source and focuses our attention in that direction. When the Green Knight does appear, the revelation of his hue to the reader is somewhat delayed; he is first mentioned in line 136, but the description logs his large size and then his courtliness before finally, in the wheel, we learn that

> ... wonder of his hwe men hade,
> Set in his semblaunt sene;

> He ferde as freke were fade,
> And oueral enker grene.
> (147–50)

Giants are fairly common in romance—so common that they have lost much of their supernatural character by this time—but his personal "hwe" gives the Green Knight an unmistakable stamp of the marvelous. The narrator emphasizes that, despite this figure's large and frightening size, his color is what arouses "wonder." In a later version, *The Greene Knight*, the titular color describes the knight's horse and apparel rather than himself, and his initial appearance is correspondingly less impressive and supernatural.[52]

The *Sir Gawain and the Green Knight* narrator underscores this Green Knight's appearance as a visual spectacle: "such a fole vpon folde, ne freke þat hym rydes, / Watz neuer *sene* in þat sale wyth *syȝt* er þat tyme / With *yȝe*" (196–98; emphasis added). The act of looking at the spectacle creates marvel—like courtly love, it is an emotion aroused through sight. But the poem also associates active looking with the process of trying to ascertain meaning: "ther watz lokyng on lenþe þe lude to beholde, / For vch mon had meruayle quat hit mene myȝt" (232–33).[53] This depiction corresponds to the late medieval shifts in the theory of vision described above: the viewers must draw inferences from the Green Knight's appearance, rather than projecting their own interpretation onto it. At the end of the description, the narrator reiterates the "wonder" felt by the court (238), perhaps guiding the reader's response into a similar emotional channel. Although the visual description is not entirely static, it does set up a contrast with the very active phase of the marvel that will soon follow, and the attention to the Green Knight's body in its initial, whole state prepares us to attend to its later disarticulation—which may, in turn, intensify interest in the dismembering of the animals in the hunting scenes.

The ensuing encounter between Gawain and the Green Knight unfolds over several stanzas, but the act of beheading and its immediate aftermath are most important for my purposes here:

> ... þe scharp of þe schalk schyndered þe bones
> And schrank þurȝ þe schyire grece and schade hit in twynne,
> Þat þe bit of þe broun stel bot on þe grounde.
> Þe fayre hede fro þe halce hit to þe erþe,
> Þat fele it foyned wyth her fete þere hit forth roled;
> Þe blod brayd fro þe body, þat blykked on þe grene.

> And nawþer faltered ne fel þe freke neuer þe helder
> Bot styþly he start forth vpon styf schonkes
> And runyschly he raȝt out þereas renkkez stoden,
> Laȝt to his lufly hed and lyft hit vp sone,
> And syþen boȝez to his blonk, þe brydel he cachchez,
> Steppez into stel-bawe and strydez alofte,
> And his hede by þe here in his honde haldez;
> And as sadly þe segge hym in his sadel sette
> As non vnhap had hym ayled, þaȝ hedlez nowe
> In stedde.
> (424–39)

There is no speech in this stanza—a striking difference from those around it, which are full of Gawain and the Green Knight's exchanges over the conditions of their agreement, the Green Knight's final headless address to Gawain and the court, and Arthur's words to Guinevere and Gawain in the aftermath. The closest stanza in the fitt to have a similar lack of speech is the one in which the court is struck silent by the Green Knight's initial appearance (232–49). Whereas that stanza focused on his figure itself as a marvel, this one focuses on the marvelous actions of that figure. The head is severed, falls, and rolls, propelled by the courtiers' feet; the blood spurts; the body moves to, reaches for, and lifts up the head and then mounts the horse. Equally significant, and noted by the narrator, is the motion that does not occur: the Green Knight "nawþer faltered ne fel." As we will learn later, it is the actions—"þat ilke gome þat gostlych speked / With his hede in his honde bifore þe hyȝe table" (2461–62)—that Morgan expected to be the effective aspect of the marvel.[54] In other texts, such as *The Turke and Sir Gawain* and *The Carle of Carlisle*, the challenger's beheading comes later and marks an end to rather than a proof of enchantment; the Carle, for instance, returns to human form after the beheading and thanks Gawain for "deliver[ing] mee / From all false witchcrafft."[55] In the wake of his beheading, on the other hand, the title character of *The Greene Knight*, who began as simply Sir Bredbeddle, truly becomes a spectacle: "all had great marvell, that they see / That he spake so merrilye / And bare his head in his hand."[56] Here, the Green Knight's appearance is more marvelous to begin with, but both the audience's anticipation and Morgan's plan culminate in the action of the beheading scene.

The quality of motion could render something a spectacle, as we saw in the case of the coronation angel;[57] Minsoo Kang's history of "self-moving, life-imitating machine[s]" highlights the persistent anxiety and fascination that such automata aroused. "The power exhibited by the self-moving object is far beyond that of inert images that can never literally reach out to stir up the deepest fear in the beholder," writes Kang. "One can always turn and walk away from a still image that disturbs, but what if that image follows, speaks, and touches?"[58] That is exactly what happens with the Green Knight: In the poem, the supernatural figure captured in the manuscript images springs into action. Although not an automaton, his headless body stuns because it is similarly "self-moving" and, we might say, death-defying rather than "life-imitating." It becomes the centerpiece of an impressive and disturbing—to borrow Kang's terminology—spectacle that is defined by movement. The spectacle of the Green Knight resembles that of the dragon lady in *Lybeaus Desconus*: she also moved, spoke, and transformed. However, the activity of her shape-shifted form happened within a single episode and was restricted to a single locale—namely, the enchanted palace. The Green Knight, functions in different contexts—in terms of both physical locations and public rather than private encounters—and reappears after a long period of time, whether we are measuring by seasons or lines. He is, we might say, not simply animated but reanimated in multiple senses, and that repetition helps to plant him firmly in the readers' and the characters' minds.

We can approach the Green Knight's first treatment in the narrative as a series of spectacles—his appearance, the moment of beheading, and the speech made with head in hand—but the poem encourages us instead to see it as a continuous and multifaceted marvel. Although it contains vivid moments, the poem emphasizes action over description, and this emphasis contributes to rather than undermines its cinematic nature. Even when depicting the Green Knight's appearance, the poem focuses on his potential actions, building anticipation for the moving spectacle to follow. His appearance causes "meruayle" (233), yet the court's deepest "wonder" focuses on "what he worch schulde" (238).

The characteristics of the marvel here—its detailed visuality and liveliness—make it memorable and thus deeply affecting. Although it is not reducible to a single image (unlike the gallery in *Sir Orfeo*, for instance), its complexity encourages readers to engage with the marvel and its moral implications. Primarily, however, the nature of the marvel appears tailored to its purposes within the narrative: it creates a more impressive and frightening test of virtue than either a human opponent or a less active or less obviously supernatural one would. The Green Knight, as critics have often observed, straddles the line between knight and wild man; like the worm with the woman's face in *Lybeaus Desconus*, he is a spectacular hybrid figure created by supernatural means. And like the serpent lady does, the Green Knight presents an extraordinary obstacle for a chivalric knight, requiring virtuous nonaction as well as action. In each case, the specific nature of the hybridity shapes the challenge; for the Green Knight, his chivalry legitimizes the ethical aspect of the test that he administers, while his supernatural qualities make that test more intense and ultimately more definitive.

The large-scale spectacle of the Green Knight also creates an unusually large-scale test: rather than simply probing the character of the hero, the Knight's initial challenge tries the reputation of Arthur's court as a whole, albeit through the mechanism of a representative. Seth Lerer identifies a "spectatorial sensibility" common by the fifteenth century in audience reactions to drama and punishment;[59] in *Sir Gawain and the Green Knight*, the beheading falls more in the category of stagecraft than penalty, but the public nature of its display has resemblances to both. The Green Knight's actions help to inspire wonder on a public scale, like the automata used in courtly displays and entertainment. The rest of the court participates in this experience, not simply as spectators but as active agents, most memorably when "Þe fayre hede fro þe halce hit to þe erþe, / Þat fele hit foyned wyth her fete þere hit forth roled" (427–28). This touch enhances the realism and credibility of the marvel—the courtiers interact with the head and demonstrate that it moves separately from the body—and sets up the spectacular moment that immediately follows when "styþly he start forth vpon styf schonkes" and takes "his lufly hed and lyft hit vp sone" so that it can speak to the court (431 and 433).

Most other detailed marvels are intimate, if not individual. Although we certainly hear of marvels performed for courtly entertainment, as in the *Franklin's Tale*, the marvels represented in these texts tend to have much smaller audiences, as in the cases of Orfeo, Lybeaus, Canacee in the *Squire's Tale*, and the knight in the *Wife of Bath's Tale*. That characteristic may help those marvels speak to the issue of how one person should relate to another, but the public nature of this spectacle is appropriate because it represents a challenge to the community of Arthur's court and to the chivalry that it espouses—in other words, to its public identity and ethics. Ultimately, however, only one knight can take up the challenge, and Gawain assumes that role. The Green Knight speaks of the knights in plural terms initially ("burnes," 259; "berdlez chylder," 280; "here ar ȝeþ mony," 284) but then shifts to the singular for the direct challenge ("if any so hardy in þis hous holdez hymseluen," 285; "if any freke be so felle," 291). With this language, the Green Knight sets up the beheading as a test of a representative of the court, as if the high mark of one knight's bravery will peg the courage of all. When no one steps forward, he again ridicules the court as a whole ("what, is þis Arþures hous?," 309), and the knights continue to react as a single entity (characterized as "alle" in lines 302 and 320). When Gawain takes over for Arthur in the challenge, that act of replacing the ruler and, one might argue, emblem of the court underscores that Gawain has become its representative. He passes this first test and thus protects the reputation of his community, but the encounter with the Green Knight initiates a moral education that quickly becomes individual. So, although the Green Knight's appearance creates a communal and spectacular marvel, it has significantly individual effects.

A different kind of marvel appears at the center of this moral education: the green girdle. Whereas the Green Knight moves from public magical spectacle to private moral agent, the girdle slides from private magical object to public moral symbol.[60] Its magical status is ultimately ambiguous, as is its status as a marvel. If it is a marvel, it lacks the visual impact and animation that make the Green Knight so obviously supernatural and impressively memorable. This lack may also explain why the girdle is not highlighted in the manuscript illustrations, which otherwise suggest an interest in the magical and moral elements of the narrative. The lady highlights the gap between the girdle's appearance and its value in her pitch to Gawain:

> "Now forsake 3e þis silke," sayde þe burde þenne,
> ["]For hit is symple in hitself? And so hit wel semez:
> Lo! so hit is littel and lasse hit is worþy.
> Bot whoso knew þe costes þat knit ar þerinne,
> He wolde hit prayse at more prys, parauenture."
> (1846–50)

As an object, the girdle's potential for animation may be different from the Green Knight's, but there is no conclusive evidence that it has any effects.[61] As a prop in the morality test, its temptation rests on its purportedly magical nature: it represents a kind of counterweight to the Green Knight's powers, a supernatural protection that levels the playing field somewhat for Gawain. What seduces him is the possibility of emulating the Green Knight's magical ability to simultaneously embrace and evade the mortal blow. In other words, the girdle temptation depends on the frightening specter of the Green Knight; in the absence of that threat, the poem implies, Gawain could have resisted.[62]

The threat that the Green Knight poses depends on his ability to manifest himself not once but twice. Although most marvels occur at the height of the narrative, as we see in the other texts in this study, the Green Knight appears at the beginning and then reappears near the end. One might argue that the first appearance is the marvel, or at least the greater marvel because it seems more spectacular, more magical, and broader in scope than the events at the Green Chapel. But, importantly, this early intervention of the marvelous into the narrative sets up the second, establishing an intensely supernatural context and, especially with the explicit promise of a future meeting, an expectation that the marvel will form a significant part of the climax. This dynamic is closest to the one that we find in *Sir Orfeo*. In both cases, the time that elapses between the marvelous interventions is meaningful and contributes to their moral aspect. Malcolm Andrew and Ronald Waldron associate these two features directly: "the presence of a moral theme in *Sir Gawain* first becomes unmistakable at the beginning of the second fitt, where the superb account of the seasons conveys a sense of the inevitable passing of time. It is here that the more serious implications of what might have seemed a macabre joke receive graver emphasis (495–9). Gawain's performance in the return bout of the beheading game becomes the focus of attention, as it emerges that the first fitt has merely been the prelude to a prolonged test of character."[63] The test is more serious, and more effective, because of the time that has passed.

The passage of time also means that the marvel is reproduced after a significant gap. Literary marvels tend to be singular rather than multiple or repeated, but, in this poem, that quality of reproducibility is significant both for the treatment of magic and for its moral effects.[64] The fact that the spectacle of the Green Knight is mobilized twice in the service of these moral tests tells us something about the magic itself. Its repetition makes this spectacle rare—indeed, as mentioned above, there is something about a marvel or spectacle that often seems to depend on its singularity. The reproducible tends to be technical or practical, involving some kind of human skill, rather than marvelous, and something that is reproduced can quickly become ordinary rather than spectacular. "Continued experience gradually removes all occasion for wonder," observes Augustine in *City of God*.[65] Nonetheless, in theory a skilled magician should be able to replicate a marvel, and the fact that this magical spectacle can be replicated suggests that the magic is both powerful and well controlled. We get a sense of not only competency, but also the intention behind the marvel; however, as I will explore below, that intention proves to be bifurcated in complicated ways.

It is possible that the magic is also more believable in its second incarnation—that the poem dispels the stunned wonder about the Green Knight as a spectacle in order to replace it with suspenseful wonder about what will happen when he meets with Gawain again. And if it is true that the poem modulates our wonder in this way, it might also be true that the secondary wonder has stronger ties to morality. Will Gawain stand his ground against the Green Knight, despite the reminders of his fearsome nature? Will the Green Knight really cut off Gawain's head? What would an appropriate chivalrous ending be, given that Gawain has kept his promise to return and demonstrated his worthiness?

As these questions suggest, the replication of the marvel of the Green Knight creates an astounding test of Gawain's virtue. Most knights face their supernatural opponents once and, upon defeating them, claim whatever reputation or reward was the result of that extraordinary test. Gawain accepts the Green Knight's challenge and cuts off his head, but then must face him again after a long delay. The second test raises the stakes: Gawain faces not only a supernatural opponent, but one whose extraordinary abilities have been memorably demonstrated, and this encounter will require Gawain to submit to that opponent without a fight. The Green Knight's beheading also plays out the fate that Gawain seems destined to suffer, minus the miraculous recovery. This parallel underscores the difference between the human and the supernatural. Gawain also projects that fate later, when he reminds the Green Knight that his wholeness will not be magically restored: "bot þaȝ my hede falle on þe stonez / I con not hit restore" (2282–83). In other words, the marvel will not be repeated. This sharp difference increases both the intensity of the test that Gawain undergoes and our sense of his courage in responding to it.

When the marvel of the Green Knight reappears, the text provides an elaborate setup that focuses on his potential cruelty. In his first manifestation at Arthur's court, the impact was built upon the unfolding of the blazon-like description of his appearance and the surprise that it offered, including the slightly delayed and therefore more effective mention of his hue. The Green Knight's potential actions were a source of wonder and trepidation, but not of terror (although many are frightened *after* those actions unfold; see lines 442–43). The second time around, we, like Gawain, know better what to expect in terms of what we will see, but the suspense over the Green Knight's course of behavior has paradoxically been heightened by our increased knowledge. The poem helps to stoke that suspense by presenting the guide's description of the cruel and frightening reputation of the knight: he is "þe worst vpon erþe," "a mon methles and mercy non vses," who happily kills anyone who strays into his realm, "be hit chorle oþer chaplayn" (2098, 2106, and 2107). If he has lost some of his edge as a visual marvel, the Green Knight's nature as an active marvel—in the sense not only of being animated, but also of acting against or in ways that affect others—has become a proportionately greater source of interest.

Although the Green Knight remains essentially the same if, in the first case, partially disassembled, his significance is slightly different. The test he represents has also changed. The first encounter tested the court's knighthood in a public context, with Gawain standing in as the representative (although the scene also suggests that Gawain's bravery outpaces the other knights', so that it is not only representative but can also be measured in relative terms as the greatest). This second encounter tests Gawain more directly—how chivalrous will he be when facing his own death?—and in isolation not just from the court but from any spectators. In between, the bedroom tests probe Gawain's courtesy as well as his courage. In the course of these tests, we discover that—when faced with the specter of the Green Knight's return and then the imminent, life-threatening blow—the hero's virtue wavers.[66]

The visual, animated, and recurring marvel of the Green Knight has simultaneously created a daunting challenge for Gawain and a memorable spectacle for the audience—one that, in both cases, encourages closer scrutiny and extended reflection.[67] Although some members of the audience may be practitioners of or adherents to chivalry, that ethical commitment is not a prerequisite; the narrative poses ethical challenges to Gawain and Arthur's court, but the questions that it raises about the nature and limits of virtue are more broadly moral. Sarah McNamer has argued that the poem "can be seen as a kind of experimental theatre, staging an affective and cognitive event that is potentially transformative." She examines how the poem gives its audience an "emotion script" for "feeling green," an affective experience that involves change, growth, and valuing one's life, and thus has moral implications;[68] she sees the poem moving its audience toward a new set of values, whereas I am interested in how its use of the marvelous opens up questions about virtue and morality that prepare the ground for such a shift. By demonstrating that even heroic virtue can falter, and showing us what it takes to make that happen, the poem invites the readers to bring their moral sensibilities to bear. This move capitalizes on the possibility that was raised by the very presence of a visual marvel, in line with the theories of vision circulating at the time.

The presence of Bertilak in the middle of the poem also becomes, in retrospect, its own source of wonder. We might marvel at the clues connecting him to the Green Knight that we missed, or simply at how the outsized supernatural figure could revert to a figure so convincingly human and natural. We might also—as I will in the next section—consider more carefully his role in creating the marvel's moral effects, if not the marvel itself. As the romance maps the limits of Gawain's virtue, Bertilak transforms not only into a marvelous figure, but also into an active and subtle moral agent. In the previous chapter, we saw that supernatural or divine agency might be required to establish moral virtue; *Sir Gawain and the Green Knight* deconstructs the moral agency at work in its marvel, conceiving of the moral agency of its readers—who have a responsibility to interpret the visual spectacles carefully—and its characters—who interact at various levels to create a comprehensive test of Gawain's virtue—in equally complex ways.

Multiple Agencies

One feature that distinguishes the marvels in *Sir Gawain and the Green Knight* from the marvels in the other texts in this study is the revelation scene. Other marvels may cultivate mystery about their source or agency—which, as I have noted, is one of the characteristics of literary marvels—but that mystery is not addressed through the type of revelation that we see in this poem.[69] Paradoxically, that revelation raises more questions than it answers about the agency and motivation behind the marvels, and about their relationship to the moral testing that Gawain has undergone. Critics remain divided about the question of female agency in the moral tests and in the poem as a whole; I suggest that it presents male and female agents as interacting to create the full slate of moral tests that Gawain faces.

The Green Knight reveals that Morgan le Fay is responsible for his shape and appearance, and that she crafted that marvel "to assay þe surquidré, ȝif hit soth were / Þat rennes of þe grete renoun of þe Rounde Table" and "to haf greued Gaynour and gart hir to dyȝe / With glopnyng of þat ilke gome þat gostlych speked / With his hede in his honde bifore þe hyȝe table" (2457–58 and 2460–62). Earlier critics debated the credibility and aesthetic appropriateness of this late revelation of Morgan's central role;[70] whether or not we accept it, this explanation is not a flattering representation of her motivations, especially in reference to her desire to frighten Guinevere to death. It does, however, include a moral dimension and specify what she seeks to examine—the pride and renown of the Round Table—which she tests through their ability to respond courageously to the challenge.[71] It also highlights the method by which her test proceeds: the communal spectacle of the Green Knight's holding "his hede in his honde" while addressing the court.

However, the Green Knight indicates that the tests after the head-in-hand speech were part of his own scheme. He explicitly claims responsibility for his wife's testing of Gawain in the bedroom scenes and for the temptation of the girdle.[72] Of course, the Green Knight, as Bertilak, does not carry out these tests alone. He explains that he sent his wife to enact them: "now know I wel þy cosses and þy costes als, / And þe wowyng of my wyf. I wroȝt hit myseluen; / I sende hir to asay þe" (2360–62). Paul Battles has demonstrated how editorial treatments of the poem have reduced our sense of the lady's agency and involvement,[73] but even with such editing, her role is clearly pivotal. Geraldine Heng rightly characterizes the Green Knight's claim as "a move that seeks to eclipse the primacy of the Lady's part and her responsibility for the stalking of Gawain."[74] Still, we might see this as a case of shared rather than usurped agency, with Bertilak instigating the tests and the lady implementing them in specific and subtle ways. In the later *Greene Knight*, the lady appears to be both completely in love with Gawain and a completely unwitting participant in his trials: her mother uses "witchcraft" to disguise her son-in-law so that he will bring Gawain to their court, and then escorts her daughter to Gawain's bed, exhorting him,

> . . . Gentle knight, awake!
> And for this faire ladies sake,
> That hath loved thee soe deere,
> Take her boldly in thine armes.[75]

Sir Gawain and the Green Knight, on the other hand, shows the lady shrewdly executing the scheme, if not conceiving of it, and the explanation—biased as it may be—reinforces that interpretation of events. Although scholars have often conflated or associated the female characters with each other,[76] this speech depicts Bertilak and his lady as the more closely connected pair, united in efforts and aims that are distinct from Morgan's.

The set of tests that they administer is more comprehensive than the one designed by Morgan: they examine Gawain's knighthood in a fuller sense, probing his courtesy more extensively, including his honesty and loyalty. We might say that they test his courage more effectively, since this is the trial in which he falls short (although, as we have seen, the compounding of the supernatural threat seems to be responsible, at least in part, for this failure). Their trials are also more individual, measuring Gawain against his own reputation rather than the Round Table's, and rely less on spectacle, although the green girdle does hearken back to the Green Knight. This last point is crucial, because it suggests that the bedroom trials are predicated on the beheading test—that the tests for which the Green Knight claims responsibility are made possible by the one that Morgan constructed. The final trial, with the second appearance of the Green Knight, ties to everything that has come before. He never explicitly claims responsibility or gives credit for this final episode, and we cannot be sure about whether it represents the final stage of Morgan's plan—since it was set up by the first appearance and its execution would seem to require her magic—or the final stage of the Green Knight's plan—since he proposed the promise to exchange blows (which resembles his later covenant, as Bertilak, with Gawain) and the outcome relies on Gawain's performance in the bedroom trials. This ambiguity encourages us to see the Green Knight and Morgan as exercising divided yet interdependent forms of agency. Randy P. Schiff has argued that Morgan's relationship to Bertilak is one of superior to inferior;[77] however, her reliance on him also circumscribes her power. Although the Green Knight has no magical powers of his own, he appears able to engineer a more comprehensive and more effective moral trial than Morgan le Fay does by harnessing and redirecting her powers, ultimately uncovering Gawain's limits. What the poem portrays, then, is both a separation and a collaboration of moral and magical agencies.[78] The marvel was created with a minor moral dimension and subsequently adapted by the subject of the marvel himself to significant moral ends.

Female sorceresses tended to raise pointed moral concerns. Although the discourse of witchcraft was not yet fully developed, the enchantress in Middle English romance was, as Corinne Saunders notes, "a deceptive or ambiguous figure, who stray[ed] across the boundary of the forbidden or the fearful."[79] As Thomas Chestre's Dame d'Amour shows, enchantresses were often morally problematic at best. The Green Knight initially suggests that Morgan is "bi craftes wel lerned," which might suggest some virtue of intelligence or dedication, but he immediately follows up with the explanation that "Þe maystrés of Merlyn mony ho hatz taken, / For ho hatz dalt drwry ful dere sumtyme / With þat conable klerk" (2447 and 2448–50). The reference to Merlin as the source of Morgan's magic and her lover casts her moral status in doubt; it also hints that Morgan's own agency is divided and dependent on, or shared with, Merlin to some degree. She is a female enchantress in a dual sense—with the power to cast magical enchantments and to enchant men like Merlin. She seems to wield that power for frivolous, or at least primarily spectacular, purposes. The division is starker in *The Greene Knight*, in which the enchantress uses her magic for obviously immoral purposes and only Sir Bredbeddle / the Green Knight shows any interest in examining Gawain's virtues, and in *William of Palerne*, in which an enchantress-queen transforms her stepson into a wolf to advance her son's interests, and only the shape-shifted wolf exhibits moral motivations or agency.

We know Morgan almost exclusively through the spectacle she creates. Retrospectively, we can see her own appearance as a type of antispectacle. As Christine Chism points out, "[the] masking of Morgan becomes even more powerful in the context of alliterative romance's centralization of spectacle. Alliterative romances both mask and communicate interior thoughts and motives through spectacular surfaces and signs—insignia, clothing, behavior, stated reputation, costuming them in order to rivet the eye and entice questions about interiors."[80] Morgan's interior remains masked, partly because she never speaks for herself in the poem, and partly because we learn relatively little about her exterior in a poem in which the visual provides such rich ground for interpretation. Our focus is redirected onto the Green Knight, a marvel with a complex life of its own.

The poem does not simply represent a division of moral and magical agency, however; between the moral trials and the confessor role that he plays for Gawain in the Green Chapel, the Green Knight / Bertilak might be seen as taking over the moral authority, or the moral center, of the poem.[81] It is relatively unusual to have a male rather than female figure transformed by magic; when considered alongside other narratives with marvels of transformation, the Green Knight's characterization reveals that moral power inheres in the shape-shifted figure rather than the shape-shifting agent. In other words, it is the shape-shifted figures that embody or enact the moral tests or functions here as well as in the *Wife of Bath's Tale* and *Lybeaus Desconus*. Each of these texts offers a different situation: In the *Wife of Bath's Tale*, the woman controls her own metamorphosis. In *Lybeaus Desconus*, male necromancers transform a captive woman's shape. And in *Sir Gawain and the Green Knight*, the woman enchants an apparently willing man's appearance. But in every case, the moral agency attaches to the shape-shifted body, regardless of its gender or degree of control over the transformation.

As supernatural characters, these figures can be attributed with accordingly enhanced knowledge and authority, and they participate in the long-standing tradition of supernatural figures as representing tests of a hero's character.

Women who inhabit a shape-shifted body, regardless of whether they effected that transformation through their own power, have deeper moral impact within and beyond their narratives than do women who exercise power primarily over others' forms. That may be in part because the correlation between the shape-shifted female body and moral agency leverages rather than transcends women's traditional physicality. Their bodies already encompass the familiar as well as the "other," and shape shifting exaggerates that hybridity by creating a spectacle that is unusual enough to be strikingly memorable but human enough to be morally relevant.[82] The Green Knight shows that the association of the shape-shifted body with moral authority can also hold true for male figures, and that a shape-shifted man can also wield moral agency. He is similar to Chaucer's loathly lady in that both engineer moral tests and possess moral authority. However, the Green Knight's moral authority and agency are mediated heavily through female characters. Without Morgan, he would lack the enchanted shape that initiates and underpins the testing; we might read her as giving away her moral agency to the Green Knight or, perhaps more precisely, as displacing it onto him. Without the lady, he would be unable to try Gawain's virtue as comprehensively and definitively. So although the Green Knight has moral agency, it derives from one woman and is enacted, at least in part, by another.

Gawain's reaction to the disclosure glosses over such nuances, suggesting that the Green Knight holds the moral authority while Morgan and the lady are active but morally compromised participants. Despite the Green Knight's implication of himself, Gawain clearly blames the women for his situation. After the Green Knight has claimed responsibility for his wife's testing but before he has explained Morgan's role, Gawain charges "boþe þat on and þat oþer, myn honoured ladyez" with having "bigyled" him (2412 and 2413), a verb that hints at magic as well as seduction.[83] A man falling for the "wyles of wymmen" is, Gawain asserts, "no ferly [marvel]" (2415 and 2414)—unlike, we must assume, the Green Knight himself. The Green Knight does not reveal Morgan's role until after Gawain asks him about his true name. It is only, in other words, when the Knight must concede that he is not a magical figure in his own right that he owns up to the source of the magic. The full disclosure—including the explanations of the correlation between the blows and the exchanges, the connection between Bertilak and the Green Knight, and the discovery that he was behind his wife's behavior—points at Bertilak as the instigator of the critical moral tests. Nonetheless, Gawain seems to blame the women (and himself) entirely. In contrast, he treats Bertilak not only as a confessor, but also as an agent whose tests of Gawain's morality were revelatory and righteous. The Green Knight taints Morgan by describing her as an enchantress with shallow aims, and although the other scheme may have been Bertilak's, it could only be carried out with his wife's cunning and deftness. So although Gawain may not be wrong in seeing the women as the active agents here, he implicitly absolves the man who claims to have designed the test that Gawain failed.

Gawain's subsequent return to court raises questions about how his experiences affect or influence the community into which he is quickly reabsorbed. In some related narratives, including *The Greene Knight*, *The Turke and Sir Gawain*, and *The Carle of Carlisle*, the opponent also returns and joins the court; in this version, with its heightened moral sensibility, however, the Green Knight's expanded role as moral tester prevents him from becoming a part of the Arthurian community. He represents the crucial mechanism of Morgan's test of the court and has taken on the responsibility of testing one of its members more extensively. Because of that first role, he cannot be absorbed into the community that he has tested without invalidating either the test or the community. Identifying him with or incorporating him into the community would change its nature, which the poem has only just established. Furthermore, and because of that second role, the Green Knight cannot be welcomed among the knights in the same way that his symbol, the green girdle, was[84]—he would be an ineluctable reminder of Gawain's shame and shortcomings, albeit in relation to what may now seem to be an unreasonable ideal.

T. McAlindon argues that Gawain's return at the end shows that "magic is not an omnipotent force."[85] However, despite the apparent revelation near the end, this poem, like all of the texts in this study, leaves readers knowing very little about the nature, workings, and limits of magic. How, exactly, did Morgan le Fay transform Bertilak into the Green Knight? Did the green girdle truly possess magical powers? The text leaves these questions unanswered. The dénouement claims to uncover the agency behind the marvel, but instead it provides a slippery identification of the purported motivation and the magical agent, pointing both back to the disguised figure of the hag and beyond her to the shadowy figure of Merlin. Although the identification of Morgan is surprising, the revelation suggests that the more significant moral agency lies with the Green Knight himself. The revelation is, one might argue, more about the moral than the magical; we certainly learn more about the former than the latter aspects of what has unfolded. The marvelous signaled the presence of the moral, and each was striking enough to engage our memories while remaining mysterious or uncertain enough to inspire our senses of wonder.

Sir Gawain and the Green Knight represents the zenith of the visual marvel in the fourteenth century. In their animation, recurrence, and divided agency, its marvels are more complex and detailed than those that come before. The marvels are also moving in other senses; they affect not only Gawain and the Round Table, but also the audience, raising moral questions about the Arthurian community and its knightly ideals. The very existence of Bertilak might teach us to look more carefully for the extraordinary in the ordinary, to resist that blunting effect of familiarity that Augustine cautioned against and instead, as both he and Jane Bennett encourage us from their different contexts and perspectives, to see the everyday world as containing and producing wonder. But at what point do natural wonders shade into the supernatural? As we will see in the next chapter, the problem of distinguishing miracle from magic dominated the medieval discourse of the marvelous. Although Richard's coronation pageant and the Cotton Nero A.x manuscript constructively mixed religious and secular elements, many philosophers and writers, including Isidore of Seville and Gervase of Tilbury, as well as Augustine himself, worked to maintain separate categories. In the *Canterbury Tales*, Chaucer does so in part by visualizing miracles while leaving the operations and outcomes of magic unseen; he draws on the now-familiar tradition of spectacular magical marvels to raise readers' expectations before substituting marvels that focus on language rather than visual representation.

CHAPTER FOUR

TALKING MAGIC
Chaucer's Spectacles of Language

As secular marvels become more spectacular and affective, they also become more like miracles—a convergence that could be disquieting or invigorating. Geoffrey Chaucer's *Canterbury Tales* offers an unusually expansive range of marvels for a literary text, cataloging the natural as well as the supernatural, the divine as well as the demonic, and the scientific as well as the saintly. This varied collection allows us to examine how the poem interacts with two different strands of influence: the relevant philosophical discourse—which stretched across the Middle Ages and underscored the problems of defining the marvelous and separating it from the miraculous—and the recent Middle English literary tradition that had established close associations among the marvelous, the visual, and the moral by this point in the fourteenth century. Over the course of the *Canterbury Tales*, a classification system takes shape that reflects medieval philosophers' concerns about distinguishing miracles, yet also shares the poetic interest in the moral potential of secular marvels.[1] The text winds these two threads together by representing secular marvels that are more morally engaging but less visual than its miracles.

One particularly vivid miracle comes from the *Man of Law's Tale*: when the knight who has framed Constance for murder swears that she is guilty, a hand appears, smiting him "upon the nekke-boon" so that he falls down and "bothe his eyen broste out of his face / In sighte of every body in that place."[2] This dramatic demonstration of God's power resolves any doubts about Constance's innocence in this specific case and about her virtuous character in general. In answering readers' questions and leaving them with a powerful image, this scene is both similar to many of the other miracles in the *Canterbury Tales* and markedly different from the depictions of secular marvels in that text.

Chaucer's depictions of magic are not as intensely visual as either his miracles or the secular marvels that we have seen in earlier Middle English texts are. We might wonder what happens when a text mobilizes readers' expectations of a climactic visual image in a narrative with pressing moral concerns only to thwart those expectations, and whether the anticipation and then absence of a visual image also have moral effects. Chaucer's tales suggest not only that this technique can be successful, but also that it works particularly well for encouraging complex questions about and analysis of moral issues rather than providing models for ethical behavior. Ethics was a significant issue in early twentieth-century Chaucer scholarship, and critics like Elizabeth Allen, Alcuin Blamires, Mark Miller, J. Allan Mitchell, and Jessica Rosenfeld have brought new perspectives to bear on it over the last decade. Blamires's *Chaucer, Ethics, and Gender* examines how Chaucer draws on moral—and especially Stoic—doctrine and how ethics are intertwined with gender in many of the same tales that this chapter will examine.[3] However, less attention has generally been paid to questions of morality in the *Canterbury Tales*, and the ways in which magic might intersect with ethics or morality have not yet been considered in detail.

With his secular marvels, Chaucer never quite gives readers who are familiar with the earlier Middle English tradition of the marvelous the singular image that they might expect in the mode of the fairy gallery, the dragon lady, or the Green Knight. He raises such expectations with the spectacles of the magical objects' arrival at court in the *Squire's Tale* and the elf queen and the dancing ladies in the *Wife of Bath's Tale*, but ultimately he evades them. In each case, Chaucer leaves us not with an image but with a space that we must fill in, and, in the process, he deeply engages readers' imaginative and moral faculties. Mark Miller identifies the "philosophical achievement" of the *Canterbury Tales* as "its refusal of easy conceptual and moral solutions" to conflicts, especially those concerning love and sexuality, and the "constant return to the rough ground of our daily engagements with them."[4] Chaucer's marvels utilize a similar strategy in the context of the extraordinary rather than the quotidian; the tales describe encounters that demand action but make ethical precedents difficult to pinpoint, generating moral questions about other kinds of relationships that cannot easily be resolved. Ultimately, this strategy offers another model by which the romance genre might lay claim to moral significance and impact. Earlier chapters showed how morality could be invoked via an emblematic marvel rendered through visual description; the *Canterbury Tales* demonstrates that spectacles registered primarily through characters' speech can also serve moral functions.

Classifying Marvels in Medieval Discourse

By juxtaposing miracles and marvels, Chaucer revives the central debate from the discourse of the marvelous: how to define the category itself. This enterprise involves significant epistemological challenges for modern scholars as well as medieval philosophers. The tide that covers the rocks and places Dorigen in Aurelius's power in the *Franklin's Tale*, for instance, might be a manufactured illusion or a natural event. For Dorigen, the outcome is simply unimaginable: "for wende I nevere by possibilitee / That swich a monstre or merveille myghte be! / It is agayns the proces of nature" (1343–45). The horse in the *Squire's Tale* that can fly, take its rider anywhere in a single day, and become invisible at the turn of a pin might be an example of practical magic or of ingenious machinery. The tale offers a lengthy description of how perplexed Cambyuskan's people are: at first they are struck silent "for merveille" at the sight of the knight riding this horse (87), but this morphs into a more active and engaged response:

> Of sundry doutes thus they jangle and trete,
> As lewed peple demeth comunly
> Of thynges that been maad moore subtilly
> Than they kan in hir lewednesse comprehende.
> (220–23)

"Thynges that been maad ... subtilly" or are "agayns the proces of nature" or beyond "possibilitee" are all possible definitions of the marvelous. The initial problem that medieval writers face in constructing that category is exactly what "thynges" to include. Many influential medieval writers—including Augustine, Thomas Aquinas, Isidore of Seville, and Gervase of Tilbury—worried about this issue, and similar concerns surfaced in household handbooks and sermon collections. The Middle English word *merveille* is capacious; it can describe an object or occurrence, which is how Dorigen uses it, or a reaction, like the people's response to the knight and his brass horse. Even in the former usage, it is defined in terms of its impact: "a thing, act, or event that causes astonishment or surprise" or a "cause for wonderment."[5] A marvel, then, would be anything that causes one to marvel.

As this tautology suggests, marvels are often defined by their mysterious nature, by the very fact that they are beyond human comprehension. From an epistemological perspective, marvels complicate both dimensions of taxonomy—namely, making distinctions as well as uncovering relationships. They draw on such a variety of discourses—religion, science, medicine, technology, visual culture and performance, etc.—that it is difficult to create coherent groupings or recognize which differences might be most meaningful. The first problem is how to distinguish the marvelous from other categories. Should the miraculous be included, or are religious marvels distinct from secular ones? How does one discern the truly supernatural from what is unfamiliar yet ordinary? The second problem is how to discriminate between different types of marvels. How does one separate well-intentioned charms from malevolent necromancy, or fairy magic from other types of enchantment? How can one identify whether a wonder is produced by magical or mechanical means? Most literary texts sidestep these questions by naming something magical or marvelous and leaving the details open to interpretation, an approach that works best when there is only one potential marvel. With a varied collection, like the one in the *Canterbury Tales*, the problem of classification becomes both more pressing and more possible to answer.

By taking up these questions, Chaucer engages with a line of thought that reaches back to the foundational text in the medieval discourse of the marvelous, *The City of God*, in which Augustine writes that marvels are "beyond all the limits of man's power."[6] Although he recognizes some natural wonders, Augustine sees most marvels as "the invention[s] of deceitful demons" and is preoccupied by their religious impact.[7] By the thirteenth century, natural marvels had become more important, and Gervase of Tilbury became a prominent promoter of their virtues. He suggests that the mysterious nature of such marvels attracts us: "when anything strange is observed we seize on it, partly because of the inversion of the natural order which surprises us, partly because of our ignorance of the cause, whose working is a mystery to us, and partly because of seeing our expectation cheated in unfamiliar circumstances of which we lack a proper understanding. . . . We call those things marvels which are beyond our comprehension . . . in fact, the inability to explain why a thing is so constitutes a marvel."[8] This definition governs the collection of marvels that he presents and allows him to include selected religious wonders alongside those from nature.

Despite their different orientations, both of these writers take up the predominant concern that emerges from the first problem of defining the marvelous in the Middle Ages: whether miracles are a type of marvel or something else altogether. Augustine is most influential in this regard; he defines miracles as "performed in order to promote the worship of the one true God" and "through simple faith and pious trust in God," whereas marvels are accomplished "by means of incantations and charms, products of an art that wickedly meddles with the occult."[9] Gervase follows his lead: "we generally call those things miracles which, being preternatural, we ascribe to divine power, as when a virgin gives birth, when Lazarus is raised from the dead, or when diseased limbs are made whole again."[10] In other words, the crucial difference is agency: miracles are the result of divine agency, while marvels encompass all other forms. This distinction is not always as firm as it might seem, since many instances of natural magic or wonders from the natural world draw on powers inherent in nature as God's creation but are considered to be part of the secular marvelous, along with sorcery, technology, and other elements. Furthermore, as we have seen in earlier chapters, marvelous agency is often ambiguous or multiple in literary texts.

This point returns us to the idea that marvels are defined by their mysterious nature; the mystery is paradoxically deepened by the fact that the agency involved is not recognizably divine. However, a complicating factor is the issue of familiarity. We can see this principle at work in texts like the *Wonders of the East* and *The Book of John Mandeville*, which present marvels from distant lands that seem marvelous in part because they are foreign. On his travels, Mandeville is introduced to a fruit that contains "a beest of flessh, blod, and boon" like "a lytel lombe withouten wolle"—this, he remarks, is a "gret mervayle." But he then offers a parallel example from his own country, "trees that bereth fruyt that bycometh bryddes fleynge." The people who find the lamb fruit unremarkable "had gret mervayle of this."[11] Each fruit is purportedly part of the natural world, but the marvel reaction in this cultural exchange arises from the observer's unfamiliarity. Gervase, whose avowed "primary purpose is to present the marvels of every province to our discerning listener," admits that if we are told of something far away, we marvel, but when "the evidence for these things is set before our eyes every day, they are held of no account, not because they are of a less marvellous character, but simply because we see them so often" (563).[12] Most of the *Canterbury Tales* marvels are set in places and times that are distant from fourteenth-century London, underscoring their unfamiliar nature.

Because marvels were so often visual, the unreliability of our sight was another significant anxiety in the discourse of the marvelous throughout the Middle Ages, second only to the related concern about the overlap between miracles and marvels. The problem was one of access (we cannot always see who or what is responsible for the marvelous effects, or how they are produced) as well as manipulation (marvels may create illusions or involve other kinds of visual deception). Further complicating the issue, miracles and divine agency require observers to trust what they cannot see; indeed, they are often visible proofs of an invisible God. Magical marvels were especially unsettling in this regard: the ability to create illusions or to transform appearances is one of the greatest powers—and greatest dangers—that magic holds. Not surprisingly, Isidore of Seville locates an etymological connection between illusion and sight in his seventh-century *Etymologies*: "they are called illusions [praestigium] because they dull [praestringere] the sharpness of one's eyes." Although magic itself may be real—and Isidore claims elsewhere that magicians can "agitate the elements, disturb the minds of people, and slay without any drinking of poison, using the violence of spells alone"—it creates illusions that are not.[13] We cannot trust what we see.

This issue creates a central tension: marvels make it hard to believe what we see, but the very fact that we have seen them nurtures our belief. If that belief is not directed toward God, it may become attached to the marvel before us, even if it is an illusion. One of Augustine's most serious condemnations of magic is that it is "a seeing that affords no sight of what really exists."[14] Although the invisible God works visible miracles that are meant, Augustine argues, to inspire our worship, he also warns that magic cannot allow access to God and that Satan uses illusions to seduce us. Later writers pick up this idea that marvels are not only deceptive, but also seductive, leading us away from God. Whereas miracles may convince us and strengthen our belief through sight, marvels can deceive us and thereby misdirect our belief by the same method.

Once a writer or philosopher has constituted the category of the marvelous itself, regardless of whether it includes the miraculous, the natural, or the merely unfamiliar, then the next challenge emerges—how to differentiate one type of marvel from another. This concern is particularly pressing for marvels that involve magic, and that seems to be the area where the most taxonomic effort is expended. These efforts seek not only to organize magic, but also, by doing so, to regain some control over it and its threatening possibilities. Agency may reappear as a consideration in this context, distinguishing not only miracles from other kinds of marvels, but also natural wonders and mechanical inventions from supernatural effects. Intention is also sometimes a basis for distinction: those who wish to heal are engaged in natural magic, for example, whereas those who seek to control another's will are practicing necromancy. In many cases, however, the defining factor is the practice that creates the magical marvel (the *how* rather than the *who* or *why*).

In the *Etymologies*, Isidore of Seville synthesizes and systematizes knowledge about a vast array of subjects, including magic, which he positions in the book on "the church and sects";[15] as Corinne Saunders notes, this was "the most widely circulated treatment of magic in the early Middle Ages."[16] Isidore identifies four categories of magic—divinations, auguries, oracles, and necromancy—but further subdivides those, noting at least ten types in the first category, for instance. An early fourteenth-century preacher's handbook also considers magic in a religious context but warns about a variety of practitioners, including palm readers, soothsayers, and those "whose art it is to look into mirrors, bowls, polished fingernails, and the like, in which they claim they see marvelous things"; these classifications coincide with Isidore's at some but not all points.[17] The distinctions drawn in the classification schemes that share an emphasis on practice still vary, especially as the Middle Ages continue.

Modern scholars have created taxonomies along similar lines, using agency to distinguish religious and secular marvels, for example, and intention and practice as the bases for marking off one type of secular marvel from another. The subcategory of medieval magic has received particular attention, with Richard Kieckhefer and other historians grappling with its complexities by developing and adapting an influential model for classifying practices as either natural or demonic: "demonic magic invokes evil spirits and rests upon a network of religious beliefs and practices, while natural magic exploits 'occult' powers within nature and is essentially a branch of medieval science."[18] As the *Canterbury Tales* shows, however, marvels are different in literary texts. Agency and intent are often obscure, so marvels must be identified and classified on the basis of representation and effect. In other words, these marvels must be read in ways similar to the literary texts themselves.

Classifying Marvels in the *Canterbury Tales*

As Caroline Walker Bynum points out, "the distinguishing of miracle and marvel as ontological categories led to the de-wondering of marvel, magic, and even of miracle. It also sometimes led to flattening—a substituting of generalized description for sharp, specific accounts of discrete and fascinating occurrences."[19] In presenting such "specific accounts" and blurring the lines between different types of marvels, the *Canterbury Tales* produces a type of "re-wondering" effect, emphasizing individual marvels and encouraging wonder-reactions. Chaucer's use of the signifying terms provides one way of tracking this dynamic. *Miracle* occurs multiple times in the Knight's, Man of Law's, Franklin's, and Second Nun's tales; the Man of Law's, the Clerk's, the Squire's, and the Franklin's tales all include multiple uses of *marvel* and/or *marvelous*; and every character except the Reeve, the Cook, the Friar, the Physician, and the Pardoner uses *wonder* in some form at least once.[20] These terms occur throughout the tales, indicating the number and range of marvels that are represented. By considering these varied marvels collectively, we can begin to see how Chaucer classifies them in three primary and often-overlapping categories—scientific, religious, and magical—and how those classifications connect to and depart from the philosophical and historical models outlined above.

The *Canterbury Tales* includes several examples that approach the line between magic and science or technology but ultimately seem to fall on the latter side; the objects that manipulate that boundary most successfully are *mirabilia*. These technological or mechanical wonders significantly increased in availability by the late thirteenth century and were popular throughout the fourteenth, as we saw in the previous chapter. Although few existed in England, King Edward II had visited the famous garden at Hesdin in 1313, and later members of the English court would likely have heard about such marvels and perhaps witnessed some while abroad. Chaucer might be alluding to them in the scene from the *Franklin's Tale* in which the clerk shows Aurelius and his brother deer-filled parks, jousting knights, and dancing ladies without leaving his study.[21] The *mirabilia* might also have inspired the disappearing brass horse from the *Squire's Tale*, which I will discuss in more detail below. Nonetheless, such inventions provoke wonder precisely because of their recognized mechanical nature. They are manmade marvels, to borrow Scott Lightsey's phrase; the exact technology is mysterious to the audience, whose wonder arises from the pleasurable paradox of something that is unknown and yet knowable. As Lightsey suggests, "the delight of the marvel was in the experience, not in the marvel itself.... These newly naturalized marvels were incapable of producing supernatural wonder."[22]

Mirabilia are similar to astrology and alchemy insofar as all three involve what we would today identify as science; as magic-like elements, however, the first is distinct from the other two. Both alchemy and astrology are about acquiring and applying knowledge (the former more concrete, the latter more abstract), whereas *mirabilia* are about the object as an embodiment of knowledge and so are closer to technology in modern parlance. In other words, in the case of *mirabilia*, medieval audiences focus less on the human role or agent—since a mechanical wonder "seeks to efface its own construction" and belongs to the "image-not-made-by-human-hands tradition"[23]—and more on the wonder of the result. That wonder is not supernatural, but instead derives from the elusiveness of an explanation that the audience believes or knows to exist; alchemy, on the other hand, is about the often-partial explanation of a process that is never proven. Whereas *mirabilia* amaze, alchemy perplexes.

The *Canterbury Tales* distinguishes *mirabilia* from astrology and alchemy because the latter two have explanations that are not only within the reach of human reasoning, but also, to some degree, present in the text. These explanations paradoxically raise and undercut the possibility that something magical is happening. Although Chaucer shows an interest in alchemy and astrology, he regards their grander claims with some skepticism—as in the *Treatise on the Astrolabe*, which differentiates knowledge of astronomy from "judicial matere [astrology] and rytes of payens, in whiche my spirit hath no feith."[24] Although the tales offer some details about astrological calculations and alchemical methods, those accounts tend to point to incomprehensible or incompletely understood causes. That aspect might make astrology and alchemy more capable than the technological marvels of arousing wonder; in her study of the causes and characteristics of wonder in the Middle Ages, Bynum argues, "the amazement discussed by philosophers, chroniclers, and travelers had a strong cognitive component; you could wonder only where you knew that you failed to understand."[25]

When this type of failure occurs in the *Canterbury Tales*, however, Chaucer casts the incomprehension as potentially temporary: a failure to understand can only follow an effort to do so, and the text hints that persistent efforts to understand might ultimately succeed. When the Canon's Yeoman fails to grasp alchemy, for instance, Chaucer preserves the possibility that its esoteric or inadequate explanations might become clear as the experiments continue. An unanticipated outcome prompts the Canon to caution the Yeoman, "be ye no thyng amased" (935), and they resolve to try again. This narrative tactic curtails the potential for wonder and any similarity to magic. Accordingly, although the *Canon's Yeoman's Tale* portrays alchemy as an "elvysshe craft" capable of causing fundamental transformations (751),[26] that reference comes during a detailed discussion about alchemical ingredients, measurements, methods, and equipment. If this exposition puzzles the audience, it likely does not inspire wonder. The astrological calculations detailed in the *Franklin's Tale* work similarly. Critical debate continues about whether the flood covering the rocks results from a natural event or astrological manipulations, but in either case Chaucer presents the causes as within the realm of human understanding and therefore not entirely magical.[27]

The *Canterbury Tales* also contains cases that interrogate the relationship between religion and magic, offering opposing views of it. In the closing tale, the Parson excoriates "malefice of sorcerie" and "thilke horrible sweryng of adjuracioun and conjuracioun, as doon thise false enchauntours or nigromanciens" (341 and 603); however, religion and magic are less in opposition to each other in Chaucer's earlier portrayals of miracles. Miracles, unlike science, eternally exceed human knowledge, but their divine agency distinguishes them from magical events.[28] The *Canterbury Tales* adheres to that distinction, representing miracles as the direct result of God's intervention, and strengthens it by portraying miracles in a markedly different register from magical or even magic-like elements: Chaucer's most significant portrayals of magic involve spectacles of language, as I will argue below, but his miracles are visual spectacles.

We have already seen this in the *Man of Law's Tale*, and several other miracles work similarly. We have another disembodied hand in the *Monk's Tale*, this time writing on a wall rather than smiting someone. In the *Second Nun's Tale*, Cecilia survives "a bath of flambes rede" (515) and preaches for several days after a messy attempted beheading. The little boy in the *Prioress's Tale* has his throat cut but continues to sing until a grain is removed from his tongue; we might think of this miracle as predominantly aural, but the emphasis on the horrific treatment of the boy's body and the importance of the physical presence of the grain also give it a strong visual dimension. In each of these cases, the miracle takes shape as a visual spectacle, and that representation relies not on the level of detail in the description but instead on the striking nature of the images presented. These spectacles encourage readers to marvel at the demonstration of divine knowledge and power but ultimately remain inscrutable. We might doubt whether Constance, Cecilia, the murdered boy, or the other characters in these tales had fair treatment or a happy ending, but there is no hint that these miracles could be understood more deeply through human powers of reasoning and investigation.

Although it may not be a miracle, Apollo's transformation of the crow in the *Manciple's Tale* seems to be accomplished through a form of divine agency: to punish the crow for revealing his wife's adultery, Apollo "made hym blak, and refte hym al his song, / And eek his speche" (305–6). Despite the human characteristics that Apollo exhibits, he is a pagan god and may therefore accomplish this end through whatever divine powers he possesses. Some medieval thinkers classified pagan gods as demons, however, and so would see this as an example of demonic magic rather than semidivine punishment.[29] In either case, Apollo's power and nature remain obscure. Also unclear is the case of the shape-shifting demon in the *Friar's Tale*. He explains his powers to the summoner:

> But whan us liketh we kan take us oon,
> Or elles make yow seme we been shape;
> Somtyme lyk a man, or lyk an ape,
> Or lyk an angel kan I ryde or go.
> (1462–65)

Nonetheless, this ability is "no wonder thyng," scoffs the fiend, "a lowsy jogelour kan deceyve thee, / And pardee, yet kan I moore craft than he" (1466–68). On one hand, this seems like the purest possible example of demonic magic. On the other hand, the "magic" is firmly positioned in hell (1459–61 and 1636–38) and worked entirely by the demon himself to achieve Satan's ends and so seems less like magic than a marvel that falls within the purview of Christianity, a partial counterweight to God's miraculous powers. At any rate, the shape shifting remains theoretical; the fiend never transforms within the narrative, and only exercises his ability to transport the summoner to hell.

If we rule out those instances in the *Canterbury Tales* in which the possibly magical elements belong more substantially to science or religion, then we are left with a number in which magic itself stands as the defining discourse. Although these cases are more clearly magical, the type of magic involved is not clear; it is neither obviously demonic (since the creation of the magic is outside the scope of the narrative) nor natural (since it seems to exceed even the occult powers inherent in nature). This ambiguity is characteristic of literary magic, which often served, at least in part, to entertain the audience in ways similar to *mirabilia* or courtly illusions. Chaucer includes some illusions of this type in his texts. In the *House of Fame*, the narrator sees

> . . . Colle tregetour
> Upon a table of sycamour

> Pleye an uncouth thyng to telle—
> Y saugh him carien a wynd-melle
> Under a walsh-note shale.
> (1277–81)

These lines seem to describe an illusion performed for courtly amusement, much like the scenes to which Aurelius's brother refers in the *Franklin's Tale*: "for ofte at feestes have I wel herd seye / That tregetours withinne an halle large / Have maad come in a water and a barge." Other reported illusions include a "grym leoun," blooming flowers, grapes on a vine, and a stone castle, each of which the magicians "voyded" as quickly as it had appeared (1142–50). The brother's references to these sights as "apparences" and his repetition of "semed" emphasize that they are illusory (1140, 1146, and 1151); the term "tregetour" may also carry the connotation of an entertainer or one who performs tricks. We could see the clerk's illusions in his study—which follow fewer than fifty lines later—as well as the brass horse from the *Squire's Tale* as courtly illusions in this vein rather than *mirabilia*. The focus on entertainment characterizes such illusions, which are often temporary and ephemeral.

The least ambiguous instances of magic in the *Canterbury Tales*—the loathly lady's transformation in the *Wife of Bath's Tale* and Canacee's ring in the *Squire's Tale*—are more substantial and enduring than the illusions, yet they have no rational explanation (mechanical, scientific, or otherwise) and do not involve divine agency. The magic has an otherworldly aspect that develops in the first tale from the reference to fairies and the implication that the loathly lady may herself be one, and in the second tale from the reception of the magical objects in Cambyuskan's court, which has already been established as an exotic space.[30] The association with a supernatural but secular otherworld marks off these tales from those that contain the more ambiguous marvels cataloged above, further signaling the magical nature of the *Wife of Bath's Tale* and the *Squire's Tale*. In addition to departing from the historical models of magic in the ways noted above, these narratives lack one of the defining characteristics of marvelous discourse: an emphasis on the visual spectacle. As the previous chapters have shown, that emphasis was particularly prominent in the literary genre that was home to many, if not most, secular marvels: romance. Although they share the romantic interest in marvels and the fourteenth-century interest in the connections among magic, morality, and spectacle, these tales imagine their marvelous spectacles differently.

Scholars interested in Chaucerian magic have recognized the connection to earlier romances but have emphasized specific correspondences, such as those between *Sir Orfeo* and the *Franklin's Tale*. They also tend to approach magic as a sign for something else, usually the analogous creative act of writing, instead of considering it on its own terms.[31] Few studies have considered Chaucer's use of magic in a context broader than a single tale.[32] In the rest of this chapter, I will examine the function of magic directly rather than as a mystification or metaphor, investigating the connections that Chaucer constructs among magic, language, and morality in the two tales that contain instances of magic that we cannot attribute to manufactured illusions, natural events, or divine intervention.

A Spectacle of Transformation: The *Wife of Bath's Tale*

A hag's transformation into a beautiful maiden is the primary magic in Chaucer's *Wife of Bath's Tale*, John Gower's "Tale of Florent," and various analogues. Although the versions involve magic to different degrees, it is consistently concentrated in the figure of the loathly lady, who provides the correct answer to the knight's quest, marries him, and then offers him a choice between having her beautiful by day or night (in Gower) or between having her be either beautiful and faithless or ugly and faithful (in Chaucer). Through his representation of the character of that magic, Chaucer reshapes the loathly lady's intervention as a conscious moral test possible only through magic; by leaving both magic and magician mysterious, he encourages readers to think more deeply about the moral questions raised by the tale regarding male-female interactions.

In Chaucer's version, magic is present from the opening lines, when the Wife describes the setting as a "land fulfild of fayerye" in "th'olde dayes of the Kyng Arthour" (859 and 857), and the loathly lady's initial appearance confirms the magical atmosphere.[33] Other versions postpone the magic; in *The Weddyng of Syr Gawen and Dame Ragnell* and *The Marriage of Sir Gawain*, the narratives establish the Arthurian setting without the additional mentions of fairies and elves,[34] and in Gower's version magic does not come into play until the wedding night, and then in the explicit form of enchantment. The knight, Florent, turns over in bed to see that his wife has become a beautiful young woman, and she then presents him with the choice regarding her nature. Her already-complete transformation operates as a temptation, or perhaps a visual aid: here is the beauty he will have and now he must choose whether to have it publicly or privately. When Florent cedes the choice to the loathly lady, she rejoices that "mi destine is overpassed" and declares that she will now be beautiful "til I be take into my grave."³⁵ She then reveals her fascinating backstory:

> The kinges dowhter of Cizile
> I am, and fell bot siththe awhile,
> As I was with my fader late,
> That my Stepmoder for an hate,
> Which toward me sche hath begonne,
> Forschop me, til I hadde wonne
> The love and sovereinete
> Of what knyht that in his degre
> Alle othre passeth of good name.³⁶

For Gower's loathly lady, the transformation from ugly to beautiful is a reversal of magic: released from her stepmother's spell, she becomes her true self. Several versions share this enchantment aspect; in *The Weddyng of Syr Gawen and Dame Ragnell*, the lady attributes her appearance to "nygramancy" and "enchauntement," and in *The Marriage of Sir Gawain*, she describes herself as "witched."³⁷ Florent's misdeed was killing another knight in battle, but he has now proven himself to be the most worthy knight and so earns his fitting reward. That reward seems to come from fate, with the stepmother as fate's proxy and the loathly lady as the prize. She moves from being the pawn of her stepmother's magic to being a symbol of Florent's virtue but possesses little control over either situation.

The emphasis on Florent's worthiness is unsurprising. Chaucer dubbed his contemporary "moral Gower," and scholars largely shared this stance until the late twentieth century; work by Diane Watt, Elizabeth Allen, and others has complicated that view of Gower as well as the implicit distinction that it creates between the two poets.³⁸ I want to argue that morality dominates Chaucer's version of the story—perhaps even more so than Gower's, despite the emphasis on Florent's virtue—and that Chaucer brings in those moral concerns not only by adding the lengthy speech on *gentilesse*, but also more subtly by refashioning the magic. In that aspect of the *Wife of Bath's Tale*, there are two key differences, which may arise from authorial invention or from an alternative set of sources: Chaucer makes different choices about the nature of the magic involved and omits the enchantment backstory.³⁹ Whatever its origin, the latter is more striking because it gives the loathly lady control over her transformation rather than making her the subject or victim of it; she is not enchanted by an evil stepmother but instead has magical powers of her own that allow her, among other things, to change from a loathly form to a lovely one. Chaucer's characterization of the loathly lady both enacts the underlying lesson of the tale—that all women desire sovereignty—and undermines it.[40] The loathly lady possesses more sovereignty as a result of her magical power and therefore gives more up when she uses it solely to satisfy her husband's pleasure, underscoring her nobility with that sacrifice. This significant change is characteristic of Chaucer's approach to the nature of magic in the narrative.

Chaucer alters the nature of the magic in part by making it something performed through language. Before Gower's loathly lady offers the choice to Florent, she transforms in instantaneous action unassociated with any direct speech.[41] In the *Wife of Bath's Tale*, however, the transformation occurs not only during but also through the lady's words. Language was crucial to magical practice outside of literary texts; acts of magic or illusion were often about significant terms or exact incantations, even when other methods, such as drawing diagrams or mixing herbal ingredients, were involved.[42] The focus on words here relates to the translation magic of the *Squire's Tale*, and may remind us of the importance of speech in *Sir Orfeo* (in which the Fairy King's promise is key) and the contrasting emphasis on actions in a magical context in *Lybeaus Desconus* and *Sir Gawain and the Green Knight* (with the fearsome kiss and nonfatal beheading, respectively). The magical knowledge that the tale has already shown the loathly lady to possess, which I will discuss below, may also make her words more powerful, and the *gentilesse* speech that immediately precedes this moment sets up readers to perceive the loathly lady's words as important and authoritative.

Here is her response after the knight has ceded the decision to her:

> "Kys me," quod she, "we be no lenger wrothe,
> For, by my trouthe, I wol be to yow bothe—
> This is to seyn, ye, bothe fair and good.
> I prey to God that I moote sterven wood,
> But I to yow be also good and trewe
> As evere was wyf, syn that the world was newe.
> And but I be to-morn as fair to seene
> As any lady, emperice, or queene,
> That is bitwixe the est and eke the west,
> Dooth with my lyf and deth right as yow lest.
> Cast up the curtyn, looke how that it is."
> (1239–49)

Language and magic are intimately bound up here; the lady promises that she will be "bothe fair and good," and she becomes so as she says so. Chaucer describes no actions and proffers no visible evidence of that marvel taking place until the end of the speech. The command to "cast up the curtyn" reinforces that the transformation has been screened from view; neither the reader nor the knight sharing the lady's bed has seen any change up to this point.[43] The speech provides the only access to the magic even as the speech acts as the agent of the magic. This is both mysterious—because no one, inside or outside the tale, sees the transformation occur, and Chaucer offers no explanation or description of it—and materially obvious, since the loathly lady says what she is doing and does what she is saying.

The magic only becomes visible when the knight sees "verraily al this, / That she so fair was, and so yong therto" (1250–51) and takes the lady into his arms and begins kissing her. The knight's reaction validates that the transformation has taken place, but it also substitutes for any depiction of the process or effects of that transformation. There is no catalog of the transformed lady's loveliness, nothing to balance the repeated references to her loathsomeness.[44] The addition of an invisible component to the choice complicates the transformation; faithfulness and fairness may well be connected, as virtue and beauty often are in medieval texts, but the latter can more easily be represented through a physical change. However, the type of choice is a further indication of magic's close association with moral qualities in this tale: Chaucer has heightened the morality of the choice itself by expanding it to include faithfulness. Because this element concerns the nature of the marriage as well as of the loathly lady herself, the change aligns with Chaucer's concern over male-female relationships. It also works with the portrayal of magic as speech rather than spectacle or, more precisely, as a spectacle of speech—a portrayal that allows the moral aspects of the choice, which are present only through the loathly lady's words, to receive at least as much emphasis as the physical aspects do.

The loathly lady's speech occupies the place in which the enchantment story occurs in the "Tale of Florent" and other versions and thus represents a significant narrative shift. The absence of that explanation puts the loathly lady in charge of her own transformation and, by extension, of the test administered to the knight. In Chaucer's version, she engineers the marriage and the choice between beauty and fidelity in order to ascertain whether the knight has learned his lesson about women's bodies and desires. Because Chaucer has reconfigured the magic as subject to the loathly lady's control, it becomes something other than a source of entertainment for the audience or a method of rewarding an otherwise unlucky but virtuous knight (as he appears to be in the analogues); magic enables the loathly lady to oversee the knight's rehabilitation, assess his morality, and determine that justice has been served for his crime. It takes a magical figure—one who has the ability to transform her physical body so that she can appear either repulsive or attractive—to carry out the definitive test of whether the knight has absorbed the lesson implicit in the quest.[45] Ultimately, the knight must put what he learned into practice, and that moral end is not just facilitated by but orchestrated entirely through magic. The tale weaves that common romance element tightly into the moral fabric of the narrative.

Magic comes into play even before the shape shifting, however; in Chaucer's version, the loathly lady's powers encompass special access to knowledge—something we also saw with the supernatural revelations of identity in the fair unknown narratives—as well as the ability to transform herself. Although the initial hint of her magical nature comes from her appearance—the knight sees some dancing ladies who disappear and then encounters the loathly lady—her magical abilities first clearly manifest themselves through her knowledge, and that knowledge, in turn, is demonstrated through her speech. She knows what all women desire; she seems, in fact, to be the only one who can produce this answer and thereby save the knight's life, although others later validate it.[46] The queen's nonmagical effort to rehabilitate the knight would have failed utterly without the loathly lady's intervention, and the narrative would have moved toward his execution unimpeded. By portraying the loathly lady as a magical being and the sole possessor of this knowledge, Chaucer indicates that the quest was supremely difficult (because only she can answer it) and that her answer is perfectly true (because it describes her as well as nonmagical women—a crossing of categories more striking than the joint affirmation of that answer by the maidens, wives, and widows at court).[47] The loathly lady is the only figure who knows "what thyng is it that wommen moost desiren" (905), and therefore she is the only one who can educate the knight and establish the moral center of the tale.

The loathly lady also knows about the knight's desires: "syn I knowe youre delit," she says to him in the pivotal bedroom scene, "I shal fulfille youre worldly appetit" (1217–18). This observation implies that her power is not limited to the two choices that she offers here; unlike the loathly ladies in the closest analogues, Chaucer's character could assume any appearance or characteristic that she wishes to, yet puts forward these options because they accord best with her husband's desires. By making the loathly lady a practitioner of magic in her own right, Chaucer has changed the nature of the magic and raised its profile within the narrative: more types of magic are possible, and magic can work in many different ways. Although Gower withheld magic until the end of his version, Chaucer makes it a critical element of the narrative throughout and associates it with the loathly lady from her first appearance.

Chaucer magnifies the moral aspect of the narrative by altering the magic, but he also leaves a pair of critical questions unanswered: why the powerful loathly lady would want to marry the knight, and whether he has truly learned his lesson. The conclusion—that very moment when modern and medieval audiences might expect the narrative to reveal its moral—offers ambiguity. The loathly lady could become anything but chooses to mold herself literally to the desires of a husband who is guilty of rape, and the tale ends by reassuring the audience that the loathly lady obeyed the knight "in every thyng / That myghte doon hym plesance or likyng" (1255–56).[48] This statement suggests that her magical powers, having served their moral purpose, have disappeared beneath her wifely submission. It creates a moral complication rather than a satisfying ending, however. Chaucer departed from other versions by making the knight guilty of such a serious crime against women while also making the loathly lady a powerful female figure who exercises authority over the knight; these two elements clash in the final moments, when she surrenders that power to him.

This clash might be resolved if we believed that the knight had learned his lesson, but the narrative is evasive on this point, and critics continue to debate it.[49] When he allows his new wife the sovereignty to make the critical choice, his concession to her "wise governance" (1231) might be a sincere and well-informed capitulation, the outcome of frustration, or, at worst, clever manipulation. The text offers little evidence to support any of those interpretations, and so we are left wondering whether the magical remediation of the knight was successful—whether a marvelous transformation, in other words, can effect a moral one. Chaucer exacerbates this uncertainty through his vagueness about the nature of the magic and the woman who uses it. When the knight and the loathly lady meet, she does not immediately specify what she wants from him, and the tale keeps the answer that she provides secret until the revelation at court; these are small but critical differences from Gower's version. The loathly lady's nature is unclear from the beginning of Chaucer's tale, and the mechanism or explanation behind her transformation (or her power to transform herself) also remains obscure.[50] This lack of explanation fuels readers' curiosity, putting us in a position analogous to the knight's in that we are unsure of what to expect from the loathly lady.

Leaving these issues unresolved has the practical result of encouraging more moral involvement from readers than the versions of the story in which the loathly lady is an enchanted maiden, the knight is a virtuous figure rather than a rapist, and her desire for him seems a natural, if not inevitable, consequence of those circumstances. The open-endedness of Chaucer's tale prevents his version—with its troubling crime and correspondingly weighty message—from becoming too didactic on the surface and reminds us that magic may be a dangerous and ambivalent partner for morality. At the same time, this approach promotes a deep engagement with the moral issues at stake, such as the central questions of what women desire and how others should respond to those desires. By cultivating ambiguity and providing evidence that could support conflicting interpretations, the tale has fostered persistent moral debates about how to interpret the ending and over Chaucer's anti- or protofeminist attitude. As we will see in the following section, Chaucer avoids determinate meanings even more determinedly through his departure from sources in the *Squire's Tale*.

A Spectacle of Translation: The *Squire's Tale*

The principal magic in the *Squire's Tale* is a linguistic rather than physical transformation: translation by means of a ring that enables communication across the species boundary. This tale appears to be the most original of the narratives within the *Canterbury Tales* that involve magical or magic-like aspects; although Chaucer draws elements from a variety of sources, none has been identified for the tale as a whole. It begins with the arrival at Cambyuskan's court of an ambassador bearing four magical objects: a horse, a sword, a mirror, and a ring. Despite an early focus on the horse, the tale shows only the ring—which deciphers avian speech for its wearer—in action.[51] Canacee, Cambyuskan's daughter, wears the magical ring and hears a falcon's love complaint; Canacee then takes the falcon back to the castle in order to care for her, but the Franklin interrupts the Squire before we learn the final resolution. As in the *Wife of Bath's Tale*, Chaucer's departure from other texts makes this version of magic, with its moral emphasis, possible. Here, the magic serves even more obvious narrative purposes because it provides the only way in which Canacee and the readers can understand the falcon's speech. Both the complaint and the magic that allows us access to it invoke concerns about intent and truthfulness, raising questions not so much about the possibility of accurate interspecies translation as about the possibility of moral communication between male and female characters.

Despite the apparent originality of the narrative, the depiction of magic in the *Squire's Tale* initially seems to be Chaucer's most conventionally romantic. In the first scene, it is mysterious and foreign, and, although not entirely visual, it does have a powerful visual component. The Squire establishes the exotic setting of Cambyuskan's court, with its "strange" foods (67) and elaborate festivities, and then introduces a knight who is so unusual that he stands out even there, among people who are already foreign to the Squire's immediate audience. The knight, in other words, is doubly strange. The narrative ties his exoticism not to his own appearance but instead to the four objects that he bears and, in one case, rides:

> In at the halle dore al sodeynly
> Ther cam a knyght upon a steede of bras,
> And in his hand a brood mirour of glas.
> Upon his thombe he hadde of gold a ryng,
> And by his syde a naked swerd hangyng;
> And up he rideth to the heighe bord.
> In al the halle ne was ther spoken a word
> For merveille of this knyght.
> (80–87)

The magical objects come closest to being spectacles in this moment, but because there is so little physical description and because they are grouped together, they function more like props in the larger spectacle of the knight's sudden arrival. In the absence of any description of the knight's own appearance, those objects must provide the basis for any conclusions about him and must be the source of the court's "merveille." This situation parallels the logic of intromission theory, which was examined in the previous chapter.

The knight gives a greeting that the narrator compares to Gawain's "olde curteisye / Though he were comen ayeyn out of Fairye" (95–96)—an additional hint about the magical nature of the knight and his gifts. However, the first speech that the tale directly represents is his explanation of those gifts and their virtues: the horse will magically transport its rider, the mirror will reveal "whan ther shal fallen any adversitee" (134), the ring will translate birds' songs, and the sword will "kerve and byte" through any armor (158), leaving a wound that can only be healed with a strike of the blunt side. What the magical objects *do* receives more emphasis than how they *look*, so the focus is on their functions and potential applications rather than on their physical natures as objects.[52]

The more standard portrayal of magic quickly becomes unconventional as Chaucer plays with literary and historical sources in these descriptions. The knight begins his explanation with the "steede of bras," which has substantial precedent in the possible sources; by mixing details from sources that address mechanical horses with details from sources that describe magical horses, however, Chaucer exceeds those precedents.[53] Critics have often interpreted his horse as primarily mechanical because it operates by a "writhyng of a pyn" (127), but, as Susan Crane points out, it seems to have been created by a form of natural magic that "predicts the oddly lifelike qualities of the steed, such as its quick eye and dancing feet."[54] Furthermore, the horse's abilities—to transport its rider anywhere within a single day, to fly, and to become invisible—seem magical, even if a mechanical action triggers that magic. The crowd's reaction to the horse at first appears to offer further evidence that it merely looks magical to the ignorant. Chaucer portrays the crowd as superstitious in their response to the magical objects, especially the horse, which fascinates them both because it is "so horsly" and because it "stant as it were to the ground yglewed" (194 and 182). It cannot be moved, the Squire says, because "they kan nat the craft" (185). Although "craft" here primarily means "method" or even "trick," it also connotes magic or witchcraft and therefore suggests that the horse is a magical as well as a mechanical object.[55]

The crowd has trouble comprehending the horse and how it works, and they employ a number of authoritative texts, both literary and scientific, in their efforts to interpret it and the other magical objects: they mention Pegasus and the Trojan horse, authorities on optics and perspective, Aristotle, Achilles, Moses, and Solomon (206–11, 228–39, and 247–51). One observer distrusts the knight's account, suspecting that the horse is a conjurer's illusion, and invokes that kind of marvel directly: "it is rather lyk / An apparence ymaad by som magyk, / As jogelours pleyen at thise feestes grete" (217–19). The Squire casts the attempts at explanation as "fantasies" and "janglyng" (205 and 257), but a substantially learned foundation exists for these precedents, and the crowd's inability to understand the horse results more from the Chaucerian combination of literary and scientific elements than from ignorance or superstition.[56] The move from fascination to attempted explanation is part of what makes the crowd's reaction "a textbook example of how wonder works," as Michelle Karnes observes.[57]

The horse, which gets the most extended physical description of all the objects, has attracted the majority of the attention not only from the people at court, but also from the scholars who are interested in the marvelous aspects of the tale. However, the ring is the object on which Chaucer focuses. The knight describes its power by saying that, if Canacee wears it,

> Ther is no fowel that fleeth under the hevene
> That she ne shal wel understonde his stevene,
> And knowe his menyng openly and pleyn,
> And answere hym in his langage ageyn.
> (149–52)

The people seem to have the least explanation for this magical power, declaring

> ... that swich a wonder thyng
> Of craft of rynges herde they nevere noon,
> Save that he Moyses and kyng Salomon
> Hadde a name of konnyng in swich art.
> (248–51)

It is no wonder that the people have trouble identifying an exact precedent for this magical object; Chaucer mixed precedents in the portrayal of the horse, but departs completely from known literary and historical traditions in his portrayal of the ring. Crucially, none of the best sources that scholars have identified for the ring has the power of translation; most are "rings of oblivion" that can make their wearers forget.[58] All three of the other magical objects have more closely related analogues for their powers, but Chaucer creates this one with the unusual power of translation, providing the foundation for another spectacle of language.

The description again downplays the visual aspect: although magical rings in romances are often set with powerful gems or bear significant inscriptions, Chaucer's ring has an unprepossessing appearance and unspectacular effects.[59] The Squire offers little description of this smallest object beyond the repeated reference to it as "queynte" (369 and 433), a term that emphasizes the ring's marvelous nature rather than providing any physical detail. Its magical effects are also on an intimate scale; they are aural rather than visual and function more as individual experience than impressive display.[60] Rather than take her somewhere (as the horse can), cause and heal external wounds (as the sword can), or show her something (as the mirror can), the ring affects Canacee's understanding. It is also the most personal magical object: rather than ride, wield, or look at it, Canacee wears it, and it works within her, causing internal rather than external effects.[61] By departing from precedent and downplaying the visual and public aspects, Chaucer raises and then violates the expectations that were established by earlier fourteenth-century representations of marvels; nonetheless, he turns this dynamic to similarly moral ends. He obliges readers to judge marvelous elements, like the ring, solely on the merits and qualities that he ascribes to them instead of securely positioning those elements in relation to other representations or traditions. Patricia Clare Ingham has recently identified the interest in the possibilities and dangers of novelty as characteristic of the tale;[62] in the case of the magic, I would add, Chaucer's radical recontextualization of it not only creates the magical objects as novelties, but also allows him to reconfigure the relationship between magic and visual spectacle and create associations among magic, language, and morality.

The other three magical objects disappear after the first section of the tale; we do not see any of them in action. In the case of the horse, this disappearance is literal: the Squire claims, "the hors vanysshed, I noot in what manere, / Out of hir sighte; ye gete namoore of me" (342–43). The ring figuratively fades from view after facilitating the encounter between Canacee and the falcon that is "the knotte why that . . . [the] tale is toold" (401). The ring makes that encounter possible, yet the two references to it during the scene are surprisingly brief. The first is indirect: after she sets out on her walk, Canacee hears birds singing and "wiste what they mente" (399), which she could only do if wearing the ring. The second is direct: after she has heard and seen the shrieking falcon but before the falcon begins her complaint, the Squire reminds us that Canacee "on hir fynger baar the queynte ryng" (433). Then we hear no more about the ring as the interaction between Canacee and the falcon unfolds. Before the Franklin interrupts and ends the tale, the Squire states, "I wol namoore as now speke of hir ryng" (652), and goes on to outline the rest of his proposed narrative, which will also include a story about Cambyuskan's son and how "ful ofte in greet peril he was, / Ne hadde he ben holpen by the steede of bras" (665–66). However, these expectations—like those that the knight's initial appearance with the four magical objects might raise—remain unfulfilled, and Canacee's use of the ring stands as the only exercise of magic.[63] Although the tale moves beyond the magical objects in many ways, the ring makes the primary action possible and, as a result, becomes important as a plot device as well as a source of magic.

The ring is not merely a narrative expedient, however; it introduces vital moral issues that are again connected to language. Rather than language serving as the means of the magic, as in the *Wife of Bath's Tale*, in which the loathly lady transforms through speech, language is the object of the magic in the *Squire's Tale*—and the powers of magic and language supersede the power of violence here as they did not in *Sir Orfeo*. The pitiable sight of the falcon's self-wounding only takes on a moral valence when the ring allows the reader as well as Canacee access to the falcon's story of betrayal, which is the central moral concern of the tale. Although the Squire hints that the falcon will get "hire love ageyn / Repentant" (654–55), the narrative represents the betrayal as a grave moral situation. The magic ring allows the falcon to give a humanized voice to that story and to contrast her lover's hypocritical protestations with her own truthful speech and ethical intent. His ability to create the illusion of love preoccupies the falcon, and she continually sounds that theme in her complaint. His falseness "was so wrapped under humble cheere, / And under hewe of trouthe in swich manere," she says, "that no wight koude han wend he koude feyne, / So depe in greyn he dyed his coloures" (507–8 and 510–11). She avers that "any womman, were she never so wys" would have been fooled, "so peynted he and kembde at point-devys / As wel his wordes as his contenaunce" (559–61). One of the moral purposes of the magic, then, is to grant a voice to the falcon as a victim of faithless behavior. Yet the magic is more than a trick of translating animal speech; it is a profoundly moral magic that goes beyond simply rendering birdsong in words to allowing the wearer to comprehend the speaker's intent—a complex and difficult undertaking, according to the falcon. The magic ring does what the falcon herself could not: it sees through the spoken words to the motivations and truths beneath. Rather than creating illusions, the magic power of the ring dispels them. Karnes has recently argued that the falcon's metaphorical language "constructs [the tercel] as a marvel for the reader" and elicits a reaction that "can fittingly be called wonder." That reaction arises from his "confounding" nature—his deception is difficult for the peregrine to perceive and for the reader to understand.[64] Although his potentially marvelous quality similarly relies on language, then, it is distinctly different from the marvelous elements in this scene that are fundamentally moral.

The falcon wounds herself, shrieks, and cries in the first moments of her encounter with Canacee, and yet the narrator claims that Canacee "hath understonde what this faucon seyde" (437). We might interpret this phrase as suggesting that Canacee understands these sounds as language, although the tale does not translate them for the readers (who, after all, are not wearing magic rings), or that Canacee and the falcon can communicate without words.[65] In either reading, I argue, the salient point is that Canacee has understood the falcon's intent. The narrative has repeatedly noted this aspect of the ring's magic, stressing that its powers are more comprehensive than basic translation. The knight explained that the ring would allow its wearer not only to "understonde [a bird's] stevene," but also to "knowe his menyng openly and pleyn" (150–51), and immediately before Canacee saw the falcon, she heard birds singing and "wiste what they mente / Right by hir song, and knew al hire entente" (399–400). Because the later phrases in each case qualify or amplify the nature of the ring's power, I read "menyng" in the first instance and "entente" in the second as referring to a deeper level of understanding than literal translation and thus to moral concerns over honest versus deceptive speech.[66] Whether language can create true representation preoccupies the *Canterbury Tales* as a whole, but the Squire has demonstrated a particular concern for this issue from the outset of his tale. He declines to describe Canacee's beauty because "it lyth nat in my tonge" and "myn Englissh eek is insufficient"; instead, he concludes, "I moot speke as I kan" (35, 37, and 41). The strange knight who brings the magical objects first speaks "after the forme used in his langage," but the Squire says he cannot represent those words: "I kan nat sowne his stile, / Ne kan nat clymben over so heigh a style" (100 and 105–6). A disjunction exists between the Squire's intent and his ability to communicate.

The tale suggests that magic can resolve such disjunctions, particularly within the context of intimate conversations. The ring allows moral communication, perfectly rendering not only what each character verbalizes, but also what they intend. Presumably, if Canacee had overheard the vows of the falcon's lover while wearing the ring, she would have perceived his true "coloures." The magic would give her access to his "entente," which he concealed so skillfully from the falcon. And we must not forget the other half of the magic: the ring also allows Canacee to speak to the falcon in her "langage" (152), creating complete two-way communication. The true rapport between these female figures contrasts with the falseness of the falcon's lover and, in the end, her relationship with him; although he had only the semblance of virtue, an issue examined in chapter 2, the falcon and Canacee have the real thing. We could see their connection as reinforcing Canacee's otherness or as hinting that such an alliance can only be formed between figures who already share the status of being outsiders. However, the narrative draws its readers into this community; we, too, are witnesses to the falcon's story and decipherers of her intent. The text suggests the possibility that the talking bird, the Tartar princess, and the audience, whether medieval or modern, recognize a common moral ground.

The mews that Canacee creates for the falcon memorializes their truthfulness and perfect understanding of each other's intentions.[67] Some scholars have interpreted it as a cage, albeit a beautiful one, but it is also a moral symbol, "covered . . . with veluettes blewe, / In signe of trouthe that is in wommen sene" and painted with "false fowles" (644–45 and 647). The ring reveals Canacee and the falcon to be moral individuals, and the mews is a "signe" of the "trouthe" that the magic makes possible. Although the magic is used for moral ends in the *Wife of Bath's Tale* to educate the knight, the magic itself is also moral in the *Squire's Tale* because it facilitates true communication; magic is a moral tool in the former instance and a moral element in the latter.

Spectacle, Romance, and Chaucer

The Wife of Bath's and the Squire's tales are the two in which we see magic at work least ambiguously, and yet we *see* very little; the text glosses over the lady's transformation from loathly to beautiful in the *Wife of Bath's Tale*, and the ring in the *Squire's Tale* works invisibly. These tales have numerous other similarities—women work the magic, the magic involves a manipulation of nature, and the narratives have courtly and romantic elements, for instance—but I propose that the most striking similarity is the relationship among magic, language, and morality. Both tales center on a moral dilemma concerning how men and women interact, and in both cases that dilemma can only be revealed or addressed through magic.[68] Partly because of their marvelous elements, both tales have been read as belonging or relevant to the romance genre. Here, Chaucer offers his own permutation of the marvel/spectacle/morality triangulation that we have found across the fourteenth century, and intervenes in a related debate—with a much longer lifespan—over the status of morality in romance.

Although textual representations of marvels are slightly less threatening than visual images, they still raise the possibility that they may seduce the audience's attention away from more important or meaningful elements of the narrative. This issue was critical to the romance genre, both because romances often featured marvels and because the ethical value of romance was a central issue in its reception. Melissa Furrow outlines the debate:

there is a deep split on ethical lines, between those ... who warn against the genre's ability to distract the reader with lies and frivolity from the pursuit of the true and the purely good, and those ... who argue that a romance should have an ethical impact on its readers and allow them to choose to pursue the good and avoid the evil. But both sides of this rift would be in agreement that the genre's moral effect on its readership was the criterion by which it should be evaluated. There are fewer voices struggling to articulate other values for romance.[69]

Furrow suggests that it is especially in the fifteenth century that romances foregrounded their "moral utility,"[70] but some in the fourteenth century made the case indirectly by showing how magical spectacles could accomplish moral ends, both within and beyond the narrative. As we saw in the second chapter, the association between magic and morality evolved as Middle English romance itself did, with magic becoming more important as a test first of love and then of courtly virtues. Although their individual methods and aims varied, then, the fourteenth-century efforts interacted with not only the discourse of the marvelous, but also the idea of the genre itself.

Romance became the foundation of the English literary tradition, and, as Christopher Cannon has demonstrated, Chaucer played a crucial role in that development. Cannon suggests that, partly because romances existed in so many variants, the "idea" or "spirit" of a given romance superseded any one material form of it. The same phenomenon existed in the genre as a whole: "romance form is not the set of words found in any particular manuscript or printed book, but rather the thought which seems to be projected—as if into the ether itself—by the aggregation of all such texts."[71] Studies of romance that cover a broad historical span can help to illuminate that "spirit," but their wide-angle view obscures smaller-scale dynamics in the evolution of romance. By considering a subset of fourteenth-century texts, this study has brought the "spirit" particular to that period into view.

Cannon sees *Sir Gawain and the Green Knight* as a turning point in the development of romance—the first text to be self-reflexive about its condition as "spirit"—and he concludes that in Chaucer's *Tale of Sir Thopas*, "the spirit of romance has finally become its own raw material, the substance of which still more romances may be made."[72] I have argued, along similar lines, that Chaucer was able to manipulate the idea of magic that he drew from earlier romances; whereas such romances—including *Sir Gawain and the Green Knight*—used visual spectacles of magic to create moral effects, Chaucer intensified the moral impact of the *Wife of Bath's Tale* and the

Squire's Tale by representing magic through spectacles of language. Cannon sees Chaucer as performing a sleight-of-hand with romance—making a new and shinier nothing out of nothing—but I suggest that Chaucer's magic spectacles represent a different kind of materiality rather than the absence of materiality, and that his tales embody and further the "spirit" that I have identified just as much as numerous other fourteenth-century examples do. It is no coincidence, I contend, that Chaucer has the first recorded uses in English of two terms vital to this "spirit"—the adjective *moral* and the noun *magic*—since, in creating spectacles of language, he focuses on the material effects of words in and beyond a magical context.[73]

Chaucer, therefore, is both typical and unusual in his treatment of marvels, morality, and spectacle. His portrayals of magic conform to the pattern of interests that I have identified, and at the same time illustrate how individual the constructions of the relationship among the three key terms can be. He had plenty of experience with spectacles—as clerk of the king's works, he helped to stage several[74]—and the *Canterbury Tales* provides abundant opportunities for marvelous descriptions in the mode of headless green knights and galleries of grotesque victims of fairy magic. However, he consistently refigures such moments to avoid dazzling displays. Although Chaucer is capable of wonderful, detailed description, he does not employ those skills when his subject is magical; his descriptions of magic are muted in comparison with both his sources and most contemporary depictions of magic. In the Wife of Bath's and the Squire's tales, Chaucer configures magical scenes that he could have rendered as visual displays to be spectacles of language instead. In the *Wife of Bath's Tale*, the loathly lady's magical transformation occurs through and under the cover of her speech to the knight; in the *Squire's Tale*, the magical ring gives Canacee—and Chaucer's audience—access to the falcon's story of betrayal. These moments are still spectacles in that they draw our attention and occupy a crucial position in the narrative, but they emphasize language and speech rather than physical or visual details.

Both of these spectacles of language involve moral concerns about how one should treat others (the loathly lady poses an ethical choice to test the knight's attitude toward women; the falcon describes her lover's betrayal and embodies its effects), and both elicit responses that seem to reveal a character's moral code (the knight gives the lady sovereignty; Canacee pities and cares for the falcon). More specifically, both tales consider the mistreatment of female characters by male ones and the difficulty that female characters have in ascertaining male characters' motivations or intentions. The magical mirror, which the knight promises will show "openly who is youre freend or foo" (136), reinforces that concern and the need for magical methods to address it. This focus hews most closely to the theological virtue of love or charity, which was discussed in the introduction, above, and Chaucer's interest in it represents his broader moral concerns.

When Edmund Spenser later completes the *Squire's Tale* in *The Faerie Queene*, he picks up on both the marvelous and the moral themes in Chaucer's tale. Spenser emphasizes the former by representing fairies and another magical ring, which stops bloodshed in battles that are conducted for the love of Canacee. He highlights the latter by placing this continuation in the middle of Book Four, which focuses on the virtue of friendship, the virtue that, in the early modern construction, resembled the one at stake in Chaucer's exploration of ethical relationships. Although Spenser's project is more overtly moral and didactic than Chaucer's (intended, as the letter to Sir Walter Raleigh records, "to fashion a gentleman or noble person in vertuous and gentle discipline"), this tale fits into that project for quite specific reasons.[75]

Yoking magic and morality presents certain challenges as a result of the ambiguous moral status of magic itself and the fact that its attractions may also distract the audience from other issues. Because the practice of magic raises ethical questions, using magic to convey or enhance a moral point can highlight the complications and ambiguities of the moral as a category; like other fourteenth-century writers, Chaucer exploits that dynamic by using magic to create moral tests and dilemmas, bring extraordinary pressures to bear on characters, and involve the readers more profoundly in moral issues.[76] By representing magic as a linguistic rather than visual phenomenon, Chaucer also discourages readers from becoming absorbed in it for its own sake and instead uses it as an aesthetic tool that can thicken a plot or magnify a moral dilemma. Although Chaucer's spectacles of language are unusual, his use of spectacle to mediate the association between the marvelous and the moral participates in a "spirit" shared by a number of fourteenth-century Middle English romances. And although Cannon perceives romance as marking the decline in "the boldness and experimentation that had characterized English writing after the conquest until the fourteenth century,"[77] I suggest that the romances under scrutiny here continued to experiment boldly within that genre before giving way to other kinds of experimentation with magic in the fifteenth century.

CONCLUSION

How Marvels Matter

Enchantment, writes Jane Bennett, begins with "a surprising encounter, a meeting with something that you did not expect and are not fully prepared to engage."[1] Imagine that you enter an unfamiliar castle and see your beloved among a gallery of people kidnapped and frozen in place by fairies, or encounter a dragon with a woman's face that approaches as if to kiss you. Imagine that your holiday feast is interrupted before it properly begins by a giant green knight who asks you to cut off his head, or that on your wedding night your wife reveals that she can transform herself (and does), or that you discover that you can understand a falcon's speech and that the two of you may be cross-species kindred spirits. At first, you can only wonder. But what do you do next?

In these cases, the marvel is so extraordinary and urgent that it pushes past the edge of existing ethical systems. The usual codes or principles are inadequate for the dilemma that the marvel presents, and yet it demands an immediate and often active response. A response that begins with wonder, which has cognitive as well as affective components, may also be moral. Caroline Walker Bynum has demonstrated that medieval wonder can itself be a moral reaction that recognizes and respects difference. The texts explored in the previous chapters are united by their interests in wonder and, even more so, in what follows—that is, what moral actions or reflections a marvel can prompt. "Without modes of enchantment," Bennett cautions, "we might not have the energy and inspiration to . . . respond generously to humans and nonhumans that challenge our settled identities."[2] Although the Middle English texts examined here do not imply that morality *requires* wonder, they do mobilize marvels as "challenge[s]" to established identities and values, exploring what generous responses might look like and what further moral consequences they might have.

By looking closely at fourteenth-century texts, this study has distinguished a strand of literary marvels that use magical spectacle to generate a wonder-reaction that can lead to moral reflections or actions within and beyond the text. *Sir Orfeo* offers a magical spectacle that reveals the fairies' moral code, guides Orfeo's appeal to recover Heurodis, and encourages readers to interrogate chivalry's investments in violence and beauty. In *Lybeaus Desconus*, an enchanted dragon lady reminds readers that the connection between appearance and virtue may be complicated, while also certifying that Lybeaus possesses not only the semblance of a virtuous knight but the true identity of Gawain's son. The *Gawain*-poet and the Cotton Nero A.x artist depict the Green Knight as a cinematic and recurring marvel; his spectacular nature allows him to investigate Arthurian chivalry, the bounds of Gawain's virtue, and the possibility of shared moral agency. In the *Canterbury Tales*, miracles are described in vivid visual detail, and magical marvels unfold largely through speech, yet the latter still function like spectacles and press characters and readers to reflect on what and how they can learn about others as well as how they should treat others.

As these and other Middle English texts experiment with the marvelous, they depart from the accepted status quo in both romance studies and magic studies. Previous scholarship on magic in medieval romance has by necessity ranged widely, examining how magic operates across many different texts to gain a sense of the landscape. Corinne Saunders's *Magic and the Supernatural in Medieval English Romance* is the definitive study in this regard; she traces how romances "pick up the complex attitudes and traditions inherited from classical culture, the Bible, Germanic and Celtic folk traditions, and learned discourses—legal, theological and philosophical"—and transform them "imaginatively to create shifting, multi-coloured tapestries of ideas and imaginings."[3] Critics who have looked at magic in individual romances have tended to approach it as satisfying generic and aesthetic expectations rather than fulfilling any narrative purpose, or as fulfilling narrative purposes primarily when its use fails or falls short—a perspective influenced by Helen Cooper's excellent 1976 essay "Magic That Does Not Work."[4] Saunders's and Cooper's conclusions are powerful precisely because they generally hold true across medieval English romance; however, a close look at the fourteenth century reveals that texts in that time period have a recognizable dynamic of their own involving magic that works within the plot and for the narrative. All of the texts examined here represent magical figures or practices, generally connected to some type of transformation. All of the poets invest in spectacle, whether visual or linguistic, to create memorable and meaningful marvels. And all of the magical spectacles have a moral aspect, encouraging characters and readers to reflect on their ethical codes and their relationships with others. The first feature is common among romances, the second less so, and the third less still; the presence of all three as an interlocking set is highly unusual.

The field of magic studies has also taken a wide-angle perspective that has overlooked these atypical cases. Cultural histories of magic tend to minimize the fourteenth century, considering that period to be one of ongoing trends rather than dramatic shifts. This time falls between the redefinition of magic and heightened attention to magic's legal repercussions in the twelfth and thirteenth centuries and the witchcraft trials that dominated in the sixteenth and seventeenth centuries, making it appear to be a transitional phase. Richard Kieckhefer points out that the fourteenth century kept developing new ideas about natural magic that had arisen earlier; Michael D. Bailey shows that "concern[s] about magic and systems of prosecution" were also increasing at the time but "had not yet achieved the full, fatal forms they would come to assume."[5] Earlier authorities, including those examined in the fourth chapter, above, heavily influenced fourteenth-century ideas about magic, and skepticism and superstition continued to coexist without taking on radical new forms or positions.[6] However, the history of magic and its representation in literature do not track exactly; something new and distinct was happening with literary portrayals of magic in England across the fourteenth century.

Other historical and literary trends of this period make it a rich and receptive context for thinking about marvels in connection with visuality and morality. Those trends include the evolving English romance tradition, the revived emphasis on chivalry, the changing understanding of vision, the rise of interest in natural rather than demonic magic, and the ongoing development of affective piety. Although these trends may have strengthened or peaked during the fourteenth century, they were also present to varying degrees before and after that period. As a result, we can locate signs of interest not only in marvels, but also in their spectacular and/or moral potential at other times and in other texts. Indeed, identifying the strong magic-spectacle-morality nexus in these fourteenth-century works can make us more attuned to those elements elsewhere. I will conclude with a few examples that highlight different treatments of these elements and thus possible directions for further study.

Other fourteenth-century marvels explore other types of connections between spectacle and morality without advancing the same theory of the marvelous, in which spectacular and secular magic provokes moral reflection. For instance, *Sir Cleges* offers a visual marvel in the form of out-of-season cherries, but the context is firmly religious, and the response to the miracle draws more on ethics than morality. The first half of *The Awntyrs off Arthur* also presents a memorable spectacle: the ghost of Guinevere's mother appears, laments her fate, and warns that Arthur's court needs to learn from her example and embrace virtue. The scene includes intense visual descriptions of the approach of darkness and the body that is "bare" and "blak to the bone, / Al biclagged in clay uncomly cladde."[7] The narrator identifies the ghost as a "mervaile" (74), but it is a supernatural visitation rather than an exercise of magic, and, fittingly, the reaction seems to contain a higher proportion of fear and disbelief than the wonder tinged with fear that is examined in the first chapter. The response closest to wonder comes from those who hear about the marvel later and are "forwondred," which the editor, Thomas Hahn, glosses as "utterly bewildered" (334). This marvel is most distinguished from those under consideration here, however, by the fact that its central spectacle offers a dire warning about immoral behavior rather than creating a moral dilemma or test that might lead to similar conclusions by indirect means. The method of delivery underscores the ominous and inescapable nature of the message: as the ghost approaches, it is "yauland and yomerand, with many loude yelle" (86).

In the tale of Jason and Medea in the *Confessio Amantis*, by contrast, John Gower offers a marvel in which he subordinates the moral implications to the spectacular magic. Drawing on Ovid, he depicts Medea's magical practice with a level of detail unusual in fourteenth-century texts. She first gives Jason a lengthy lesson in sacrifice and enchantment so that he can safely retrieve the Golden Fleece.[8] When Jason requests that she use her "art magique" to renew his father's youth, the narrator assures us that "what sche dede in that matiere / It is a wonder thing to hiere, / Bot yit for the novellerie / I thenke tellen a partie" (V.3947, 3953–56). This "partie" takes up more than two hundred lines, and includes specifics about the words, ingredients, and actions involved; Medea does everything from making herself invisible (V.4028) to cackling like a hen (V.4101). Genius frames this extended description as wondrous and novel and therefore engaging; in the economy of the tale, this episode seems to overshadow the moral message, which warns "what sorwe it doth / To swere an oth which is noght soth" (V.4223–24). The audience is encouraged to linger over Medea's magical actions rather than her murderous ones, and Jason's apparently lesser crimes form the basis of the moral lesson for Amans.

This approach is in keeping with recent critical interpretations of Gower's moral interests as complex and ambiguous, and it represents a different take on the relationship among magic, spectacle, and morality than we have seen in the preceding chapters. Gower seems more interested in the agent of the magic than are the authors of most medieval literary texts, and that ties into a different strand in the history of magic: the evolution of witchcraft. We know little about how the Fairy King, the *Lybeaus* necromancers, Morgan le Fay, and the loathly lady effected their enchantments; the texts represent the spectacular results, not the step-by-step process. Gower, however, dwells on the process at much greater length than he does on the result. This direction of attention past the marvel to its agent might foreshadow the rise of witchcraft, with its emphasis on fear of the powerful magical figure rather than on wonder at a marvelous outcome. Indeed, the tale presents Medea herself as a greater source of marvel than it does her accomplishment of the magical restoration of an old man's youth.

Interest in marvels, spectacle, and/or morality continued into the fifteenth century, although not in the consistently and tightly interconnected form that we saw in the case studies at the center of this project. The term *marvel* appears throughout *Le Morte d'Arthur* in connection with a variety of secular and religious elements, for example. In some cases, the marvels seem to be primarily aesthetic or atmospheric elements; in other cases, they have strong moral or, interestingly, immoral overtones. The most well-known examples of the latter show how wonder can go wrong in complicated ways. With Merlin's help, Uther disguises himself in the form of Igrayne's husband and rapes her; when she discovers that her husband was already dead, she can only "merveill[e] who that myghte be that laye with her in lykenes of her lord." The Lady of the Lake later charms Merlin figuratively and literally, trapping him beneath a "grete stone" by asking him to share with her "the mervayles there."[9] As those two episodes suggest, magical spectacles are vital to certain, particularly early, parts of the narrative, and they can carry great moral weight. In the text as a whole, however, the functions and associations of marvels are characterized by their range and flexibility rather than by a unifying interest in the relationship among magic, spectacle, and morality.

The status of marvels in *Le Morte d'Arthur* largely reinforces the work of those literary scholars and historians who have considered representations of magic across the sweep of medieval English romance and determined that it is most frequently an aesthetic or generic feature. Malory and the other sources examined here show that the varied connections between the marvelous and the moral warrant further investigation, as the field of magic studies continues to develop. *Middle English Marvels* has pursued one line of investigation by identifying a cluster of texts that go against the dominant trends in medieval English romance. These texts diverge from the trends by representing magic that works both as a marvel and as a critical plot element and by exploring the multistage moral reactions that such marvels could inspire, from wonder to action to reflection. Middle English marvels constitute a robust countertrend that does not undo the prevailing scholarly narrative about magic in medieval romance but adds a significant new dimension to it. They suggest that other clusters of texts or countertrends might exist and that exploring those possibilities would be a productive exercise in scholarly wonder.

Notes

Introduction

1. A more detailed discussion of this angel can be found in chapter 3.
2. This is not to say, however, that all marvels in Middle English texts demonstrate the same combination of features. Many of them—as I will discuss throughout the book—are marvelous and spectacular but lack the moral aspect.
3. The two terms overlap significantly in Middle English, and Michelle Sweeney argues that this may represent a conscious strategy in romance: "in coming to terms with the use of magic in the romances, it is important to appreciate the idea of the marvellous, as the terms *magical* and *marvellous* were often used interchangeably in the texts. It is arguable that romance writers did this deliberately owing to the need for an acceptable place for magic in their works. In softening the lines between magic and the marvellous, the potentially negative aspects of magic were downplayed. . . . *Wonder* functioned in a similar manner to *marvellous*, in that its use softened any potentially negative connotations to the word *magic*" (*Magic in Medieval Romance*, 31).
4. Le Goff, *Medieval Imagination*, 27–44.
5. Although not involved in all marvels, imagination was common to a variety of them, including dreams, illusions, prophecy, bewitchment, and weather-related marvels. Karnes, "Marvels in the Medieval Imagination," 330–31.
6. On technological marvels in a literary context, see especially Lightsey, *Manmade Marvels*, and Patricia Clare Ingham, "Little Nothings."
7. Le Goff, *Medieval Imagination*, 31; emphasis in original.
8. Kieckhefer, *Magic in the Middle Ages*, chap. 1.
9. Kieckhefer, *Forbidden Rites*; Fanger, *Rewriting Magic*; Klaassen, *Transformations of Magic*; Page, *Magic in the Cloister*. See also Fanger, *Conjuring Spirits* and—for an examination of popular magic as reflected in legal, theological, and medical texts—Catherine Rider, *Magic and Impotence*.
10. Cooper, *English Romance in Time*, chap. 3. This chapter is a revised version of Cooper, "Magic That Does Not Work."
11. Chaucer, *Riverside Chaucer*, lines 1203–4.
12. As Lightsey suggests, "the delight of the [manmade] marvel was in the experience, not in the marvel itself. . . . These newly naturalized marvels were incapable of producing supernatural wonder" (*Manmade Marvels*, 57).
13. *Sir Gawain and the Green Knight*, ed. Andrew and Waldron, line 147.
14. Lambeth Palace MS 306, lines 2064–65, in *Lybeaus Desconus*, ed. Mills.
15. Especially because these marvels often take the form of transformations that were connected in some way to the human, they inspire a wonder that lends itself to connections with human morality rather than the kind of awestruck wonder that is usually associated with the sublime. For more on the sublime in the Middle Ages, see Jaeger, *Magnificence and the Sublime*.
16. "Merveille (n.)," *Middle English Dictionary*.
17. Bynum, "Wonder," 24; see also Bynum, "Miracles and Marvels." Brewer's *Wonder and Skepticism* considers medieval wonder as an emotion, focusing specifically on the period from 1100 to 1300. Important work on wonder in related historical periods includes Greenblatt, *Marvelous Possessions*, and Onians, "I Wonder." Onians, an art historian, offers a "natural history" of wonder, which recognizes five key eras: "New Kingdom Egypt," "Assyria between the eleventh and the ninth century BC," "the Hellenistic world," "the early Roman Empire," and the "sixteenth and seventeenth centuries" (11 and 26). Dennis Quinn includes

medieval wonder in his "synoptic history" but focuses on the Christian framework (*Iris Exiled*, chap. 4).

18. Jane Bennett, *Enchantment of Modern Life*, 3–4. Bennett conceptualizes ethics as affective and embodied rather than as "a code to which one is obligated," and her use of "ethical" hews closely to the Middle English understanding of "moral," which I will explore in more detail below.

19. Ibid., 4.

20. Jane Bennett, *Vibrant Matter*, vii; see also xi–xiii.

21. Sweeney, *Magic in Medieval Romance*, 49. Sweeney identifies "the core formula of characters being evaluated through magical trials" as consistent from twelfth-century French romance to later insular romances such as *Sir Tristrem*, *Ywain and Gawain*, *Syr Launfal*, and the *Franklin's Tale* (169). As she points out, "once a character can conquer the need for magic or pass a marvellous test unscathed, it signals in the romance that he or she has emerged from the learning process. The character has achieved a secure social standing or has come to terms with the personal conflict which had been inhibiting growth and maturity" (49).

22. Watkins, "Fascination and Anxiety," 55.

23. On the debates about the moral value of romance, see Furrow, *Expectations of Romance*, especially chap. 1.

24. "Moral (adj.)" and "etik, (n.(1))," *Middle English Dictionary*. These usages seem most appropriate for these texts and their contexts, but Alcuin Blamires has differentiated the key terms more sharply in his work on Chaucer, reserving "ethics" for "that part of the behavioural code that was inherited from antiquity and roughly associated, by the later Middle Ages at least, with the *Ethics* of Aristotle and with Roman Stoicism which later succeeded it" and employing "morality" to designate "the Christian moral schema" (*Chaucer, Ethics, and Gender*, 7–8). For more on medieval ethics and literature, see Rosenfeld, *Ethics and Enjoyment*; Mark Miller, *Philosophical Chaucer*; and J. Allan Mitchell, *Ethics and Exemplary Narrative* and *Ethics and Eventfulness*.

25. These concerns do not map exactly onto schemata such as the Ten Commandments or the seven deadly sins, but they do accord with the description of love (or charity), which was the greatest of the three theological virtues, according to Paul, and indispensable for relationships of all types. Described as one of the gifts of the Holy Ghost in the fourteenth-century *Book of Vices and Virtues*, love includes the qualities of consideration, mutual help, and empathy, among others (*Book of Vices and Virtues*, 143–48). This book is one of a number of translations of the French text, but I have singled it out because it is contemporary with the other texts under consideration here.

26. For a fuller interpretation of the *Canterbury Tales* as a marvel collection, see Williams, "Ellesmere Dragons."

27. McNamer, *Affective Meditation*, 14.

Chapter 1

An earlier version of this chapter was published as Williams, "Fairy Magic, Wonder, and Morality in *Sir Orfeo*."

1. On this point, see especially Bynum, "Wonder," and, for an examination of wonder in relation to the sublime, Jaeger, "Richard of St. Victor." On the ways in which medieval discourse also "de-wondered" marvels and miracles through categorization and natural explanation, see Bynum, "Miracles and Marvels."

2. See introduction, above, for the operating definition of *moral* in this project.

3. On the Celtic or folkloric context, see Dorena Allen, "Orpheus and Orfeo"; Clark, "*Sir Orfeo:* The Otherworld"; Jirsa, "In the Shadow of the Ympe-tre"; Miyares, "Wonder Tale Pattern"; and Vicari, "Sparagmos." On the Christian or biblical context, see Byrne, *Otherworlds*, 93–96; John Block Friedman, *Orpheus in the Middle Ages*, chap. 5 (parts of which appeared in an earlier form as John Block Friedman, "Eurydice"); and Jeffrey, *Houses of the Interpreter*, chap. 10. On the classical context, see Davies, "Classical Threads in 'Orfeo'"; Dronke, "Return of Eurydice"; Giaccherini, "From *Sir Orfeo*"; Knapp, "Meaning of *Sir Orfeo*"; Liuzza, "*Sir Orfeo*"; Jeff Rider, "Receiving Orpheus"; and Severs, "Antecedents of Sir Orfeo." On the historical context, see Dominique Battles, "*Sir Orfeo* and English Identity," and Falk, "Son of Orfeo." Many of these studies, of course, examine overlapping contexts for the poem.

4. See especially Cartlidge, "Sir Orfeo in the Otherworld," and Fletcher, "*Sir Orfeo*."

5. See D'Arcy, "Faerie King's *Kunstkammer*"; Lerer, "Artifice and Artistry in *Sir Orfeo*"; Liuzza, "*Sir Orfeo*"; Longsworth,

"*Sir Orfeo*"; Ronquist, "Powers of Poetry"; and Seaman, "Disconsolate Art." As Ronquist notes, however, the aesthetic dimension of the poem does not imply a corresponding lack of ethical or conceptual significance; in fact, he points out, poetry proves to wield the "power of ethical speculation" ("Powers of Poetry," 112; see also 103).

6. There are two main issues associated with the ending: its happy outcome, which departs from the major if not the minor classical versions of the legend, and the interpolation of the final episode with the steward. Many, if not most, critics discuss the happy ending; Kooper does so in particular detail in "Twofold Harmony." Critics who examine the interpolated steward episode include Miyares, "Wonder Tale Pattern"; Riddy, "Uses of the Past"; Severs, "Antecedents of Sir Orfeo"; and Taylor, "Sir Orfeo and the Minstrel King." The critical context for the gallery scene is taken up later in this chapter.

7. The issue of Orfeo's kingship complicates the enduring questions about the poem because it raises the stakes in his encounters with the Fairy King and in his return to the human world. See, for example, Babich, "Power of the Kingdom"; Evans, "*Sir Orfeo* and Bare Life"; Falk, "Son of Orfeo"; Hazell, *Poverty*, 49–56; Kendall, "Family, *Familia*, and the Uncanny"; Kooper, "Twofold Harmony"; and Taylor, "Sir Orfeo and the Minstrel King."

8. Gender-related concerns complicate the central questions by drawing attention to the troubled representation of Heurodis through both her kidnapping and her recovery. See, for example, Caldwell, "Heroism of Heurodis," and Christina M. Carlson, "'Minstrel's Song of Silence.'"

9. Green, *Elf Queens and Holy Friars*, 71 and 72.

10. Bynum, "Wonder," 15. Bynum does not specifically consider the wonder associated with or invoked by fairies.

11. Gower, *English Works*, II.964.

12. Auchinleck MS, lines 147–48, 151, 159, and 161, in *Sir Orfeo*, ed. Bliss. Future references will be parenthetical.

13. "Fairie, (n.)," *Middle English Dictionary*.

14. Latham, *Elizabethan Fairies*, 41–48, and Lewis, *Discarded Image*, 122–38. See also Briggs, *Anatomy of Puck*, chap. 2.

15. Saunders, *Magic and the Supernatural*. "Romances repeatedly raise questions of intention and morality in relation to otherworldly encounters," writes Saunders, "and draw attention to the difficulties of distinguishing different aspects of the supernatural—divine, demonic, and faery" (180).

16. Wade, *Fairies in Medieval Romance*, 3. This intense focus allows him to examine each text on its own terms but leads him to construct interpretations that rely heavily on authorial intention. He argues explicitly for a "new intentionality, a revitalized and nuanced discussion of the world-constructing powers of the author" (7). See also Byrne, *Otherworlds*, 12–23, for a thoughtful examination of the term "otherworld" and its uneasy adaptation to medieval concepts; Byrne considers the structural similarities across otherworld encounters and descriptions but does not explicitly take up questions of magic.

17. See, for example, Jeff Rider, "Other Worlds of Romance," and Huot, "Others and Alterity."

18. Cooper, *English Romance in Time*, 174.

19. Zipes, *Why Fairy Tales Stick*, 130–31. Elsewhere, Zipes makes a similar point about medieval fairy tales specifically: "contained in chivalric romances, heroic sagas and epics, chronicles, sermons, poems, lais, and primers during the European Middle Ages, the fairy tale was often a story about miraculous encounters, changes, and initiations illustrating a particular didactic point that the writer wished to express in an entertaining manner" ("Introduction," xxi).

20. Wade offers a typical formulation of the "amoral" perspective: "fairies, within the text-worlds of their romances, are free from the moral scruples humans are expected to abide by and operate within" (*Fairies in Medieval Romance*, 14). See also Cooper, *English Romance in Time*, 197–207; Kieckhefer, *Magic in the Middle Ages*, 108; and Salla, "Disappearing Fairies."

21. See the introduction, above, and chapter 4 for more on these foundational categories.

22. *Sir Gawain and the Green Knight*, ed. Andrew and Waldron, line 240. The enchantment is revealed to be the work of Morgan le Fay; *fay* and *fairy* work similarly.

23. Seth Lerer has recently proposed an emendation that underscores this sense of mystery in the fairy hunting scene: he suggests that line 285 should describe what Orfeo hears not as a "dim cri" but as a "'derne cri,' a secret

or magical sound of fairy hunting" ("*Sir Orfeo,* Line 285," 322).

24. See, for example, Riddy, "Uses of the Past," 11.

25. Cooper, *English Romance in Time,* 189.

26. Bruce Mitchell, "Faery World of *Sir Orfeo.*" Versions of the detailed catalog of victims appear in Auchinleck and Ashmole 61 but not Harley 3810.

27. In addition to Lerer's "Artifice and Artistry," Riddy's "Uses of the Past" has been influential on this issue.

28. On the lack of morality in the gallery, see D'Arcy, "Faerie King's *Kunstkammer,*" and Fletcher, "*Sir Orfeo.*" More broadly, Vicari argues that the fairies are "incomprehensible in human, ethical terms" ("Sparagmos," 76), whereas Cartlidge connects the "lack of any moral framework" in the fairy world to the poem itself ("Sir Orfeo in the Otherworld," 200n14). Saunders suggests that *Sir Orfeo*'s "denouement is characterized by game-playing and amorality" (*Magic and the Supernatural,* 204). Other critics comment on the ambiguous role of morality in the poem as a whole. Dieter Mehl argues that it has "a deeper truth" but exhibits "a complete absence of didactic and moralizing" (*Middle English Romances,* 43). Longsworth concurs, stating that "no lesson is pointed: the poem is certainly not heterodox but neither is it explicitly moralistic" ("*Sir Orfeo,*" 6).

29. Fletcher, "*Sir Orfeo,*" 165.

30. Beyond characterizing the people "liggeand wiþ-in þe wal" of the fairy castle as "meruails," the poet offers no other collective description of the group. Out of necessity, scholars have adopted various terms, including "catalogue," "assembly," "collection," "tableau," and "gallery" (see, respectively, Lerer, "Artifice and Artistry," 107; Dorena Allen, "Orpheus and Orfeo," 103; Davies, "Classical Threads in 'Orfeo,'" 163; and Riddy, "Uses of the Past," 6 and 9). Despite the fact that the word itself did not appear until the sixteenth century, "gallery" has become perhaps the most popular choice, and has been used in this context since at least Felicity Riddy's 1976 work on the poem. Although all of the possible terms have some aesthetic connotations, the associations of "gallery" have been particularly mined by Fletcher, who chooses the term "to emphasize the sense of their being displayed like so many statues in an exhibition," and D'Arcy, who reads the "numinous power of this outdoor sculptural gallery" against contemporary suspicion of sculpture in the round (Fletcher, "*Sir Orfeo,*" 142n4, and D'Arcy, "Faerie King's *Kunstkammer,*" 10). My rationale is similar to Fletcher's: I wish to underscore the poet's presentation of this scene as a visual spectacle—for the reader as well as for Orfeo—with strong aesthetic overtones.

31. Riddy, "Uses of the Past," 6.

32. Beckerman, "Spectacle in the Theatre," 9.

33. Those critics who explicitly follow Allen include Babich, "Power of the Kingdom"; Fletcher, "*Sir Orfeo*"; and Foster, "Fantasy and Reality."

34. Dorena Allen, "Orpheus and Orfeo," 105. She does not, however, examine this possibility in detail.

35. John Block Friedman, *Orpheus in the Middle Ages,* 193–94. Friedman focuses on the fairies' motivations and agency rather than their morality.

36. "Tales possunt tam homines quam mulieres in alias naturas transformare [et] secum ducere apud *eluenlond*" (*Fasciculus Morum,* ed. and trans. Wenzel, 578–79). Fletcher discusses this evidence, but ultimately rejects the idea that the fairies created the figures: "any ghastly transformation suffered by the people in the gallery happened first in the real world, not at the hands of the fairies" ("*Sir Orfeo,*" 161).

37. Despite his emphasis on the threat to Heurodis as an explanation for the figures in the gallery, John Block Friedman is vague as to how she escaped punishment: "presumably Heurodis did not struggle against the fairy king, perhaps in part because of her identification with a Eurydice who, as natural prey for Satan, was destined for a demon world, and in part because of the narrative requirement that she be eventually restored to the world of man by Sir Orfeo" (*Orpheus in the Middle Ages,* 194).

38. D'Arcy reads this line as suggesting that Orfeo reacted with wonder ("Faerie King's *Kunstkammer,*" 11), but the characterization of the "meruails" comes from the narrator rather than Orfeo himself.

39. Keeping one's word, or *trouthe,* is an essential virtue in romances. In both the *Franklin's Tale* and *Sir Gawain and the Green Knight,* a magical spectacle becomes a test of that virtue; in *Sir Orfeo,* the spectacle is instead a testament to it.

40. Ronquist, "Powers of Poetry," 108–9. Ronquist characterizes this as a "moral response" (110), but examines it through Orfeo's moral code rather than the Fairy King's.

41. Suzanne M. Edwards also reads *Sir Orfeo* as having ethical import; her reading focuses on Heurodis's ravishment and how the poem "shift[s] the moral stakes of sexual violence—so often associated with women's deaths and the triumph of justice in medieval culture—to favor survival" (*Afterlives of Rape*, 130).

42. Chivalry did not require violence and cannot be reduced to a dynamic between aggression and honor; romances tended not only to emphasize that aspect, but also to grapple with it in complex ways. As Richard Kaeuper observes, "almost without fail these works [of chivalric literature] give prominence to acts of disruptive violence and problems of control," and yet their "attitudes about violence come strongly mixed" (*Chivalry and Violence*, 22). See also Saul, *Chivalry in Medieval England*, 196; for more detail about the complex ways in which knightly violence was reconciled with religious ideology, see Kaeuper, *Holy Warriors*.

43. W. J. T. Mitchell, *Picture Theory*, 5.

44. "Image (n.)," *Middle English Dictionary*.

45. Camille, "Before the Gaze," 216. See also, for example, the first chapter of Kolve, *Chaucer and the Imagery of Narrative*; Brantley, "Vision, Image, Text"; and Brown, "Images."

46. Carruthers also points out that the activities of reading and seeing were inseparable. See Carruthers, *Book of Memory*, chap. 7; *Craft of Thought*; and "Moving Images in the Mind's Eye." For more on the modern-day memory training of mental athletes, see Foer, *Moonwalking with Einstein*.

47. Carruthers, *Book of Memory*, 11 and 14. This emphasis on moral character correlates with the Middle English distinction between ethics—which mobilized codes and systems developed through reason—and morality, which involved affective responses and virtuous actions of the kind motivated by memorable images.

48. Minnis, "Medieval Imagination and Memory," 240–41. Minnis details the foundation for this connection: "Aristotle also explored the moral implications of imagination. In the sphere of practical reason it plays an important part in helping to regulate conduct, in large measure due to its ability to produce images of things past or absent and indeed images relating to future things" (240). However, Aristotle was not the sole source of these ideas; as Carruthers explains, "scholars writing before the full revival of Aristotle also saw the connection between memory and the molding of moral character" (*Book of Memory*, 89). On the importance of imagery to the imagination in the Middle Ages, see also Karnes, *Imagination, Meditation, and Cognition*, chaps. 1–3, and Watson, "Phantasmal Past." This discussion of the moral utility of the imagination complicates the later view that associated the Middle Ages—and especially medieval romance—pejoratively with that faculty and its use of images, as explored in Simpson, "Rule of Medieval Imagination."

49. Minnis, "Medieval Imagination and Memory," 270. See also Carruthers, *Book of Memory*, chap. 7. Some forms of magic used images to bypass the actions of learning and access the memory directly. Michael Camille studies the images of the Ars Notoria, for example, which were designed to communicate knowledge of the liberal arts magically, and points out that "these images did not need to be memorized in the traditional way, since their magical effect linked the operator directly to the celestial powers responsible for the enhancement of memory" ("Visual Art in Two Manuscripts," 117). In the same volume, see Watson, "John the Monk's *Book*," and Fanger, "Plundering the Egyptian Treasure."

50. See, for example, Dimmick et al., *Images, Idolatry, and Iconoclasm*, and Stanbury, *Visual Object of Desire*. Indeed, vision itself could be understood as a moral process (or as a process with moral significance); see, for example, Peter of Limoges, *Moral Treatise on the Eye*, especially chaps. 6–7.

51. Gayk, *Image, Text, and Religious Reform*, 8.

52. Bynum, "Wonder," 21.

53. For an overview of this evolution of wonder, see Greenblatt, "Resonance and Wonder," especially 49–52; for a more detailed consideration, see Daston and Park, *Wonders and the Order of Nature*.

54. Felski, *Uses of Literature*, 54.

55. Jane Bennett, *Enchantment of Modern Life*, 5.

56. For more detail about the distinction between these reactions and how they might

figure in the future of historicist literary study, see Williams, "Enchanted Historicism."

57. Bynum, "Wonder," 25.

58. Daston and Park, *Wonders and the Order of Nature*, 14.

59. Philip Fisher, *Wonder*, 6–7.

60. "Et unde, quaeso, admiratio nisi ex inopinato incredibilique spectaculo?... Sed rei novitatem quanto magis miramur, tanto diligentius attendimus; et quanto attentius perspicimus, tanto plenius cognoscimus" (original and translation quoted in Jaeger, "Richard of St. Victor," 162–63). Jaeger adapts his translation from Richard of St. Victor, *Twelve Patriarchs*, 316.

61. Greenblatt, "Resonance and Wonder," 42. See also Jaeger, *Enchantment*; however, because Jaeger understands enchantment to result from the charisma exercised by visual and literary works of art, his concept of enchantment is both more overwhelming and more individual than the one that I am developing here.

62. Philip Fisher, *Wonder*, 17 and 21. For Fisher, visuality is so important that wonder is a reaction more common to the visual arts than to literature in the twentieth century; however, as we have seen, reading and seeing were much more closely associated in the Middle Ages.

63. Jane Bennett, *Enchantment of Modern Life*, 1. As discussed in the introduction, Bennett's use of "ethical" corresponds more closely to "moral" in Middle English.

64. Ibid., 17.

65. Ibid., 29.

66. McNamer, *Affective Meditation*, 19; see also 137. Although McNamer considers *behold* in the context of affective piety, similar connotations might be at work here, especially given the parallels that I have outlined between sacred and secular marvels and the particular resonances that these suffering bodies might have with Christ's.

67. Bennett's focus on the positive possibilities of enchantment as an alternative to cynicism or disenchantment prevents her from exploring in detail the ways in which enchantment might go awry. However, she does acknowledge this problem implicitly, describing enchantment as having moral potential rather than ensuring a moral outcome.

68. Biernoff, *Sight and Embodiment*, 137.

69. Falk does problematize the ending, though for reasons different than those that I present here. He notes Heurodis's barrenness and suggests that "the steward's succession is a personal catastrophe for Orfeo and an atrocity for the institution of feudal monarchy" ("Son of Orfeo," 261). For a more positive reading of the succession, see Kendall, "Family, *Familia*, and the Uncanny."

70. On the eleventh-century versions with a happy ending, see Dronke, "Return of Eurydice." On classical versions with a happy ending, see Dorena Allen, "Orpheus and Orfeo," 109, and Liuzza, "Poetics of Performance," 274–79. Bliss discusses the evidence for an Old French or Anglo-Norman source in the Introduction to *Sir Orfeo* (ix–li, xl–xli).

71. Caldwell and Christina M. Carlson are two exceptions, but they rely on evidence outside the narrative to interpret Heurodis as an inspiring example of marital fidelity (Caldwell, "Heroism of Heurodis") or as unable to reconcile speech in any form with beauty or queenship (Carlson, "Minstrel's Song of Silence").

72. In a fairy story recorded by Walter Map, we encounter a similar spectacle of a dead or near-dead wife, but her body does not seem to signify in the same way or have moral undertones. When her husband encounters her, "he marvelled and was afraid, and when he saw her whom he had buried, alive again, he could not trust his eyes, and doubted what the fairies (fates) could be doing [Miratur et metuit, et cum rediuiuam uideat quam sepelierat, non credit oculis, dubius quid a fatis agatur]" (*De Nugis Curialium*, 344–45). The two reunite, and go on to have children together.

73. Bynum, *Holy Feast and Holy Fast*. Bynum argues that "medieval efforts to discipline and manipulate the body should be interpreted more as elaborate changes rung upon the *possibilities* provided by fleshliness than as flights from physicality" and uncovers "the extent to which religious women derived their basic symbols from such ordinary biological and social experiences as giving birth, lactating, suffering, and preparing and distributing food" (6).

74. Simons, "Reading a Saint's Body," 12.

75. For example, Michael Camille points out that John of Salisbury's famous conception of the state as a body in his twelfth-century *Policraticus* "was not visualised by an artist until the mid-fourteenth century" ("Image and the Self," 68).

76. Camille, "Image and the Self," 66. The image that directly prompts Camille's observation is from a French manuscript—a miniature showing "the interior of a fashionable residence" where "a university doctor points out to a fashionably dressed nobleman a picture [of a naked human body] on the wall above a little dog on a bench" (Ibid.). However, his point is relevant to Western medieval culture more broadly.

77. Caldwell also argues that Heurodis's mutilated body is central to the poem but reads it as an attempt to preserve her chastity; Caldwell further speculates that the Fairy King rapes Heurodis despite this attempt ("Heroism of Heurodis," 294–96).

78. Christina M. Carlson makes a similar point about Orfeo's recognition of the clothes in the service of her argument about Heurodis as "completely passive, totally silent, and thoroughly embodied" ("Minstrel's Song of Silence," 71); Carlson sees Heurodis's speech after the dream as a transgression of that model that destabilizes Orfeo's kingship.

79. Elliot Kendall identifies a slightly different critique here; he brings the Freudian concept of the uncanny to bear, reading the fairy world as representing the dark realities of patriarchy and patrilineage. He suggests that the poem illustrates "patriarchy's capacity to limit rather than to enable female political agency," but nonetheless reads the ending as marking a positive "structural shift from patrilineage to a merit-based politics of the wider household" ("Family, *Familia*, and the Uncanny," 311 and 326–27).

80. See, for example, Babich, "Power of the Kingdom"; Caldwell, "Heroism of Heurodis"; Falk, "Son of Orfeo"; and Peter J. Lucas, "Earlier Verse Romance."

81. Nakley, "Sovereignty Matters."

82. Corinne Saunders considers how suffering is written on the bodies of Orfeo as well as Heurodis but comes to a different conclusion, suggesting that "the restoration of the bodies of the king and his wife are synonymous with the restoration of social order, and their integrity asserts the power of human love and loyalty even in the face of incomprehensible, seemingly inevitable, supernatural forces.... The body, seized and unmade through the sinister, unruly forces of desire, is regained, remade through virtuous love" ("Affective Body," 91–92).

Chapter 2

1. On the popularity of the romance as measured by manuscript copies, see Field, *Malory: Texts and Sources*, 291.

2. Mills, "Composition and Style," 109. Chaucer's allusion to "sir Lybeux" in his parodic *Tale of Sir Thopas* may also have affected modern readers' perceptions (*Riverside Chaucer*, line 900).

3. A few decades after Mills, W. A. Davenport was more even-handed, identifying Chestre's work as both "providing a fair register of what Chaucer found absurd in contemporary English romance" and demonstrating "why Chaucer found romance a genre worth his serious attention" (*Chaucer and His English Contemporaries*, 107). Renée Ward, responding directly to Mills, worked to redeem Chestre's reputation by contending that "a re-examination of Chestre's *Lybeaus Desconus* reveals that Chestre is not ... inept and inadequate ... but rather a writer who redefines the popular romance hero and thus the genre through his version of the story of the fair unknown" ("Challenging the Boundaries," 119).

4. See, for instance, Salisbury, "*Lybeaus Desconus*," and Weldon, "'Naked as She Was Bore.'"

5. In this light, *Lybeaus* may be a better fit with the moral texts in the fifteenth-century Ashmole manuscript than critics have recognized; for instance, Lynne S. Blanchfield contrasts *Lybeaus* with all of "the other entertaining stories [that] have some obvious moral point" ("Rate Revisited," 213). James Wade suggests that the romance may have had some moral interest, primarily because of Lybeaus's shortcomings: "the fundamental incongruity of an ungallant romance hero might also have been what morally minded readers would have found most interesting about these texts [*Lybeaus* and *Thomas of Erceldoune*], their moral messiness exposing the tensions between the chivalric ideal and the complexities of lived experience" ("Ungallant Knights," 218). Although the Ashmole context is particularly interesting from this perspective, the Lambeth Palace manuscript is the most-often cited version, and so this chapter works primarily with that text.

6. As Eve Salisbury and James Weldon point out, the question of authorship has not been entirely resolved ("Introduction," 10–11). Despite the inconclusive evidence, scholars

generally refer to Thomas Chestre as the poet, and I have followed that convention here.

7. Bliss, *Naming and Namelessness in Medieval Romance*, 108. Bliss notes this use of "Lybeaus Desconus" as part of a pattern of interest in names and naming that she identifies in the romance (107–12); I am similarly interested in its connections to the issue of identity, but I am also interested in what constitutes sufficient proof of identity.

8. *Squire of Low Degree*, lines 75, 77–78, and 613–32. However, this fifteenth-century romance repeatedly refers to the standard of "a *venturous* knyght" (e.g., lines 250, 478, 558, 576, and 590; emphasis added), which we might see as a slight shift in emphasis from a *virtuous* knight whose key virtue is "doughtiness," as in *Lybeaus* itself.

9. See, for example, Sweeney, *Magic in Medieval Romance*. Sweeney is also interested in the moral implications magic may have, but she focuses on the relationship of magic to the development or revelation of character (see 19).

10. Finlayson, "Marvellous in Middle English Romance," 364.

11. Cooper, *English Romance in Time*, 143 and 146.

12. This phenomenon might be part of the reason that magical elements often show up in Arthurian texts, where courtly love tends to be central; however, I would suggest that this subgenre draws on a narrative that has been associated with magic from earlier incarnations—such as Geoffrey of Monmouth's *History of the Kings of Britain*—and thus it becomes an expectation that Arthurian stories include magic. In fact, in such texts, magic is more often atmospheric than critical to the plot (*Ywain and Gawain* is one good example), which suggests that it appears more often because of the expectations of the subgenre than because it performs integral work in the narrative.

13. *Partonope of Blois*, line 743.

14. Ibid., lines 3 and 11. The prologue goes on to assert the moral relevance of these stories: "in thys boke shalle ye fynde wrytte / Both goode and euelle. I do yow to wytte: / The goode taketh, the euelle leve" (lines 60–62). See also Ihle, "English *Partonope of Blois*," especially 304–5.

15. *William of Palerne*, lines 119, 120, and 137.

16. See Barron, "Alliterative Romance and the French Tradition."

17. Salisbury and Weldon outline these changes in their "Introduction," 4–5.

18. Cooper, *English Romance in Time*, 142–43.

19. Bynum, *Metamorphosis and Identity*, 32.

20. Some medieval readers likely saw some romances as having a more fundamental ethical potential, serving "as a tool for learning, a record for the edification of the reader of the wise and foolish actions of men and women of the past, from which we of the present can learn" (Furrow, *Expectations of Romance*, 16).

21. Yearley, *Mencius and Aquinas*, 21.

22. *Book of Vices and Virtues*, 21.

23. "Il n'y regardent profit, ne avantage pour leurs amis, ne a la grant grevance de leurs ennemis, mais sanz conseil donner ne prendre fierent des esperons et a po d'arroy, et font d'armes assez de leur main et moult de fois plus a leur domage que a leur profit, mais de l'onneur de la main font il assez, et en ceste maniere se sont il trouvez en pluseurs bonnes journees sanz autre estat ne maniere de le faire; mais contre l'onnour de hardiesce ne leur peut l'en rienz reprouver; et a ceuls qui tant de bonnes journees ont veues et esté aidant de si bon ouvrage de la main et de leurs corps comme il y ont fait, l'en les doit bien appeller preux, combien que, quant a estre preus a droit, l'en y pourroit encores miex faire" (*Book of Chivalry*, 150–51).

24. Herdt, *Putting on Virtue*, 46.

25. "Se ce n'est purement de la droite grace de Nostre Seigneur et de sa tres douce mere et de sa glorieuse court" (*Book of Chivalry*, 156–57).

26. Knight, "Social Function" 99 and 114.

27. Mills's introduction nicely summarizes the general position: Chestre "shares with other ME redactors a fondness for sharpening the moral focus of his narrative where this was traditionally ambiguous.... In LD both Maugys and the Dame d'Amore are presented very much in terms of black and white; the first becomes an aggressor of the most repulsive kind; the second, a heartless seductress for whom Lybeaus does not spare a thought once he is out of her clutches" ("Introduction," 62).

28. *Sir Launfal*, lines 46–48. All references to this text hereafter will be cited parenthetically by line number.

29. Dinah Hazell explores the sociohistorical context for Chestre's moral interests in "Blinding of Gwennere." Although she does

not connect these moral considerations to his use of magic in detail, Hazell does consider the tradition of supernatural moral agents (137–38).

30. Lambeth Palace MS 306, in *Lybeaus Desconus*, ed. Mills, lines 5–9. All references to this text hereafter will be cited parenthetically by line number.

31. We see this tension in *Sir Perceval of Galles* and Malory's "Tale of Gareth"; in both narratives, the hero's identity is known but his knighthood remains to be proven. In the former, Arthur clarifies when the ultimate test is about to occur (after some agitation on Perceval's part), and in the latter, Malory extends the testing into the realm of the bedroom.

32. *Book of Vices and Virtues*, 79 and 81.

33. Ibid., 161. The text goes on to detail the "seuene bowes" of doughtiness (170–88).

34. Ibid., 83.

35. McDonald, "Polemical Introduction," 15.

36. One exception is *Perceval of Galles*, where magic may undermine the proofs of Perceval's knighthood. We discover near the end of the text that a magic ring he took from a lady has protected him throughout.

37. Mills, "Composition and Style," 92, and Finlayson, "Marvellous in Middle English Romance," 396.

38. Saunders contrasts the clerks' necromancy with the "explicitly faery magic" of the Dame d'Amore, noting that the latter is a "rare" example of a "conspicuous witch" (*Magic and the Supernatural*, 171 and 188).

39. *Lybeaus Desconus* in *Codex Ashmole 61*, line 1515.

40. The same might be said of music. It is associated not only with the Dame and the clerks, but also with Theodeley, the dwarf who accompanies Lybeaus and Elene on the quest. The poem introduces this character, who is largely portrayed positively, with reference to his musical abilities: "mekyll he couthe of game, / Sotill, sawtrye in same, / Harpe, fethill and crowthe" (145–47).

41. *Lybeaus Desconus* in *Codex Ashmole 61*, 1986–87.

42. Mills, "Introduction," 57.

43. While the giants that Lybeaus has fought might be seen as supernatural figures, they are not directly associated with magic, and their defining characteristic seems to be physical size. Similarly, the clerks' poisoning of the swords seems to be a human trick rather than a supernatural act. The one encounter that might also be seen to invoke magic is Lybeaus's battle with Maugys; it immediately precedes the first definitive mention of magic with the Dame d'Amore and, because it wins Lybeaus access to a beautiful woman who is associated with magic, structurally parallels the fight with the necromancers. Furthermore, the giant's name might call to mind the term *magus*. These associations are largely speculative, however, and Maugys's credentials as a giant are themselves in question (as Mills points out in the notes to lines 1291–93, Maugys retains characteristics in common with the cruel but human knight Malgiers in *Le Bel Inconnu*).

44. Weldon, "'Naked as She Was Bore,'" 69.

45. Crane, *Gender and Romance*, 85, 87, and 150–51; Salisbury, "*Lybeaus Desconus*."

46. Knight, "Social Function," 108.

47. In the legend of Melusine, written in French in the late fourteenth century and translated into English circa 1500, we find an interesting counterexample. Melusine's body presents a similar spectacle: one day a week, she turns into a serpent from the waist down. However, she seeks to keep that spectacle private and makes her husband, Raymondin, promise not to see her on those days. Lybeaus must be courageous enough to confront the spectacle, whereas Raymondin must be loyal and courteous enough to allow it to go unseen; only Lybeaus succeeds. After many years and ten children, Raymondin finally gives into temptation and spies on his wife through a hole in the door. His trespass—and later condemnation of her—leads to suffering and separation.

48. This scene may also recall Rymenhild's kissing of Horn in one of the earliest English romances:

Heo makede him faire chere
And tok him abute the swere.
Ofte heo him custe,
So wel so hire luste.
"Horn," heo sede, "withute strif,
Thu schalt have me to thi wif."

(*King Horn*, lines 407–12)

49. Crane, *Gender and Romance*, 191.

50. *Book of Vices and Virtues*, 161.

51. *Book of John Mandeville*, lines 309–10, 312–13, 315, 335–36, and 340–41.

52. Ulrich von Zatzikhoven, *Lanzelet*, 116, 117, and 118.

53. "Kinde (n.)," *Middle English Dictionary*.

54. In one version, Gawain certifies his son's identity directly to the lady ("Y gat . . .

him by a forest syde / On a gentil lady"), and then Lybeaus goes to his father and kisses him, whereupon his father tells everyone to call him "Gengelayne" (*Lybeaus Desconus*, ed. Mills, p. 275); in another, Lybeaus's mother recognizes him ("sche knew Lybeus wele be sy3ht") and tells Gawain "thys is owre chyld so fre" (p. 285; see also the Naples manuscript, lines 2232–67, in *Lybeaus Desconus*, ed. Salisbury and Weldon). In the analogues, the knight finds out his identity in different episodes altogether (p. 242). The versions with the parental revelation(s) can be regarded as part of a distinct strand of the textual tradition in which a scribe made substantial enough revisions, in Salisbury and Weldon's view, to be described as a "co-author" ("Introduction," 18).

55. Salisbury, *"Lybeaus Desconus,"* 80.

56. In a conference paper at the 2011 International Congress on Medieval Studies, James Weldon noted the unusually active role the lady plays after her disenchantment, arguing that she does not transform into a typical beautiful maiden but instead maintains an empowering liminal position.

57. Crane, *Gender and Romance*, 28.

58. Cooper, *English Romance in Time*, 332.

59. Mitchell-Smith, "Defining Violence"; see especially 157.

60. Zaerr, "Music and Magic"; and Weldon, "'Naked as She Was Bore,'" 73.

61. For a more detailed discussion of the invocation of Eve in this scene, see Weldon, "'Naked as She Was Bore,'" 74–75.

62. Burns, "Snake-Tailed Woman," 197.

63. Sarah Alison Miller, *Medieval Monstrosity and the Female Body*, 138. Miller does not specifically discuss monstrosity in romance, but focuses instead on representations of femaleness as "an Ovidian body, a medicalized body, or a mystical body" (5).

64. Crane, *Gender and Romance*, 91.

65. Salisbury made this point in a conference presentation at the 2011 International Congress on Medieval Studies.

66. If the ending hints at any problems, those would seem to be related to the lack of heirs rather than to the lady's enchanted past.

67. Cohen, "Monster Culture," 6. Although I am most interested in how an individual monstrous form might challenge identity categories, the same potential exists with "monstrous races," which John Block Friedman explores in *Monstrous Races*.

68. Sarah Alison Miller, *Medieval Monstrosity*, 144. For an overview of this aspect of monstrosity, see Urban, *Monstrous Women*, 8–13. On medieval monsters in a broader context, see Jones and Sprunger, *Marvels, Monsters, and Miracles*, and Bildhauer and Mills, *Monstrous Middle Age*.

Chapter 3

1. E. R. Truitt traces this evolution of courtly marvels from textual to material phenomena in *Medieval Robots*, chap. 5.

2. For discussions of the Hesdin marvels and their connections to textual marvels, see Daston and Park, *Wonders and the Order of Nature*, 95–108; Sherwood, "Magic and Mechanics in Medieval Fiction"; Truitt, *Medieval Robots*, 122–37; and Van Buren, "Reality and Literary Romance."

3. Kipling, "Sumptuous Pageants," 83.

4. Jefferson, "Language and Vocabulary," 209–10.

5. "In summitate castelli, quæ ad modum tholi inter quatuor turres elevata fuerat, positus erat angelus aureus, tenens auream coronam in manibus, qui tali ingenio factus fuerat, ut adventanti regi coronam porrigeret inclinando. Adinventa sunt illo die in civitate et alia multa in honorem regis, quæ numerare per singula longum foret" (*Chronicon Angliae*, 155; translation from Maidstone, *Concordia*, Appendix 2, 104). The *Anonimalle Chronicle* provides a similar, if less detailed, description: "enmy la dite toure fuist fait une petit clocher et amount le clocher fuist esteaunt une aungelle portaunt une corone dore et moustraunt al dit prince pur luy comforter [within the said tower had also been built a small belfry, and on the belfry stood an angel, bearing a golden crown, holding it out towards the said prince, to do him comfort]" (*Anonimalle Chronicle*, 108; translation from *Concordia*, Appendix 2, 105–6).

6. Lightsey, *Manmade Marvels*, 53.

7. See, for example, Eamon, "Technology as Magic."

8. Jefferson, "Language and Vocabulary," 180; Osberg, "Goldsmiths' 'Chastell.'"

9. *Chronicon Angliae*, 155, and *Concordia*, Appendix 2, 104.

10. Kipling, "Sumptuous Pageants," 88; see also Kipling, "'He That Saw It,'" 52–57. The popularity of this motif continues into the early modern period and was recorded as a key

precedent in queen consort processions in the *Ryalle Booke* (see Hunt, *Drama of Coronation*, 57–58).

11. Maidstone, *Concordia*, appendix 1 passim.

12. "Descendunt ab ea iuvenis, simul ipsaque virgo; / Nulla fuit scala, nec patuere gradus. / Nubibus inclusi veniunt, et in ethere pendent, / Quo tamen ingenio nescio, crede michi!" (ibid. lines 285–88).

13. "Singula testatur fulgida materies. / Materiam superavit opus: patet hoc et in artis / Et simul artificis subtilitate nova" (ibid. lines 292–94).

14. Lightsey, *Manmade Marvels*, 50–51.

15. Kipling, "Sumptuous Pageants."

16. Stanbury, *Visual Object of Desire*, 5.

17. For a discussion of how this "economy of wonder" functioned in political and literary contexts, see Lightsey, "Chaucer's Secular Marvels," and *Manmade Marvels*, chap. 2. Although they were depicted in earlier texts, actual automata did not appear in medieval Europe until this point because of the state of mechanical knowledge and, perhaps, concerns over idolatry (see Truitt, "Knowledge and Automata," 169–70, and Kang, *Sublime Dreams of Living Machines*, 62–63).

18. Gordon Kipling, for example, stresses that civic triumphs had "ritual and dramatic purposes" as well as "political meaning," and argues for "the royal entry as a serious late medieval art form" (*Enter the King*, 3). Kim Phillips shows that ritual and spectacle often worked to similar ends (e.g., to display power and dramatize nobility) in private settings as well as public ones ("Invisible Man").

19. See, for example, Dimmick et al., *Images, Idolatry, and Iconoclasm*, and Stanbury, *Visual Object of Desire*. Political or courtly spectacles could also include a moral dimension; civic triumphs, for instance, often invoked biblical imagery or allusions (Kipling, *Enter the King*, chap. 1).

20. Gregory the Great, *Letters*, 11.10, p. 745. "Nam quod legentibus scriptura, hoc idiotis praestat pictura cernentibus, quia in ipsa ignorantes uident quod sequi debeant, in ipsa legunt qui litteras nesciunt" (Gregory the Great, *Registrum Epistularum, Libri VIII–XIV*, 874).

21. Camille, "Before the Gaze," 207.

22. Chaucer, *Riverside Chaucer*, lines 232–34.

23. Sarah Stanbury works through the relationship between visual poetics and visual theory thoughtfully in the conclusion to *Seeing the "Gawain"-Poet*.

24. Bynum, *Christian Materiality*.

25. Barbara Newman argues that a religious vision, for instance, "was never supposed to be an end in itself, at least not in principle: it was valued because it could lead the soul into deeper contrition, purer devotion, more perfect knowledge, and greater intimacy with God" ("What Does It Mean," 14).

26. Hanawalt and Reyerson, "Introduction," ix.

27. See Tony Davenport, "Abbreviation."

28. As we will see in chapter 4, Geoffrey Chaucer's *Squire's Tale* includes a similar scene of self-wounding, but with a bird rather than a hybrid swan/human. There, the focus of the marvel is the avian speech, which Canacee understands via the magic ring.

29. *Romance of the Cheuelere Assigne*, vii–ix.

30. Stanbury, *Visual Object of Desire*, 6 (emphasis in original).

31. *St. Erkenwald* is didactic in a different way and to a different end: it uses an auditory marvel (when the bishop compels the body to speak) that is bookended by visual descriptions (of the uncorrupted body and then of its accelerated decay) to illustrate spiritual doctrine (about the redeeming power of baptism).

32. Reichardt, "Paginal Eyes," 24 and 27.

33. *Sir Gawain and the Green Knight*, ed. Andrew and Waldron, lines 1805–7. All poems in this edition are hereafter cited parenthetically by line number.

34. See the introduction, above, and—on how chivalry as an ethical system frames a magical spectacle that nonetheless demands a moral reaction in *Lybeaus Desconus*—chapter 2.

35. Gilbert, "Arthurian Ethics," 154–55.

36. Critics who address the moral or ethical dimension of the poem include Ganim, "Disorientation, Style, and Consciousness"; Kamps, "Magic, Women, and Incest"; Kindrick, "Gawain's Ethics"; Lander, "Convention of Innocence"; Mann, "Courtly Aesthetics and Courtly Ethics"; Mark Miller, "Ends of Excitement"; and Putter, *Sir Gawain*.

37. I will focus on the secular aspects of the marvel in *Sir Gawain and the Green Knight*, but as Corinne Saunders points out, "the power of the Green Knight to survive beheading evokes both the pagan celebration of regeneration of

the seasons, and the Christian hope for salvation and resurrection" ("Religion and Magic," 208).

38. Carruthers, *Book of Memory*, 292.
39. Scott, *Later Gothic Manuscripts*, 66–67.
40. Reichardt, "'Several Illuminations, Coarsely Executed,'" 130 and 129.
41. These images are now available in color online, as part of the Cotton Nero A.x project, at http://gawain.ucalgary.ca/ or in black and white in *Pearl, Cleanness, Patience, and Sir Gawain*, intro. Gollancz.
42. J. R. R. Tolkien and E. V. Gordon make this point in their edition of the poem: "a curious feature of the illustrations is that they fail to illustrate some of the most significant features of the text" (introduction to *Sir Gawain and the Green Knight*, ed. Tolkien and Gordon, xiii).
43. Lee, "Illuminating Critic," 19. The issues of who was responsible for the subjects of the illustration and how well the illustrator might have known the poem continue to be contentious; for views opposed to Lee's on those points, see A. S. G. Edwards, "Manuscript," and Scott, *Later Gothic Manuscripts*, 67. My argument is that, regardless of whether the artist or the owner was responsible, the images comprise a visual interpretation of the poem. For other discussions of the relationship between the text and the images, see Doyle, "Manuscripts," and Horrall, "Notes."
44. Reichardt, "'Several Illuminations, Coarsely Executed,'" 136. Although he does not name marvels as another theme, he does note the central placement of the image of the disembodied hand at Belshazzar's feast (125–28).
45. Hilmo, "Power of Images," 185. Ann Astell suggests a specific correspondence to the life of St. John the Baptist as represented in a wall painting in Idsworth (*Political Allegory*, 135–37).
46. Hilmo, "Power of Images," 186.
47. The absence of Bertilak in his human form may suggest his parallel role as the other primary agent behind the scenes of Gawain's moral testing.
48. Hilmo, *Medieval Images*, 159.
49. On the operating distinction between ethics and morality in this project, see the introduction, above.
50. Lynn Arner, for example, invokes magic but primarily focuses on other interpretive issues ("Ends of Enchantment"). Barbara Kline, conversely, examines the magic in the context of Tzvetan Todorov's concept of the fantastic but does not engage substantially with the wider critical history of the poem ("Duality, Reality, and Magic").
51. Renoir, "Descriptive Technique," 132; Stanbury, *Seeing the "Gawain"-Poet*. Stanbury demonstrates that the poem engages with readers visually in complex ways, requiring readers to become "visual participants" who "see from composite and even contradictory points of view" (101). I build on this idea of the active involvement of the readers through the visual by exploring how that mode allows the marvelous to work to moral ends.
52. *Greene Knight*, in *Sir Gawain: Eleven Romances and Tales*, line 80. Gillian Rogers examines some other crucial differences between these versions ("Grene Knight").
53. Stanbury also notes the evaluative aspect of these gazes in *Seeing the "Gawain"-Poet*, chap. 5.
54. We might note here that the specific words spoken seem irrelevant to Morgan's plan. This detail lends credence to the argument later in this chapter that the Green Knight is the central moral agent of the narrative, since it leaves open the possibility that exacting the promise of a return encounter was part of his agenda rather than Morgan's.
55. *Carle of Carlisle*, in *Sir Gawain: Eleven Romances*, lines 402–3.
56. *Greene Knight*, in *Sir Gawain: Eleven Romances*, lines 199–201.
57. For a consideration of animated devotional images, and specifically the figure of Christ, see the third section of Stanbury's *Visual Object of Desire*.
58. Kang, *Sublime Dreams of Living Machines*, 8 and 36. For more on specifically medieval automata, see Truitt, *Medieval Robots*.
59. Lerer, "Culture of Spectatorship," 31.
60. For an influential analysis of the girdle in the context of feminine desire rather than magic and morality, see Heng, "Feminine Knots." For commentary on the girdle in a commercial and chivalric context, see Shoaf, *Poem as Green Girdle*.
61. Helen Cooper offers a persuasive basis for assumptions that the girdle is a dud: the poem "would be much less exciting if the girdle were indeed what the lady says it is, a talisman of invulnerability. It is true that Gawain is not killed while he is wearing it; but if he, and we, really believed in its magical powers, his bravery

in finally facing the Green Knight would dissolve, and the episode would lose both its suspense and its significance" ("Supernatural," 278).

62. Although Gawain rejects the girdle as a love offering, he relents when the lady tells him of its protective powers:

Þen kest þe knyȝt, and hit come to his hert
Hit were a juel for þe jopardé þat hym jugged were:
When he acheued to þe chapel his chek for to fech,
Myȝt he haf slypped to be vnslayn þe sleȝt were noble.
(1855–58)

63. Introduction to *Sir Gawain and the Green Knight*, ed. Andrew and Waldron, 23.

64. We might also identify multiple instances of magic in the *Wife of Bath's Tale* if we include her initial appearance. However, we do not witness the same type of magic in this scene and the later transformation.

65. Augustine, *City of God Against the Pagans*, vol. 7, 21. "Assiduitas experiendi paulatim subtrahit admirationis incitamentum" (Augustine, *De Civitate Dei*, vol. 2, 763).

66. I read the evidence about the magical nature of the girdle as ultimately ambiguous. However, the lady makes much of the disparity between its appearance and its virtues, suggesting that it is much less of a visual marvel than the Green Knight himself. Additionally, the girdle is tempting only insofar as the Green Knight is terrifying—it is a way for Gawain to gain a supernatural advantage and thus even the playing field against his supernatural opponent.

67. Here we might pause to consider how these tests stack up against those of Lybeaus Desconus (who is, after all, Gawain's son). Both knights encounter enchanted figures and have to mount a chivalric response, but the details differ. Whereas Lybeaus knows that he is entering a magical situation, the magic initially makes a surprise appearance at Gawain's home court. And whereas the enchanted figure recurs in Gawain's tests, Lybeaus faces a number of opponents and obstacles, but only one magical test. As I argued in the previous chapter, the enchantment involved makes that last test the only one that can definitively resolve the question of Lybeaus's identity. In Gawain's case, it is his reputation rather than his identity that is at stake (and, indeed, the ethical discourse on which his reputation depends); those stakes may explain why his tests are multiple. Additionally, *Lybeaus Desconus* explores the nature of true virtue, whereas *Sir Gawain and the Green Knight* seems concerned with its limits.

68. McNamer, "Feeling," 252 and 253.

69. The certification of Lybeaus Desconus's identity may be the closest parallel, but that revelation is more about the character than the magic.

70. Those who question Morgan's centrality often draw on Kittredge; see, for example, Albert B. Friedman ("Morgan le Faye"). For those supporting it, see Baughan, "Role of Morgan le Fey"; Carson, "Morgain la Fée"; Moore, "Making Sense of an Ending"; and Twomey, "Morgain la Fée."

71. Michelle Sweeney raises the possibility that Morgan is a moral agent: "the disturbing question for the audience becomes, is Morgan powerful enough to test Camelot's moral status and initiate Gawain's education? She is described as a goddess; could this mean that her desire to see Arthur humiliated and Gaynour extinguished is the driving moral force of the poem (2446–55)?" ("Making Meaning from Magic," 145–46).

72. On this point, I disagree with Sheila Fisher, who argues that "in her bedroom testings of Gawain, [the lady] is not acting on behalf of a man. Rather, she refers to Morgan and to Morgan's power" ("Taken Men and Token Women," 79). As Fisher points out, the poem acknowledges Morgan's agency behind the scheme as a whole, and the lady herself does not mention her husband; however, Bertilak identifies himself rather than Morgan as the agent behind the seduction scheme, which tests Gawain according to the virtues that concern Bertilak (courage, loyalty, honesty, etc.) rather than the one virtue associated with Morgan's part of the test (pride).

73. Paul Battles, "Amended Texts, Emended Ladies"; see especially 324–31.

74. Heng, "Feminine Knots," 508.

75. *Greene Knight* in *Sir Gawain, Eleven Romances,* lines 50 and 372–76.

76. See, for example, Heng, "Feminine Knots," and Sheila Fisher, "Taken Men and Token Women."

77. Schiff, *Revivalist Fantasy*, chap. 3; see especially 83–89. Schiff also suggests that their sights are set on different types of goals: "Morgan leaves the games of venery and courtly love to

her inferior agents, and instead concentrates on fashioning the trans-regional message of her independent power" (99). Although I see Morgan as more focused on Arthur's court and Bertilak as more interested in Gawain as an individual, I do not see this as a split between superior and inferior, since their efforts are complementary.

78. Michael W. Twomey acknowledges this relationship in broader terms: "in one sense she and Bertilak are collaborators, while in another sense his is the social power as owner of the castle, and in yet another sense hers is the underlying power as magician and moral force that sets the adventure in motion" ("Morgan le Fay at Hautdesert," 114).

79. Saunders, "Erotic Magic," 40. Saunders suggests that both Morgan and Bertilak's wife can be seen as menacing enchantresses (46–47); Heidi Breuer considers Morgan as part of a medieval tradition representing witches (*Crafting the Witch*, chap. 3). The enchantress and female witch may be bound up with ideas about maidens as both alluring and deadly; see Judith Bennett, "Death and the Maiden," especially 293–94.

80. Chism, *Alliterative Revivals*, 92.

81. Here I depart from Bonnie Lander, who also sees the Green Knight as testing the limits of chivalry but characterizes Hautdesert as "not amoral but intelligently immoral," representing a sophistication that contrasts with Gawain's simplistic understanding of chivalry ("Convention of Innocence," 44).

82. From this perspective, we might see Morgan's disguised appearance at Bertilak's court—as "an auncian" with "Rugh ronkled chekez" and a "body . . . schort and þik"—as posing a preliminary test of courtesy, which Gawain passes by bowing to her before turning to the "loueloker" lady (948, 953, 966, and 973)—although, as with the Green Knight, he fails to recognize her true identity.

83. Some critics agree with Gawain in granting Bertilak's lady independent agency, but they often do so by associating her with magic—either collapsing her and Morgan into a single figure or suggesting that the lady has her own sources of magic as a fairy mistress. For an example of the former interpretation, see Carson, "Morgain la Fée"; for examples of the latter, see Puhvel, "Art and the Supernatural," and Whitaker, "Otherworld Castles."

84. The adoption of the girdle by the court at the end seems to suggest the communicability of the moral experience it signifies. It may also be that, by adopting the girdle, the other knights dilute the shame that it signifies to Gawain; in other words, his individual failure cannot be removed, but it can be reconfigured when he is re-enfolded into the community, a process visually signified by the adoption of the girdle as a common signal that no longer singles out Gawain. At the end of the poem, his relationship to the community is remade: he is no longer its representative but one of its members.

85. McAlindon, "Magic, Fate, and Providence," 121.

Chapter 4

Parts of this chapter appeared in an earlier form as Williams, "Magic."

1. Michelle Karnes has also noted connections between philosophical discourse on the marvelous and Chaucer's writing. She argues that the *Squire's Tale* shows that Chaucer and natural philosophers share an "interest in the natural causes of marvels" as well as "a common fascination with the power of mental images" ("Wonder, Marvels, and Metaphor," 462).

2. Chaucer, *Riverside Chaucer*, lines 669 and 671–72. All references to the poetic works in this edition hereafter will be cited parenthetically by line number.

3. In the course of his consideration of the relationship between gender and ethics in Chaucer, Blamires does treat two of the tales containing marvels, but he focuses on specific virtues (e.g., credulity and vision as well as liberality in the *Wife of Bath's Tale*, and liberality as well as patience and equanimity in the *Franklin's Tale*) rather than the more general connection between magic and morality that I sketch out in this chapter (*Chaucer, Ethics, and Gender*, chaps. 2, 5, and 6).

4. Mark Miller, *Philosophical Chaucer*, 248.

5. "Merveille (n.)," *Middle English Dictionary*.

6. Augustine, *City of God Against the Pagans*, vol. 3, 307. "Humanae facultatis excedant" (Augustine, *De Civitate Dei*, vol. 1, X.xii, 286).

7. Augustine, *City of God Against the Pagans*, vol. 3, 293. "Fallacium daemonum esse commenta" (Augustine, *De Civitate Dei*, vol. 1, X.x, 283).

8. "Que inaudita percipiuntur amplectimur, tum ex mutatione cursus naturalis quam

admiramur, tum ex ignorancia cause cuius ratio nobis est imperscrutabilis, tum ex assuetudine nostra quam in aliis uariari sine cognitione iudicii iusti cernimus. . . . Mirabilia uero dicimus que nostre cognicioni non subiacent . . . sed et mirabilia constituit ignorantia reddende rationis quare sic sit" (Gervase of Tilbury, *Otia Imperialia*, 558–59).

9. Augustine, *City of God Against the Pagans*, vol. 3, X.ix, 287. "Fiebant ad commendandum unius Dei ueri cultum. . . . Fiebant autem simplici fide atque fiducia pietatis" and "incantationibus et carminibus nefariae curiositatis arte compositis" (Augustine, *De Civitate Dei*, vol. 1, 281).

10. "Porro miracula dicimus usitatius que preter naturam diuine uirtuti ascribimus, ut cum uirgo parit, cum Lazarus resurgit, cum lapsa membra reintegrantur" (Gervase, *Otia Imperialia*, 558–59).

11. *Book of John Mandeville*, lines 2344–48.

12. "Propositi nostri principium est mirabilia singularium prouinciarum deliciosis auribus inferre" and "quia uero ante oculos nostros cotidiana de hiis documenta uersantur, non genere minus mirabili, sed ipsa uisus assiduitate uilescunt" (Gervase, *Otia Imperialia*, 558–59 and 562–63).

13. "Dictum autem praestigium, quod praestringat aciem oculorum" and "hi et elementa concutiunt, turbant mentes hominum, ac sine ullo veneni haustu violentia tantum carminis interimunt" (*"Etymologies" of Isidore of Seville*, 183 and 182; Isidore of Seville, *Etymologiarvm*, VIII.ix.33 and VIII.ix.9).

14. Augustine, *City of God Against the Pagans*, vol. 3, 289. "In qua non ea uidentur, quae uere sunt" (Augustine, *De Civitate Dei*, vol. 1, X.ix, 282).

15. Isidore, "De Ecclesia et Sectis" (*"Etymologies" of Isidore of Seville*, 36; Isidore, *Etymologiarvm*, VIII).

16. Saunders, *Magic and the Supernatural*, 99.

17. "Quorum ars est inspicere in speculis, pelvibus, et unguibus politis, et huiusmodi, [in quibus] vident ut dicunt mirabilia" (*Fasciculus Morum*, 578–79).

18. Kieckhefer, *Magic in the Middle Ages*, 1. See also Bailey, "Meanings of Magic." Other sources offering broad summaries of medieval magical practices include Duffy, *Stripping of the Altars*, chap. 8; Flint, *Rise of Magic*, and Jolly et al., *Witchcraft and Magic in Europe*. They build on some earlier sources, most notably Thomas, *Religion and the Decline of Magic*, and Thorndike, *History of Magic*. Catherine Rider gives a helpful overview of the different attitudes toward magic and religion in *Magic and Religion*. More specialized historical considerations of medieval magic can be found in During, *Modern Enchantments*, chap. 1; Fanger, *Conjuring Spirits*; Page, *Magic in the Cloister*; and Watkins, *History and the Supernatural*. Works focusing on particular manuscript representations of medieval magic include Kieckhefer, *Forbidden Rites*; Kieckhefer, *Hazards of the Dark Arts*; and Page, *Magic in Medieval Manuscripts*. For magic in a legal context, and an examination of the relationship between medieval ideas of the magician and early modern ideas of the witch, see Peters, *Magician, the Witch, and the Law*. For generally accessible overviews, see Bailey, *Magic and Superstition in Europe*, chaps. 3–4; Flint, "A Magic Universe"; and Lawrence-Mathers and Escobar-Vargas, *Magic and Medieval Society*.

19. Bynum, "Miracles and Marvels," 809.

20. For a full listing of usages, see "miracle," "merveille," "merveillen," "merveillous," "wonder (adv.)," " wonder (n.)," "wonderful," "wonderli," "wondren," and "wondringe" in Benson, *Glossarial Concordance to the Riverside Chaucer*. As I have argued elsewhere, the presence of two marginal dragons in the Ellesmere manuscript also underscores the presence and variety of marvels in the *Canterbury Tales* (Williams, "Ellesmere Dragons").

21. Mary Flowers Braswell interprets this display, as well as others in the tale, as "correspond[ing] with medieval automata" and suggests that it might have been produced by means of a kind of rotating stage ("Magic of Machinery," 106). Similarly, Anthony E. Luengo argues that "the 'diverse apparences' conjured up by the Orléans clerk . . . are instances not of supernatural magic but of stage magic" ("Magic and Illusion in *The Franklin's Tale*," 1). Laura Hibbard Loomis was among the first to provide the historical context to support this interpretation ("Secular Dramatics"), and Merriam Sherwood provided the historical context for automata in medieval romance more broadly ("Magic and Mechanics in Medieval Fiction"). See also Lightsey, *Manmade Marvels*, chap. 2.

22. Lightsey, *Manmade Marvels*, 57.

23. Camille, *Gothic Idol*, 249.

24. *Treatise on the Astrolabe,* in Chaucer, *Riverside Chaucer,* II.4, p. 671. However, Jonathan Hughes makes the case that alchemy was key to not only philosophical and scientific but also political and cultural discourse during the fourteenth century (*Rise of Alchemy*).

25. Bynum, "Wonder," 23–24. Bynum's scope is broader than a study of magic, but it is one of the possible sources of wonder.

26. On interpretations of this phrase, see Patterson, "Perpetual Motion"; Green, "Changing Chaucer"; and Lightsey, *Manmade Marvels,* chap. 3.

27. Scholars have favored the former interpretation. Luengo argues that "the clerk merely calculated mathematically the period of an upcoming high tide which will *cover* the rocks" and that the illusion is "in fact, a perfectly natural event" ("Magic and Illusion," 12). It is, D. Vance Smith suggests, "an illusion that is not, in fact, an illusion"—that is, "the appearance of an appearance" (*Arts of Possession,* 43). Angela M. Lucas specifically suggests that the presence of this explanation in the tale distinguishes its "magic" from what is generally found in Breton lays (see "Keeping Up Appearances," especially 21–23). For a detailed examination of medieval knowledge of tides that supports this position, see Wood, *Chaucer and the Country of the Stars,* chap. 6. For more on astrology throughout Chaucer's canon, see North, *Chaucer's Universe.*

28. It may also be that miracles were received with less wonder than magic; Bynum suggests that "miracles, portents, and oddities are sites and stagings of wonder less often than we might suppose" ("Wonder," 17).

29. Kieckhefer, *Magic in the Middle Ages,* 10.

30. Although the *Franklin's Tale* might seem to raise similar expectations with its identification of the story as a Breton lay, it largely violates those expectations rather than building on them (see Angela M. Lucas, "Keeping Up Appearances").

31. On *Sir Orfeo* and the *Franklin's Tale,* see, for instance, Cook, "Chaucer's Franklin's Tale and *Sir Orfeo.*" For a recent example of a study that employs the magic-as-figure approach effectively, see Fumo, *Legacy of Apollo,* chap. 4.

32. For two important exceptions, see Lightsey, *Manmade Marvels,* chap. 2 (an earlier version of which was published as "Chaucer's Secular Marvels"), and Saunders, "Magic, Science, and Romance." Saunders offers a treatment of the supernatural across Chaucer's canon and its historical context that is more comprehensive than mine; whereas I seek to distinguish the different types of marvels in his texts, she examines their commonalities.

33. Although I will not consider the Arthurian setting in detail here, other scholars have explored that magical aspect of the tale. See, for instance, Ingham, "Pastoral Histories," and, on the broader context of romance and fantasy, Fradenburg, "Wife of Bath's Passing Fancy." On the fairy world specifically, see Fein, "Other Thought-Worlds," and Laskaya, *Chaucer's Approach to Gender,* 184–86.

34. Withrington and Field, "*Wife of Bath's Tale,*" 420 and 442.

35. Gower, *English Works,* I.1835 and 1838.

36. Ibid., I.1841–49.

37. Withrington and Field, "*Wife of Bath's Tale,*" p. 437, lines 691 and 693, and p. 447, line 179.

38. Elizabeth Allen, *False Fables and Exemplary Truth,* chaps. 3–5, and Watt, *Amoral Gower.*

39. This choice may tie back to one strand of earlier versions that portray the hag as a magical figure, as P. J. C. Field discusses ("What Women Really Want," 63).

40. In her reading of the *Wife of Bath's Tale* and its analogues, Crane argues that "two problems complicate the effort to find agency and self-definition in masquerade: most of the plots in question identify the shapeshifter with her beautiful rather than her grotesque body, and most shapeshifters finally claim that they were not responsible for their grotesque forms" (*Gender and Romance,* 87). By removing the latter problem, Chaucer casts the former in doubt as well; his loathly lady thus possesses remarkably more "agency and self-definition" because she controls her "masquerade" through magic.

41. When Florent has reluctantly climbed into bed with his loathly bride, she speaks to him, but Gower does not directly represent that speech: "evere in on sche spak and preide, / And bad him thenke on that he seide, / Whan that he tok hire be the hond" (*English Works,* I.1795–97). She then immediately becomes beautiful, before offering him the choice. In *The Weddyng of Syr Gawen and Dame Ragnell,* she speaks directly, but that speech is unconnected to her transformation, which is sudden and surprising. In *The Marriage of Sir Gawain,* there is a gap in the text at this moment (Withrington

and Field, "*Wife of Bath's Tale*," 436 and 446). Chaucer reinforces that the loathly lady is still loathly as she and the knight lie in bed together, noting that, as he tosses and turns, "his olde wyf lay smylynge everemo" (1086).

42. See the examples described in Kieckhefer, *Magic in the Middle Ages*, 6–8.

43. Susan Carter also briefly comments on how the language here is "performing the promise to be both fair and good and true, even as it acts as a distracting screen," but contends that "the sexual act" has also occurred in the space of this speech ("Coupling the Beastly Bride," 338–39). Thomas A. Van suggests that change has happened not only to the loathly lady, but also to the knight: "when she invites her husband to lift the curtain and see how lovely she has become, he is of course discovering her true beauty through the accumulated changes in his own powers of observation. The eyes watching now are not the same eyes which saw the woman he raped" ("False Texts and Disappearing Women," 190). Although the knight may also have undergone a change, I would argue that Chaucer challenges the idea that what is revealed is the lady's "true beauty."

44. As Lorraine Stock points out, Chaucer's description of her loathsomeness is understated relative to descriptions in other versions of the story ("Just How"); nonetheless, it exceeds the description of her loveliness. Kathryn L. McKinley interprets the absence of detail in the latter case as an aesthetic choice: "for Chaucer to provide details at this point would be to diminish the literary and dramatic moment he has so carefully constructed" ("Silenced Knight," 369).

45. Sandra M. Salla notes that this shift makes the loathly lady's "primary function" to serve "as the traditional fairy-educator of the knight" and connects this to specific conventions in fairy narratives ("Disappearing Fairies," 289); I am interested in the more local context of other Chaucerian displays of magic.

46. In the "Tale of Florent," the matron reacts to the correct answer by crying "treson" and denouncing the one who "hast thus told the privite, / Which alle wommen most desire" (Gower, *English Works*, I.1659 and 1660–61), implying that the loathly lady was not the only one able to supply the answer but instead the only one who was willing to do so.

47. "Upon my lyf, the queene wol seye as I," the loathly lady assures the knight (1016).

Chaucer's characterization makes the loathly lady a more fitting proxy for the Wife of Bath, since the Wife also seems to see herself as possessing powerful knowledge about men's and women's desires.

48. Elaine Tuttle Hansen has memorably remarked on this: "the rapist not only saves his life but is also rewarded by the promise of that impossible being, an unfailingly beautiful, faithful, and obedient wife; the hag who gave him the answer, who had all the power, gives it up, and transforms herself into a Constance or Griselda" (*Chaucer and the Fictions of Gender*, 33); see also Saunders, *Rape and Ravishment*, 305–9. Jill Mann interprets this moment more positively, proposing that "obeyed" is used here "in a sexual context that gives it wholly new connotations ... [as] an expression of the instinctive desire to give pleasure" (*Feminizing Chaucer*, 74). Suzanne M. Edwards suggests that contemporary readers might have understood the rape itself and questions of both male and female desire to be more ambiguous than has previously been recognized. However, she concludes, "in the lesson the knight learns, rape remains a terrible harm because it is a violation of a female body and will" ("Rhetoric of Rape and the Politics of Gender," 19; see also the revised version in Suzanne M. Edwards, *Afterlives of Rape*, chap. 3).

49. Some of the most well-known readings of the tale do not make a definitive claim about this issue, focusing on the lady's reaction rather than the knight's answer; see, for example, Dinshaw, *Chaucer's Sexual Poetics*, 128–29, and Elaine Tuttle Hansen, *Chaucer and the Fictions of Gender*, 33. Those who do make a claim carefully qualify their interpretations. Susan Crane suggests that "unless [the knight] is 'glosing' her like Jankyn, which is unlikely in view of his thoughtful sigh ... the old wife has talked him into loving and respecting her" (*Gender and Romance*, 37). Jill Mann characterizes "the transformation of a rapist into a meekly submissive husband" as "miraculous" and "even more magical" than the loathly lady's transformation, "something that *can* only be told as fairy-tale" (*Feminizing Chaucer*, 70). Most recently, Susanne Sara Thomas has pointed out how the difficulties with defining sovereignty in the tale problematize the scene of the knight's submission ("Problem of Defining *Sovereynetee*," especially 92–96).

50. Arthur Lindley suggests that the loathly lady's unknown motivations for desiring the knight are another piece of this puzzle: "She wants him because she wants him.... She is mysterious precisely because she is entirely self-contained" ("'Vanysshed Was This Daunce,'" 13).

51. As Maidie Hilmo points out, the Squire's Ellesmere portrait on f. 115v also shows a ring (Hilmo, *Medieval Images*, 182–83).

52. John M. Fyler comments on the linked purposes of these magical objects: "their purpose is to make the distant or obscure accessible or the exotic familiar, to unmask doubleness or hypocrisy" ("Domesticating the Exotic," 3).

53. See DiMarco, "Squire's Tale," especially 182–86, and Berry, "Flying Sources."

54. Crane, *Animal Encounters*, 148. On the horse as mechanical object, see, for example, Lionarons, "Magic, Machines, and Deception."

55. "Craft (n.(1))," *Middle English Dictionary*.

56. Robert S. Haller similarly notes that the "conjectures of the *lewed* show a surprisingly learned familiarity with classical myth and classical learning" but suggests that the Squire "would insist that these wonders must be taken as more subtle than either scientific explanation or classical literary precedent.... He assumes that such wonders are a way of separating the noble from the vulgar heart" ("Chaucer's 'Squire's Tale,'" 290).

57. Karnes, "Wonder, Marvels, and Metaphor," 469.

58. DiMarco, "Squire's Tale," 195–200. Elsewhere, DiMarco suggests that the power of forgetfulness might play a role in the reconciliation of the falcon and her lover that remains untold ("Note on Canacee's Magic Ring," 405).

59. Not all medieval magic rings were spectacular in appearance or effects; protective rings, such as those in *Ywain and Gawain*, *King Horn*, or *Floris and Blancheflour*, might be seen as another counterexample. For more on magic rings, see Kieckhefer, *Magic in the Middle Ages*, 106–111 and 171; Page, *Magic in Medieval Manuscripts*, 29–30; and Cooper, *English Romance in Time*, 146–51.

60. The scene that the ring enables does have powerful visual elements—most notably, the falcon wounding herself "til the rede blood / Ran endelong the tree ther-as she stood" (415–16)—but these are neither magical nor connected to the ring directly.

61. The ring has an additional magical power that features less prominently in the narrative: "and every gras that groweth upon roote / She shal eek knowe, and whom it wol do boote, / Al be his woundes never so depe and wyde" (153–55). This power is similar in character to the ring's power of translation in that it works within Canacee, although it arguably has more significant external effects. Canacee alludes to this power in her first speech to the falcon, offering, "herbes shal I right ynowe yfynde / To heel with youre hurtes hastily" (470–71). Later, Canacee does treat the falcon by wrapping her "softely in plastres" and making "salves newe / Of herbes preciouse and fyne of hewe / To heelen with this hauk" (636 and 639–41).

62. Ingham, "Little Nothings."

63. The disappearance of the horse is a possible exception here, but readers do not witness the moment of its disappearance; instead, we hear about it after it has already happened.

64. Karnes, "Wonder, Marvels, and Metaphor," 474.

65. In her consideration of the depiction of animals in the tale, Susan Crane supports the latter reading: "at first it seems Canacee will need the magic ring, a perfect manifestation of animal orientalizing, a decoder of strange avian meanings. Instead, Canacee and the formel turn out not entirely to need it" ("For the Birds," 33; see also Crane, *Animal Encounters*, chap. 5). Elsewhere, Crane also argues that "the spectacle of self-wounding communicates before speech" (*Gender and Romance*, 76).

66. "Entente (n.)" and "mening(e) (ger.(1))," *Middle English Dictionary*. The *Middle English Dictionary* confirms that the definitions of "entente" as one's will, desire, or mental attitude and of "menyng" as interpretation or hidden meaning were not only current when Chaucer was writing, but also utilized in some of his other texts.

67. Sara Deutch Schotland offers broader discussions of the friendship between Canacee and the falcon ("Talking Bird and Gentle Heart" and "Avian Hybridity"). For a perspective on the relationship as a "failure," see Gutman, "Chaucer's Chicks."

68. Interestingly, although this dynamic is strongest in these two most clearly magical texts, it extends beyond them; the connection between magical or magic-like elements and morality is characteristic of the *Canterbury Tales* as a whole. For example, the illusory magic

in the *Franklin's Tale* undermines truth but still has a potent moral impact, and the semidivine or demonic magic in the *Manciple's Tale* enforces a questionable punishment that raises broader ethical concerns. Both narratives also tie morality to love and social relationships.

69. Furrow, *Expectations of Romance*, 41.

70. Ibid., 23. See also 140.

71. Cannon, *Grounds of English Literature*, 175.

72. Ibid., 205.

73. See "magik(e) (n.)," and "moral (adj.)" *Middle English Dictionary*, and "magic, n." and "moral, adj.," *Oxford English Dictionary*, If we arrange by date of composition rather than manuscript date, Richard Rolle may have an earlier usage of "moral." Chaucer is also credited with the first use of the noun "magicien" (*Middle English Dictionary*) / "magician" (*Oxford English Dictionary*). Middle English offered several other extant possibilities for talking about something magical (as a "merveille," the result of "sorcerie" or "nigromancie," or an effect produced by a "tregetour," for example).

74. Here, I include the physical symbols of royal power that Chaucer was in charge of renovating or rebuilding (including the Tower Wharf and the St. George chapel at Windsor) as well as performances such as the tournament at Smithfield in 1390. See David R. Carlson, *Chaucer's Jobs*, 26–31.

75. Spenser, *Faerie Queene*, 714.

76. Chaucer's penchant for posing moral questions rather than providing answers has been noted by Blamires, *Chaucer, Ethics, and Gender*, 1–2 and 17–19; Kane, *Liberating Truth*, 16–17; and Mann, *Feminizing Chaucer*, xiv–xv and xvii.

77. Cannon, *Grounds of English Literature*, 172.

Conclusion

1. Jane Bennett, *Enchantment of Modern Life*, 5.

2. Ibid., 174.

3. Saunders, *Magic and the Supernatural*, 12.

4. Cooper's own thoughtfully nuanced argument suggests that "sidelining" magic or "diverting its wonder elsewhere" can be "one particular way of making magic central to romance" (*English Romance in Time*, 138). An important exception is Michelle Sweeney, who in *Magic in Medieval Romance* does consider the function of magic in a wide range of romances. However, my argument departs from hers by focusing on Middle English texts and particularly on wonder and on the moral implications beyond the text.

5. Kieckhefer, *Magic in the Middle Ages*, 12, and Michael D. Bailey, "Age of Magicians," 17. For more information about how this set the stage for the later focus on witchcraft, see Bailey, "From Sorcery to Witchcraft."

6. For more on skepticism, see Brewer, *Wonder and Skepticism*; Kamerick, "Shaping Superstition"; and Finlayson, "Marvellous in Middle English Romance," 363–74. This attitude was bolstered by the most significant writer to address magic-related issues during the fourteenth century, Nicole Oresme, who sought to explain the natural causes behind apparent marvels; see Bert Hansen, *Nicole Oresme*.

7. *Awntyrs off Arthur*, in *Sir Gawain: Eleven Romances*, lines 105–6. All references to this text hereafter will be cited parenthetically by line number.

8. Gower, *English Works*, V.3575–3622. Hereafter cited parenthetically.

9. Malory, *Works of Sir Thomas Malory*, vol. I, 9 and 126.

Bibliography

Allen, Dorena. "Orpheus and Orfeo: The Dead and the *Taken*." *Medium Aevum* 33 (1964): 102–11.

Allen, Elizabeth. *False Fables and Exemplary Truth in Later Middle English Literature*. New York: Palgrave Macmillan, 2005.

The Anonimalle Chronicle, 1333 to 1381. Edited by V. H. Galbraith. Manchester: Manchester University Press, 1927.

Arner, Lynn. "The Ends of Enchantment: Colonialism and *Sir Gawain and the Green Knight*." *Texas Studies in Literature and Language* 48, no. 2 (2006): 79–101.

Astell, Ann. *Political Allegory in Late Medieval England*. Ithaca: Cornell University Press, 1999.

Augustine. *The City of God Against the Pagans*. Vol. 3, *Books VIII–XI*. Translated by David S. Wiesen. Cambridge, Mass.: Harvard University Press, 1968.

———. *The City of God Against the Pagans*. Vol. 7, *Books XXI–XXII*. Translated by William M. Green. Cambridge, Mass.: Harvard University Press, 1972.

———. *De Civitate Dei*. Vol. 1, *Libri I–X*. Edited by Bernardus Dombart and Alphonsus Kalb. Corpus Christianorum Series Latina XLVII. Turnhout: Brepols, 1955.

———. *De Civitate Dei*. Vol. 2, *Libri XI–XXII*. Edited by Bernardus Dombart and Alphonsus Kalb. Corpus Christianorum Series Latina XLVIII. Turnhout: Brepols, 1955.

The Awntyrs off Arthur. In *Sir Gawain: Eleven Romances and Tales*, edited by Thomas Hahn. Kalamazoo, Mich.: Medieval Institute Publications, 1995.

Babich, Andrea G. Pisani. "The Power of the Kingdom and the Ties that Bind in *Sir Orfeo*." *Neophilologus* 82 (1998): 477–86.

Bailey, Michael D. "The Age of Magicians: Periodization in the History of European Magic." *Magic, Ritual, and Witchcraft* 3 (2008): 1–28.

———. "From Sorcery to Witchcraft: Clerical Conceptions of Magic in the Later Middle Ages." *Speculum* 76, no. 4 (2001): 960–90.

———. *Magic and Superstition in Europe: A Concise History from Antiquity to the Present*. Lanham, Md.: Rowan and Littlefield, 2007.

———. "The Meanings of Magic." *Magic, Ritual, and Witchcraft* 1 (2006): 1–23.

Barron, W. R. J. "Alliterative Romance and the French Tradition." In *Middle English Alliterative Poetry and Its Literary Background: Seven Essays*, edited by David Lawton, 70–87. Cambridge, England: D. S. Brewer, 1982.

Battles, Dominique. "*Sir Orfeo* and English Identity." *Studies in Philology* 107, no. 2 (2010): 179–211.

Battles, Paul. "Amended Texts, Emended Ladies: Female Agency and the Textual Editing of *Sir Gawain and the Green Knight*." *Chaucer Review* 44, no. 3 (2010): 323–43.

Baughan, Denver Ewing. "The Role of Morgan le Fey in *Sir Gawain and*

the Green Knight." *ELH* 17, no. 4 (1950): 241–51.
Beckerman, Bernard. "Spectacle in the Theatre." *Theatre Survey* 25, no. 1 (1984): 1–13.
Bennett, Jane. *The Enchantment of Modern Life: Attachments, Crossings, and Ethics*. Princeton: Princeton University Press, 2001.
———. *Vibrant Matter: A Political Ecology of Things*. Durham: Duke University Press, 2010.
Bennett, Judith. "Death and the Maiden." *Journal of Medieval and Early Modern Studies* 42, no. 2 (2012): 269–305.
Benson, Larry D., ed. *A Glossarial Concordance to the Riverside Chaucer*. Vol. 1. New York: Garland, 1993.
Berry, Craig A. "Flying Sources: Classical Authority in Chaucer's *Squire's Tale*." *ELH* 68, no. 2 (2001): 287–313.
Biernoff, Suzannah. *Sight and Embodiment in the Middle Ages*. New York: Palgrave Macmillan, 2002.
Bildhauer, Bettina, and Robert Mills, eds. *The Monstrous Middle Ages*. Toronto: University of Toronto Press, 2003.
Blamires, Alcuin. *Chaucer, Ethics, and Gender*. Oxford: Oxford University Press, 2006.
Blanchfield, Lynne S. "Rate Revisited: The Compilation of Narrative Works in MS Ashmole 61." In *Romance Reading on the Book: Essays on Medieval Narrative Presented to Maldwyn Mills*, edited by Jennifer Fellows, Rosalind Field, Gillian Rogers, and Judith Weiss, 208–20. Cardiff: University of Wales Press, 1996.
Bliss, Jane. *Naming and Namelessness in Medieval Romance*. Cambridge: D. S. Brewer, 2008.
The Book of Vices and Virtues: A Fourteenth Century English Translation of the Somme le Roi of Lorens D'Orléans. Edited by W. Nelson Francis. EETS 217. London, 1942.
Brantley, Jessica. "Vision, Image, Text." In *Middle English*, edited by Paul Strohm, 315–34. Oxford Twenty-First Century Approaches to Literature. Oxford: Oxford University Press, 2007.
Braswell, Mary Flowers. "The Magic of Machinery: A Context for Chaucer's *Franklin's Tale*." *Mosaic* 18, no. 2 (1985): 101–10.
Breuer, Heidi. *Crafting the Witch: Gendering Magic in Medieval and Early Modern England*. New York: Routledge, 2009.
Brewer, Keagan. *Wonder and Skepticism in the Middle Ages*. London: Routledge, 2016.
Briggs, K. M. *The Anatomy of Puck: An Examination of Fairy Beliefs Among Shakespeare's Contemporaries and Successors*. London: Routledge and Kegan Paul, 1959.
Brown, Peter. "Images." In *A Companion to Medieval English Literature and Culture, c. 1350–c. 1500*, edited by Peter Brown, 307–21. Malden, Mass.: Blackwell, 2007.
Burns, E. Jane. "A Snake-Tailed Woman: Hybridity and Dynasty in the *Roman de Mélusine*." In *From Beasts to Souls: Gender and Embodiment in Medieval Europe*, edited by E. Jane Burns and Peggy McCracken, 185–220. Notre Dame: University of Notre Dame Press, 2013.
Bynum, Caroline Walker. *Christian Materiality: An Essay on Religion in Late Medieval Europe*. New York: Zone Books, 2011.
———. *Holy Feast and Holy Fast: The Religious Significance of Food to Medieval Women*. Berkeley: University of California Press, 1987.
———. *Metamorphosis and Identity*. New York: Zone Books, 2001.

———. "Miracles and Marvels: The Limits of Alterity." In *Vita religiosa im Mittelalter*, edited by Franz Felton and Nikolas Jaspert, 799–817. Berlin: Duncker & Humblot, 1999.

———. "Wonder." *American Historical Review* 102, no. 1 (1997): 1–26.

Byrne, Aisling. *Otherworlds: Fantasy and History in Medieval Literature*. Oxford: Oxford University Press, 2016.

Caldwell, Ellen M. "The Heroism of Heurodis: Self-Mutilation and Restoration in *Sir Orfeo*." *Papers on Language and Literature* 43, no. 3 (2007): 291–310.

Camille, Michael. "Before the Gaze: The Internal Senses and Late Medieval Practices of Seeing." In *Visuality Before and Beyond the Renaissance: Seeing as Others Saw*, edited by Robert S. Nelson, 197–223. Cambridge: Cambridge University Press, 2000.

———. *Gothic Idol: Ideology and Image-Making in Medieval Art*. Cambridge: Cambridge University Press, 1989.

———. "The Image and the Self: Unwriting Late Medieval Bodies." In *Framing Medieval Bodies*, edited by Sarah Kay and Miri Rubin, 62–99. Manchester: Manchester University Press, 1994.

———. "Visual Art in Two Manuscripts of the Ars Notoria." In *Conjuring Spirits: Texts and Traditions of Medieval Ritual Magic*, edited by Claire Fanger, 110–39. University Park: Pennsylvania State University Press, 1998.

Cannon, Christopher. *The Grounds of English Literature*. Oxford: Oxford University Press, 2004.

Carlson, Christina M. "'The Minstrel's Song of Silence': The Construction of Masculine Authority and the Feminized Other in the Romance *Sir Orfeo*." *Comitatus* 29 (1998): 62–75.

Carlson, David R. *Chaucer's Jobs*. New York: Palgrave Macmillan, 2004.

Carruthers, Mary. *The Book of Memory: A Study of Memory in Medieval Culture*. 2nd ed. Cambridge: Cambridge University Press, 2008.

———. *The Craft of Thought: Meditation, Rhetoric, and the Making of Images, 400–1200*. Cambridge: Cambridge University Press, 2000.

———. "Moving Images in the Mind's Eye." In *The Mind's Eye: Art and Theological Argument in the Middle Ages*, edited by Jeffrey F. Hamburger and Anne-Marie Bouché, 287–305. Princeton: Department of Art and Archaeology, Princeton University, in association with Princeton University Press, 2006.

Carson, Mother Angela, O.S.U. "Morgain la Fée as the Principle of Unity in *Gawain and the Green Knight*." *Modern Language Quarterly* 23 (1962): 3–16.

Carter, Susan. "Coupling the Beastly Bride and the Hunter Hunted: What Lies Behind Chaucer's *Wife of Bath's Tale*." *Chaucer Review* 37, no. 4 (2003): 329–45.

Cartlidge, Neil. "Sir Orfeo in the Otherworld: Courting Chaos?" *Studies in the Age of Chaucer* 26 (2004): 195–226.

Charny, Geoffroi de. *The Book of Chivalry of Geoffroi de Charny: Text, Context, and Translation*. Edited by Richard W. Kaeuper and Elspeth Kennedy. Philadelphia: University of Pennsylvania Press, 1996.

Chaucer, Geoffrey. *The Riverside Chaucer*. Edited by Larry D. Benson. Boston: Houghton Mifflin, 1987.

Chism, Christine. *Alliterative Revivals*. Philadelphia: University of Pennsylvania Press, 2002.

Chronicon Angliae. Edited by Edward Maunde Thompson. London: Longman, 1874.

Clark, Rosalind. "*Sir Orfeo:* The Otherworld vs. Faithful Human Love." *Proceedings of the Medieval Association of the Midwest* II (1993): 71–80.

Cleanness. In *The Poems of the Pearl Manuscript*, edited by Malcolm Andrew and Ronald Waldron. 5th ed. Exeter: University of Exeter Press, 2007.

Cohen, Jeffrey Jerome. "Monster Culture (Seven Theses)." In *Monster Theory: Reading Culture*, edited by Jeffrey Jerome Cohen, 3–25. Minneapolis: University of Minnesota Press, 1996.

Cook, Robert. "Chaucer's Franklin's Tale and *Sir Orfeo*." *Neuphilologische Mitteilungen* 95, no. 3 (1994): 333–36.

Cooper, Helen. *The English Romance in Time: Transforming Motifs from Geoffrey of Monmouth to the Death of Shakespeare*. Oxford: Oxford University Press, 2004.

———. "Magic That Does Not Work." *Medievalia et Humanistica* 7 (1976): 131–46.

———. "The Supernatural." In *A Companion to the "Gawain"-Poet*, edited by Derek Brewer and Jonathon Gibson, 277–91. Rochester, N.Y.: D. S. Brewer, 1997.

Crane, Susan. *Animal Encounters: Contacts and Concepts in Medieval Britain*. Philadelphia: University of Pennsylvania Press, 2013.

———. "The Biennial Chaucer Lecture: For the Birds." *Studies in the Age of Chaucer* 29 (2007): 23–41.

———. *Gender and Romance in Chaucer's "Canterbury Tales."* Princeton: Princeton University Press, 1994.

D'Arcy, Anne Marie. "The Faerie King's *Kunstkammer:* Imperial Discourse and the Wondrous in *Sir Orfeo*." *Review of English Studies* 58, no. 233 (2007): 10–33.

Daston, Lorraine, and Katharine Park. *Wonders and the Order of Nature, 1150–1750*. New York: Zone Books, 1998.

Davenport, Tony. "Abbreviation and the Education of the Hero in *Chevalere Assigne*." In *The Matter of Identity in Medieval Romance*, edited by Phillipa Hardman, 9–20. Cambridge, England: D. S. Brewer, 2002.

Davenport, W. A. *Chaucer and His English Contemporaries: Prologue and Tale in "The Canterbury Tales."* New York: St. Martin's Press, 1998.

Davies, Constance. "Classical Threads in 'Orfeo.'" *Modern Language Review* 56 (1961): 161–66.

DiMarco, Vincent. "A Note on Canacee's Magic Ring." *Anglia* 99, nos. 3–4 (1981): 399–405.

———. "The Squire's Tale." In *Sources and Analogues of the "Canterbury Tales*,*"* vol. 1, edited by Robert M. Correale and Mary Hamel, 169–209. Cambridge, England: D. S. Brewer, 2002.

Dimmick, Jeremy, James Simpson, and Nicolette Zeeman, eds. *Images, Idolatry, and Iconoclasm in Late Medieval England: Textuality and the Visual Image*. Oxford: Oxford University Press, 2002.

Dinshaw, Carolyn. *Chaucer's Sexual Poetics*. Madison: University of Wisconsin Press, 1989.

Doyle, A. I. "The Manuscripts." In *Middle English Alliterative Poetry and Its Literary Background: Seven Essays*, edited by David Lawton, 88–100. Woodbridge, Suffolk: D. S. Brewer, 1982.

Dronke, Peter. "The Return of Eurydice." *Classica et Mediaevalia* 23 (1962): 198–215.

Duffy, Eamon. *The Stripping of the Altars: Traditional Religion in England,*

1400–1580. New Haven: Yale University Press, 1992.
During, Simon. *Modern Enchantments: The Cultural Power of Secular Magic.* Cambridge, Mass.: Harvard University Press, 2002.
Eamon, William. "Technology as Magic in the Late Middle Ages and the Renaissance." *Janus* 70, nos. 3–4 (1983): 170–212.
Edwards, A. S. G. "The Manuscript: British Library MS Cotton Nero A.x." In *A Companion to the "Gawain"-Poet,* edited by Derek Brewer and Jonathon Gibson, 197–219. Rochester, N.Y.: D. S. Brewer, 1997.
Edwards, Suzanne M. *The Afterlives of Rape in Medieval English Literature.* New York: Palgrave Macmillan, 2016.
———. "The Rhetoric of Rape and the Politics of Gender in the *Wife of Bath's Tale* and the *1382 Statute of Rapes.*" *Exemplaria* 23, no. 1 (2011): 3–26.
Evans, Ruth. "*Sir Orfeo* and Bare Life." In *Medieval Cultural Studies: Essays in Honour of Stephen Knight,* edited by Ruth Evans, Helen Fulton, and David Matthews, 198–212. Cardiff: University of Wales Press, 2006.
Falk, Oren. "The Son of Orfeo: Kingship and Compromise in a Middle English Romance." *Journal of Medieval and Early Modern Studies* 30 (2000): 247–74.
Fanger, Claire, ed. *Conjuring Spirits: Texts and Traditions of Medieval Ritual Magic.* University Park: Pennsylvania State University Press, 1998.
———. "Plundering the Egyptian Treasure: John the Monk's *Book of Visions* and Its Relation to the *Ars Notoria* of Solomon." In *Conjuring Spirits: Texts and Traditions of Medieval Ritual Magic,* edited by Claire Fanger, 216–49. University Park: Pennsylvania State University Press, 1998.
———. *Rewriting Magic: An Exegesis of the Visionary Autobiography of a Fourteenth-Century French Monk.* University Park: Pennsylvania State University Press, 2015.
Fasciculus Morum: A Fourteenth-Century Preacher's Handbook. Edited and translated by Siegfried Wenzel. University Park: Pennsylvania State University Press, 1989.
Fein, Susanna. "Other Thought-Worlds." In *A Companion to Chaucer,* edited by Peter Brown, 336–41. Oxford: Blackwell, 2002.
Felski, Rita. *Uses of Literature.* Malden, Mass.: Blackwell, 2008.
Field, P. J. C. *Malory: Texts and Sources.* Cambridge, England: D. S. Brewer, 1998.
———. "What Women Really Want: The Genesis of Chaucer's *Wife of Bath's Tale.*" *Arthurian Literature* 27 (2010): 59–85.
Finlayson, John. "The Marvellous in Middle English Romance." *Chaucer Review* 33, no. 4 (1999): 363–408.
Fisher, Philip. *Wonder, the Rainbow, and the Aesthetics of Rare Experiences.* Cambridge, Mass.: Harvard University Press, 1998.
Fisher, Sheila. "Taken Men and Token Women in *Sir Gawain and the Green Knight.*" In *Seeking the Woman in Late Medieval and Renaissance Writings: Essays in Feminist Contextual Criticism,* edited by Sheila Fisher and Janet E. Halley, 71–105. Knoxville: University of Tennessee Press, 1989.
Fletcher, Alan J. "*Sir Orfeo* and the Flight from the Enchanters." *Studies in the Age of Chaucer* 22 (2000): 141–77.
Flint, Valerie J. "A Magic Universe." In *A Social History of England, 1200–1500,* edited by Rosemary Horrox and W. Mark Ormrod, 340–55. Cambridge: Cambridge University Press, 2006.

———. *The Rise of Magic in Early Medieval Europe*. Princeton: Princeton University Press, 2001.

Foer, Joshua. *Moonwalking with Einstein: The Art and Science of Remembering Everything*. New York: Penguin, 2011.

Foster, Edward E. "Fantasy and Reality in *Sir Orfeo*." *Ball State University Forum* 14, no. 4 (1973): 22–29.

Fradenburg, Louise O. "The Wife of Bath's Passing Fancy." *Studies in the Age of Chaucer* 8 (1986): 31–58.

Friedman, Albert B. "Morgan le Faye in *Sir Gawain and the Green Knight*." *Speculum* 35, no. 2 (1960): 260–74.

Friedman, John Block. "Eurydice, Heurodis, and the Noon-Day Demon." *Speculum* 41, no. 1 (1966): 22–29.

———. *The Monstrous Races in Medieval Art and Thought*. Cambridge, Mass.: Harvard University Press, 1981.

———. *Orpheus in the Middle Ages*. Cambridge, Mass.: Harvard University Press, 1970.

Fumo, Jamie C. *The Legacy of Apollo: Antiquity, Authority, and Chaucerian Poetics*. Toronto: University of Toronto Press, 2010.

Furrow, Melissa. *Expectations of Romance: The Reception of a Genre in Medieval England*. Woodbridge, Suffolk: D. S. Brewer, 2009.

Fyler, John M. "Domesticating the Exotic in the *Squire's Tale*." *ELH* 55, no. 1 (1988): 1–26.

Ganim, John M. "Disorientation, Style, and Consciousness in *Sir Gawain and the Green Knight*." *PMLA* 91, no. 3 (1976): 376–84.

Gayk, Shannon. *Image, Text, and Religious Reform in Fifteenth-Century England*. Cambridge: Cambridge University Press, 2010.

Gervase of Tilbury. *Otia Imperialia: Recreation for an Emperor*. Edited and translated by S. E. Banks and J. W. Binns. Oxford: Clarendon Press, 2002.

Giaccherini, Enrico. "From *Sir Orfeo* to 'Schir Orpheus': Exile, and the Waning of the Middle Ages." In *Displaced Persons: Conditions of Exile in European Culture*, edited by Sharon Ouditt, 1–10. Burlington, Vt.: Ashgate, 2002.

Gilbert, Jane. "Arthurian Ethics." In *The Cambridge Companion to the Arthurian Legend*, edited by Elizabeth Archibald and Ad Putter, 154–70. Cambridge: Cambridge University Press, 2009.

Gower, John. *The English Works of John Gower*. 2 vols. Edited by G. C. Macaulay. EETS Extra Series 81 and 82. 1900–1901. London: Oxford University Press, 1901–2. Reprinted 1957.

Green, Richard Firth. "The Biennial Chaucer Lecture: Changing Chaucer." *Studies in the Age of Chaucer* 25 (2003): 27–52.

———. *Elf Queens and Holy Friars: Fairy Beliefs and the Medieval Church*. Philadelphia: University of Pennsylvania Press, 2016.

Greenblatt, Stephen. *Marvelous Possessions: The Wonder of the New World*. Chicago: University of Chicago Press, 1991.

———. "Resonance and Wonder." In *Exhibiting Cultures: The Poetics and Politics of Museum Display*, edited by Ivan Karp and Steven Lavine, 42–56. Washington, D.C.: Smithsonian, 1991.

The Greene Knight. In *Sir Gawain: Eleven Romances and Tales*, edited by Thomas Hahn. Kalamazoo, Mich.: Medieval Institute Publications, 1995.

Gregory the Great. *The Letters of Gregory the Great*. Vol. 3. Translated by John R. C. Martyn. Toronto: Pontifical Institute of Mediaeval Studies, 2004.

———. *Registrum Epistularum, Libri VIII–XIV, Appendix*. Edited by Dag

Norberg. Corpus Christianorum Series Latina CXL A. Turnhout: Brepols, 1982.

Gutman, Sara. "Chaucer's Chicks: Feminism and Falconry in 'The Knight's Tale,' 'The Squire's Tale,' and *The Parliament of Fowls*." In *Rethinking Chaucerian Beasts*, edited by Carolynn Van Dyke, 69–83. New York: Palgrave Macmillan, 2012.

Haller, Robert S. "Chaucer's 'Squire's Tale' and the Uses of Rhetoric." *Modern Philology* 62, no. 4 (1965): 285–95.

Hanawalt, Barbara A., and Kathryn L. Reyerson. "Introduction." In *City and Spectacle in Medieval Europe*, edited by Barbara A. Hanawalt and Kathryn L. Reyerson, ix–xx. Minneapolis: University of Minnesota Press, 1994.

Hansen, Bert. *Nicole Oresme and the Marvels of Nature: A Study of His "De causis mirabilium" with Critical Edition, Translation, and Commentary*. Toronto: Pontifical Institute of Mediaeval Studies, 1985.

Hansen, Elaine Tuttle. *Chaucer and the Fictions of Gender*. Berkeley: University of California Press, 1992.

Hazell, Dinah. "The Blinding of Gwennere: Thomas Chestre as Social Critic." *Arthurian Literature* 20 (2003): 123–43.

———. *Poverty in Late Middle English Literature: The "Meene" and the "Riche."* Dublin: Four Courts Press, 2009.

Heng, Geraldine. "Feminine Knots and the Other *Sir Gawain and the Green Knight*." *PMLA* 106, no. 3 (1991): 500–514.

Herdt, Jennifer A. *Putting on Virtue: The Legacy of the Splendid Vices*. Chicago: University of Chicago Press, 2008.

Hilmo, Maidie. *Medieval Images, Icons, and Illustrated English Literary Texts: From the Ruthwell Cross to the Ellesmere Chaucer*. Burlington, Vt.: Ashgate, 2004.

———. "The Power of Images in the Auchinleck, Vernon, *Pearl*, and Two *Piers Plowman* Manuscripts." In Kathryn Kerby-Fulton, Maidie Hilmo, and Linda Olson, *Opening Up Middle English Manuscripts: Literary and Visual Approaches*, chap. 3. Ithaca: Cornell University Press, 2012.

Horrall, Sarah M. "Notes on British Library, MS Cotton Nero A.x." *Manuscripta* 30, no. 3 (1986): 191–98.

Hughes, Jonathan. *The Rise of Alchemy in Fourteenth-Century England: Plantagenet Kings and the Search for the Philosopher's Stone*. London: Continuum, 2012.

Hunt, Alice. *The Drama of Coronation: Medieval Ceremony in Early Modern England*. Cambridge: Cambridge University Press, 2008.

Huot, Sylvia. "Others and Alterity." In *The Cambridge Companion to Medieval French Literature*, edited by Simon Gaunt and Sarah Kay, 238–50. Cambridge: Cambridge University Press, 2008.

Ihle, Sandra. "The English *Partonope of Blois* as Exemplum." In *Courtly Literature: Culture and Context: Selected Papers from the 5th Triennial Congress of the International Courtly Literature Society*, edited by Keith Busby and Erik Kooper, 301–11. Amsterdam: John Benjamins, 1990.

Ingham, Patricia Clare. "Little Nothings: *The Squire's Tale* and the Ambition of Gadgets." *Studies in the Age of Chaucer* 31 (2009): 53–80.

———. "Pastoral Histories: Utopia, Conquest, and the *Wife of Bath's Tale*." *Texas Studies in Literature and Language* 44, no. 1 (2002): 34–46.

Isidore of Seville. *Etymologiarvm Sive Originvm*. 2 vols. Edited by

W. M. Lindsay. London: Oxford University Press, 1962.

———. *The "Etymologies" of Isidore of Seville*. Translated by Stephen A. Barney, W. J. Lewis, J. A. Beach, and Oliver Berghof. Cambridge: Cambridge University Press, 2006.

Jaeger, C. Stephen. *Enchantment: On Charisma and the Sublime in the Arts of the West*. Philadelphia: University of Pennsylvania Press, 2012.

———, ed. *Magnificence and the Sublime in Medieval Aesthetics: Art, Architecture, Literature, Music*. New York: Palgrave Macmillan, 2010.

———. "Richard of St. Victor and the Medieval Sublime." In *Magnificence and the Sublime in Medieval Aesthetics: Art, Architecture, Literature, Music*, edited by C. Stephen Jaeger, 157–78. New York: Palgrave Macmillan, 2010.

Jefferson, Lisa. "The Language and Vocabulary of the Fourteenth- and Early Fifteenth-Century Records of the Goldsmiths' Company." In *Multilingualism in Later Medieval Britain*, edited by D. A. Trotter, 175–212. Rochester, N.Y.: D. S. Brewer, 2000.

Jeffrey, David Lyle. *Houses of the Interpreter: Reading Scripture, Reading Culture*. Waco: Baylor University Press, 2003.

Jirsa, Curtis R. H. "In the Shadow of the Ympe-tre: Arboreal Folklore in *Sir Orfeo*." *English Studies* 89, no. 2 (2008): 141–51.

Jolly, Karen, Catharina Raudvere, and Edward Peters. *Witchcraft and Magic in Europe*. Vol. 3, *The Middle Ages*. Philadelphia: University of Pennsylvania Press, 2002.

Jones, Timothy S., and David A. Sprunger, eds. *Marvels, Monsters, and Miracles: Studies in the Medieval and Early Modern Imaginations*. Kalamazoo, Mich.: Medieval Institute Publications, 2002.

Kaeuper, Richard. *Chivalry and Violence in Medieval Europe*. Oxford: Oxford University Press, 1999.

———. *Holy Warriors: The Religious Ideology of Chivalry*. Philadelphia: University of Pennsylvania Press, 2009.

Kamerick, Kathleen. "Shaping Superstition in Late Medieval England." *Magic, Ritual, and Witchcraft* 3, no. 1 (2008): 29–53.

Kamps, Ivo. "Magic, Women, and Incest: The Real Challenges in *Sir Gawain and the Green Knight*." *Exemplaria* 1, no. 2 (1989): 313–36.

Kane, George. *The Liberating Truth: The Concept of Integrity in Chaucer's Writings*. London: Athlone Press, 1980.

Kang, Minsoo. *Sublime Dreams of Living Machines: The Automaton in the European Imagination*. Cambridge, Mass.: Harvard University Press, 2011.

Karnes, Michelle. *Imagination, Meditation, and Cognition in the Middle Ages*. Chicago: University of Chicago Press, 2011.

———. "Marvels in the Medieval Imagination." *Speculum* 90, no. 2 (2015): 327–65.

———. "Wonder, Marvels, and Metaphor in the *Squire's Tale*." *ELH* 82, no. 2 (2015): 461–90.

Kendall, Elliot. "Family, *Familia*, and the Uncanny in *Sir Orfeo*." *Studies in the Age of Chaucer* 35 (2013): 289–327.

Kieckhefer, Richard. *Forbidden Rites: A Necromancer's Manual of the Fifteenth Century*. University Park: Pennsylvania State University Press, 1998.

———, trans. *Hazards of the Dark Arts: Advice for Medieval Princes on Witchcraft and Magic*. University Park: Pennsylvania State University Press, 2017.

———. *Magic in the Middle Ages*. Canto. Cambridge, Mass: Cambridge University Press, 2000.

Kindrick, Robert L. "Gawain's Ethics: Shame and Guilt in *Sir Gawain and the Green Knight*." *Annuale Mediaevale* 20 (1981): 5–32.

King Horn. In *Four Romances of England*, edited by Ronald B. Herzman, Graham Drake, and Eve Salisbury. Kalamazoo, Mich.: Medieval Institute Publications, 1999.

Kipling, Gordon. *Enter the King: Theatre, Liturgy, and Ritual in the Medieval Civic Triumph*. Oxford: Oxford University Press, 1998.

———. "'He That Saw It Would Not Believe It': Anne Boleyn's Royal Entry into London." In *Civic Ritual and Drama*, edited by Alexandra F. Johnston and Wim N. M. Hüsken, 39–79. Amsterdam: Rodopi, 1997.

———. "Richard II's Sumptuous Pageants and the Idea of the Civic Triumph." In *Pageantry in the Shakespearean Theater*, edited by David M. Bergeron, 83–103. Athens: University of Georgia Press, 1985.

Klaassen, Frank. *The Transformations of Magic: Illicit Learned Magic in the Later Middle Ages and Renaissance*. University Park: Pennsylvania State University Press, 2013.

Kline, Barbara. "Duality, Reality, and Magic in *Sir Gawain and the Green Knight*." In *Functions of the Fantastic: Selected Essays from the Thirteenth International Conference on the Fantastic in the Arts*, edited by Joseph L. Sanders, 107–14. Westport, Conn.: Greenwood Press, 1995.

Knapp, James F. "The Meaning of *Sir Orfeo*." *Modern Language Quarterly* 29 (1968): 263–73.

Knight, Stephen. "The Social Function of the Middle English Romances." In *Medieval Literature: Criticism, Ideology, and History*, edited by David Aers, 99–122. New York: St. Martin's Press, 1986.

Kolve, V. A. *Chaucer and the Imagery of Narrative: The First Five Canterbury Tales*. Stanford: Stanford University Press, 1984.

Kooper, Erik. "The Twofold Harmony of the Middle English *Sir Orfeo*." In *Companion to Early Middle English Literature*, 2nd ed., edited by N. H. G. E. Veldhoen and H. Aertsen, 115–32. Amsterdam: VU University Press, 1995.

Lander, Bonnie. "The Convention of Innocence and *Sir Gawain and the Green Knight*'s Literary Sophisticates." *Parergon* 24, no. 1 (2007): 41–66.

Laskaya, Anne. *Chaucer's Approach to Gender in the "Canterbury Tales."* Rochester, N.Y.: D. S. Brewer, 1995.

Latham, Minor White. *The Elizabethan Fairies: The Fairies of Folklore and The Fairies of Shakespeare*. New York: Columbia University Press, 1930.

Lawrence-Mathers, Anne, and Carolina Escobar-Vargas. *Magic and Medieval Society*. New York: Routledge, 2014.

Lee, Jennifer A. "The Illuminating Critic: The Illustrator of Cotton Nero A.x." *Studies in Iconography* 3 (1977): 17–46.

Le Goff, Jacques. *The Medieval Imagination*. Translated by Arthur Goldhammer. Chicago: University of Chicago Press, 1988.

Lerer, Seth. "Artifice and Artistry in *Sir Orfeo*." *Speculum* 60, no. 1 (1985): 92–109.

———. "'Representyd Now in Yower Syght': The Culture of Spectatorship in Late-Fifteenth-Century England." In *Bodies and Disciplines: Intersections of Literature and History in Fifteenth-Century England*, edited by Barbara A. Hanawalt and David Wallace,

29–62. Minneapolis: University of Minnesota Press, 1996.

———. "*Sir Orfeo*, Line 285: An Emendation." *Notes & Queries* 59, no. 3 (2012): 320–22.

Lewis, C. S. *The Discarded Image: An Introduction to Medieval and Renaissance Literature*. Cambridge: Cambridge University Press, 1964.

Lightsey, Scott. "Chaucer's Secular Marvels and the Medieval Economy of Wonder." *Studies in the Age of Chaucer* 23 (2001): 289–316.

———. *Manmade Marvels in Medieval Literature and Culture*. New York: Palgrave Macmillan, 2007.

Lindley, Arthur. "'Vanysshed Was This Daunce, He Nyste Where': Alisoun's Absence in the Wife of Bath's Prologue and Tale." *ELH* 59, no. 1 (1992): 1–21.

Lionarons, Joyce Tally. "Magic, Machines, and Deception: Technology in the *Canterbury Tales*." *Chaucer Review* 27, no. 4 (1993): 377–86.

Liuzza, Roy Michael. "*Sir Orfeo:* Sources, Traditions, and the Poetics of Performance." *Journal of Medieval and Renaissance Studies* 21, no. 2 (1991): 269–84.

Longsworth, Robert M. "*Sir Orfeo*, the Minstrel, and the Minstrel's Art." *Studies in Philology* 79, no. 1 (1982): 1–11.

Loomis, Laura Hibbard. "Secular Dramatics in the Royal Palace, Paris, 1378, 1389, and Chaucer's 'Tregetoures.'" *Speculum* 33, no. 2 (1958): 242–55.

Lucas, Angela M. "Keeping Up Appearances: Chaucer's Franklin and the Magic of the Breton Lay Genre." In *Literature and the Supernatural: Essays for the Maynooth Bicentenary*, edited by Brian Cosgrove, 11–32. Dublin: Columba Press, 1995.

Lucas, Peter J. "Earlier Verse Romance." In *Readings in Medieval Texts: Interpreting Old and Middle English Literature,* edited by David F. Johnson and Elaine Treharne, 229–40. Oxford: Oxford University Press, 2005.

Luengo, Anthony E. "Magic and Illusion in *The Franklin's Tale*." *Journal of English and Germanic Philology* 77 (1978): 1–16.

Lybeaus Desconus. Edited by M. Mills. EETS 261. London: Oxford University Press, 1969.

Lybeaus Desconus. Edited by Eve Salisbury and James Weldon. Kalamazoo, Mich.: Medieval Institute Publications for TEAMS, 2013.

Lybeaus Desconus. In *Codex Ashmole 61: A Compilation of Popular Middle English Verse*, edited by George Shuffelton. Kalamazoo, Mich.: Medieval Institute Publications, 2008.

Maidstone, Richard. *Concordia: The Reconciliation of Richard II with London*. Edited by David R. Carlson. Translated by A. G. Rigg. Kalamazoo, Mich.: Medieval Institute Publications, 2003.

Malory, Thomas. *The Works of Sir Thomas Malory*. 3 vols. 3rd ed. Edited by Eugene Vinaver. Revised by P. J. C. Field. Oxford: Clarendon Press, 1990.

Mandeville, John. *The Book of John Mandeville*. Edited by Tamarah Kohanski and C. David Benson. Kalamazoo, Mich.: Medieval Institute Publications, 2007.

Mann, Jill. "Courtly Aesthetics and Courtly Ethics in *Sir Gawain and the Green Knight*." *Studies in the Age of Chaucer* 31 (2009): 231–65.

———. *Feminizing Chaucer*. Cambridge, England: D. S. Brewer, 2002. Originally published as *Geoffrey Chaucer*, 1991.

Map, Walter. *De Nugis Curialium*. Edited and translated by M. R. James. Revised by C. N. L. Brooke and R. A. B. Mynors. Oxford: Clarendon Press, 1983.

McAlindon, T. "Magic, Fate, and Providence in Medieval Narrative and *Sir Gawain and the Green Knight*." *Review of English Studies* 16, no. 62 (1965): 121–39.

McDonald, Nicola. "A Polemical Introduction." In *Pulp Fictions of Medieval England: Essays in Popular Romance*, edited by Nicola McDonald, 1–21. Manchester: Manchester University Press, 2004.

McKinley, Kathryn L. "The Silenced Knight: Questions of Power and Reciprocity in the *Wife of Bath's Tale*." *Chaucer Review* 30, no. 4 (1996): 359–78.

McNamer, Sarah. *Affective Meditation and the Invention of Medieval Compassion*. Philadelphia: University of Pennsylvania Press, 2010.

———. "Feeling." In *Middle English*, edited by Paul Strohm, 241–57. Oxford Twenty-First Century Approaches to Literature. Oxford: Oxford University Press, 2007.

Mehl, Dieter. *The Middle English Romances of the Thirteenth and Fourteenth Centuries*. New York: Barnes and Noble, 1969.

Middle English Dictionary. Edited by Hans Kurath, Sherman Kuhn, and Robert E. Lewis. Ann Arbor: University of Michigan Press, 1952–95. http://quod.lib.umich.edu/m/med/.

Miller, Mark. "The Ends of Excitement in *Sir Gawain and the Green Knight*: Teleology, Ethics, and the Death Drive." *Studies in the Age of Chaucer* 32 (2010): 215–56.

———. *Philosophical Chaucer: Love, Sex, and Agency in the "Canterbury Tales*." Cambridge: Cambridge University Press, 2004.

Miller, Sarah Alison. *Medieval Monstrosity and the Female Body*. New York: Routledge, 2010.

Mills, M. "The Composition and Style of the 'Southern' *Octavian, Sir Launfal*, and *Libeaus Desconus*." *Medium Aevum* 31, no. 1 (1962): 88–109.

———. "Introduction." In *Lybeaus Desconus*, edited by M. Mills, 1–70. EETS 261. London: Oxford University Press, 1969.

Minnis, Alastair. "Medieval Imagination and Memory." In *The Cambridge History of Literary Criticism*, vol. 2, *The Middle Ages*, edited by Alastair Minnis and Ian Johnson, 239–74. Cambridge: Cambridge University Press, 2005.

Mitchell, Bruce. "The Faery World of *Sir Orfeo*." *Neophilologus* 48 (1964): 155–59.

Mitchell, J. Allan. *Ethics and Eventfulness in Middle English Literature*. New York: Palgrave Macmillan, 2009.

———. *Ethics and Exemplary Narrative in Chaucer and Gower*. Cambridge, England: D. S. Brewer, 2004.

Mitchell, W. J. T. *Picture Theory: Essays on Verbal and Visual Representation*. Chicago: University of Chicago Press, 1994.

Mitchell-Smith, Ilan. "Defining Violence in Middle English Romances: 'Sir Gowther' and 'Libeaus Desconus.'" *Fifteenth-Century Studies* 34, no. 1 (2009): 148–61.

Miyares, Rubèn Valdès. "The Wonder Tale Pattern of *Sir Orfeo*." *SELIM* 3 (1993): 117–48.

Moore, Dennis. "Making Sense of an Ending: Morgan le Faye in *Sir Gawain and the Green Knight*." *Mediaevalia* 10 (1984): 213–33.

Nakley, Susan. "Sovereignty Matters: Anachronism, Chaucer's Britain, and England's Future's Past." *Chaucer Review* 44, no. 4 (2010): 368–96.

Newman, Barbara. "What Does It Mean to Say 'I Saw'? The Clash Between Theory and Practice in Medieval

Visionary Culture." *Speculum* 80, no. 1 (2005): 1–43.

North, J. D. *Chaucer's Universe*. Oxford: Oxford University Press, 1988.

Onians, John. "I Wonder: A Short History of Amazement." In *Sight and Insight: Essays on Art and Culture in Honour of E. H. Gombrich at 85*, edited by John Onians, 11–33. London: Phaidon Press, 1994.

Osberg, Richard H. "The Goldsmiths' 'Chastell' of 1377." *Theatre Survey* 27, nos. 1–2 (1986): 1–15.

Oxford English Dictionary. Oxford: Oxford University Press. http://www.oed.com.

Page, Sophie. *Magic in Medieval Manuscripts*. Toronto: University of Toronto Press, 2004.

———. *Magic in the Cloister: Pious Motives, Illicit Interests, and Occult Approaches to the Medieval Universe*. University Park: Pennsylvania State University Press, 2013.

Partonope of Blois. Edited by A. Trampe Bodtker. EETS Extra Series 109. London: K. Paul, Trench, Trubner & Co., 1912.

Patience. In *The Poems of the Pearl Manuscript*, edited by Malcolm Andrew and Ronald Waldron. 5th ed. Exeter: University of Exeter Press, 2007.

Patterson, Lee. "Perpetual Motion: Alchemy and the Technology of the Self." *Studies in the Age of Chaucer* 15 (1993): 25–57.

Pearl. In *The Poems of the Pearl Manuscript*, edited by Malcolm Andrew and Ronald Waldron. 5th ed. Exeter: University of Exeter Press, 2007.

Pearl, Cleanness, Patience, and Sir Gawain: Reproduced in Facsimile. Introduced by Sir Israel Gollancz. EETS 162. London: Oxford University Press, 1923.

Peter of Limoges. *The Moral Treatise on the Eye*. Translated by Richard Newhauser. Toronto: Pontifical Institute of Mediaeval Studies, 2012.

Peters, Edward. *The Magician, the Witch, and the Law*. Philadelphia: University of Pennsylvania Press, 1978.

Phillips, Kim. "The Invisible Man: Body and Ritual in a Fifteenth-Century Noble Household." *Journal of Medieval History* 31 (2005): 143–62.

Puhvel, Martin. "Art and the Supernatural in *Sir Gawain and the Green Knight*." *Arthurian Literature* 5, no. 1 (1985): 1–69.

Putter, Ad. *"Sir Gawain and the Green Knight" and French Arthurian Romance*. Oxford: Clarendon Press, 1995.

Quinn, Dennis. *Iris Exiled: A Synoptic History of Wonder*. Lanham, Md.: University Press of America, 2002.

Reichardt, Paul F. "Paginal Eyes: Faces Among the Ornamented Capitals of MS Cotton Nero A.x, Art. 3." *Manuscripta* 36, no. 1 (1992): 22–36.

———. "'Several Illuminations, Coarsely Executed': The Illustrations of the *Pearl* Manuscript." *Studies in Iconography* 18 (1997): 119–42.

Renoir, Alain. "Descriptive Technique in *Sir Gawain and the Green Knight*." *Orbis Litterarum* 13 (1958): 126–32.

Richard of St. Victor. *The Twelve Patriarchs; The Mystical Ark; Book Three of the Trinity*. Translated by Grover A. Zinn. New York: Paulist Press, 1979.

Riddy, Felicity. "The Uses of the Past in *Sir Orfeo*." *Yearbook of English Studies* 6 (1976): 5–15.

Rider, Catherine. *Magic and Impotence in the Middle Ages*. Oxford: Oxford University Press, 2006.

———. *Magic and Religion in Medieval England*. London: Reaktion, 2012.

Rider, Jeff. "The Other Worlds of Romance." In *The Cambridge Companion to Medieval Romance*, edited by Roberta L. Krueger,

115–31. Cambridge: Cambridge University Press, 2000.

———. "Receiving Orpheus in the Middle Ages: Allegorization, Remythification, and *Sir Orfeo*." *Papers on Language and Literature* 24, no. 4 (1988): 343–66.

Rogers, Gillian. "The Grene Knight." In *A Companion to the "Gawain"-Poet*, edited by Derek Brewer and Jonathon Gibson, 365–72. Rochester, N.Y.: D. S. Brewer, 1997.

The Romance of the Cheuelere Assigne. Edited by Henry H. Gibbs. EETS Extra Series 6. London: Early English Text Society, 1868.

Ronquist, E. C. "The Powers of Poetry in *Sir Orfeo*." *Philological Quarterly* 64, no. 1 (1985): 99–117.

Rosenfeld, Jessica. *Ethics and Enjoyment in Late Medieval Poetry: Love After Aristotle*. Cambridge: Cambridge University Press, 2011.

Salisbury, Eve. "*Lybeaus Desconus*: Transformation, Adaptation, and the Monstrous-Feminine." *Arthuriana* 24, no. 1 (2014): 66–85.

Salisbury, Eve, and James Weldon. "Introduction." In *Lybeaus Desconus*, edited by Eve Salisbury and James Weldon, 1–29. Kalamazoo, Mich.: Medieval Institute Publications for TEAMS, 2013.

Salla, Sandra M. "Disappearing Fairies in the *Wife of Bath's Tale*." *Mediaevalia* 21, no. 2 (1997): 281–93.

Saul, Nigel. *Chivalry in Medieval England*. Cambridge, Mass.: Harvard University Press, 2011.

Saunders, Corinne. "The Affective Body: Love, Virtue, and Vision in English Medieval Literature." In *The Body and the Arts*, edited by Corinne Saunders, Ulrika Maude, and Jane Macnoughton, 87–102. New York: Palgrave Macmillan, 2009.

———. "Erotic Magic: The Enchantress in Middle English Romance." In *The Erotic in the Literature of Medieval Britain*, edited by Amanda Hopkins and Cory Rushton, 38–52. Rochester, N.Y.: D. S. Brewer, 2007.

———. *Magic and the Supernatural in Medieval English Romance*. Cambridge, England: D. S. Brewer, 2010.

———. "Magic, Science, and Romance: Chaucer and the Supernatural." In *Medieval English Literary and Cultural Studies: SELIM XV*, edited by Juan Camilo Conde Silvestre and Ma Nila Vázquez González, 121–43. Murcia: Universidad de Murcia, 2004.

———. *Rape and Ravishment in the Literature of Medieval England*. Cambridge, England: D. S. Brewer, 2001.

———. "Religion and Magic." In *The Cambridge Companion to the Arthurian Legend*, edited by Elizabeth Archibald and Ad Putter, 201–17. Cambridge: Cambridge University Press, 2009.

Schiff, Randy P. *Revivalist Fantasy: Alliterative Verse and Nationalist Literary History*. Columbus: Ohio State University Press, 2011.

Schotland, Sara Deutch. "Avian Hybridity in 'The Squire's Tale': Uses of Anthropomorphism." In *Rethinking Chaucerian Beasts*, edited by Carolynn Van Dyke, 115–30. New York: Palgrave Macmillan, 2012.

———. "Talking Bird and Gentle Heart: Female Homosocial Bonding in the *Squire's Tale*." In *Friendship in the Middle Ages and Early Modern Age: Explorations of a Fundamental Ethical Discourse*, edited by Albrecht Classen and Marilyn Sandidge, 525–41. New York: Walter de Gruyter, 2010.

Scott, Kathleen L. *Later Gothic Manuscripts, 1390–1490*. Vol. 2, *Catalogue and Indexes*. A Survey of Manuscripts Illuminated in the

British Isles 6. London: H. Miller, 1996.

Seaman, Myra. "Disconsolate Art." In *Dark Chaucer: An Assortment*, edited by Myra Seaman, Eileen Joy, and Nicola Masciandaro. Brooklyn, N.Y.: Punctum Books, 2012.

Severs, J. Burke. "The Antecedents of Sir Orfeo." In *Studies in Medieval Literature in Honor of Professor Albert Croll Baugh*, edited by MacEdward Leach, 187–207. Philadelphia: University of Pennsylvania Press, 1961.

Sherwood, Merriam. "Magic and Mechanics in Medieval Fiction." *Modern Philology* 44, no. 4 (1947): 567–92.

Shoaf, R. A. *The Poem as Green Girdle: Commercium in "Sir Gawain and the Green Knight."* Gainesville: University Press of Florida, 1984.

Simons, Walter. "Reading a Saint's Body: Rapture and Bodily Movement in the *Vitae* of Thirteenth-Century Beguines." In *Framing Medieval Bodies*, edited by Sarah Kay and Miri Rubin, 10–23. Manchester: Manchester University Press, 1994.

Simpson, James. "The Rule of Medieval Imagination." In *Images, Idolatry, and Iconoclasm in Late Medieval England: Textuality and the Visual Image*, edited by Jeremy Dimmick, James Simpson, and Nicolette Zeeman, 4–24. Oxford: Oxford University Press, 2002.

Sir Gawain: Eleven Romances and Tales. Edited by Thomas Hahn. Kalamazoo, Mich.: Medieval Institute Publications, 1995.

Sir Gawain and the Green Knight. Edited by J. R. R. Tolkien and E. V. Gordon. Revised by Norman Davis. Oxford: Clarendon Press, 1967.

Sir Gawain and the Green Knight. In *The Poems of the Pearl Manuscript*, edited by Malcolm Andrew and Ronald Waldron. 5th ed. Exeter: University of Exeter Press, 2007.

Sir Launfal. In *Middle English Breton Lays*, edited by Anne Laskaya and Eve Salisbury. Kalamazoo, Mich.: Medieval Institute Publications, 1995.

Sir Orfeo. Edited by A. J. Bliss. 2nd ed. Oxford: Clarendon Press, 1966.

Smith, D. Vance. *Arts of Possession: The Middle English Household Imaginary*. Minneapolis: University of Minnesota Press, 2003.

Spenser, Edmund. *The Faerie Queene*. Edited by A. C. Hamilton, Hiroshi Yamashita, and Toshiyuki Suzuki. Revised 2nd edition. London: Routledge, 2013.

The Squire of Low Degree. In *Sentimental and Humorous Romances*, edited by Erik Kooper. Kalamazoo, Mich.: Medieval Institute Publications for TEAMS, 2005.

Stanbury, Sarah. *Seeing the "Gawain"-Poet: Descriptions and the Act of Perception*. Philadelphia: University of Pennsylvania Press, 1991.

———. *The Visual Object of Desire in Late Medieval England*. Philadelphia: University of Pennsylvania Press, 2008.

Stock, Lorraine. "Just How Loathly Is the 'Wyf'? Deconstructing Chaucer's 'Hag' in *The Wife of Bath's Tale*." In *Magistra Doctissima: Essays in Honor of Bonnie Wheeler*, edited by Dorsey Armstrong, Ann W. Astell, and Howell Chickering, 34–42. Kalamazoo, Mich.: Medieval Institute Publications, 2013.

Sweeney, Michelle. *Magic in Medieval Romance from Chretien de Troyes to Chaucer*. Dublin: Four Courts Press, 2000.

Sweeney, Mickey. "*Sir Gawain and the Green Knight*: Making Meaning from Magic." *Mediaevalia* 23 (2002): 137–57.

Taylor, Paul Beekman. "Sir Orfeo and the Minstrel King." *ANQ* 13, no. 1 (2000): 12–16.

Thomas, Keith. *Religion and the Decline of Magic: Studies of Popular Beliefs in Sixteenth and Seventeenth Century England*. New York: Scribner, 1971. Paperback edition 1997.

Thomas, Susanne Sara. "The Problem of Defining *Sovereynetee* in the *Wife of Bath's Tale*." *Chaucer Review* 41, no. 1 (2006): 87–97.

Thorndike, Lynn. *A History of Magic and Experimental Science*. 8 vols. New York: Macmillan, 1923–58.

Truitt, E. R. *Medieval Robots: Mechanism, Magic, Nature, and Art*. Philadelphia: University of Pennsylvania Press, 2015.

———. "'Trei poëte, sages dotors, qui mout sorent di nigromance': Knowledge and Automata in Twelfth-Century French Literature." *Configurations* 12, no. 2 (2004): 167–93.

Twomey, Michael W. "Morgain la Fée in *Sir Gawain and the Green Knight*: From Troy to Camelot." In *Text and Intertext in Medieval Arthurian Literature*, edited by Norris J. Lacy, 91–115. New York: Garland, 1996.

———. "Morgan le Fay at Hautdesert." In *On Arthurian Women: Essays in Memory of Maureen Fries*, edited by Bonnie Wheeler and Fiona Tolhurst, 103–19. Dallas: Scriptorium Press, 2001.

Ulrich von Zatzikhoven. *Lanzelet*. Translated by Thomas Kerth with additional notes by Kenneth G. T. Webster and Roger Sherman Loomis. New York: Columbia University Press, 2005.

Urban, Misty. *Monstrous Women in Middle English Romance: Representations of Mysterious Female Power*. Lewiston, N.Y.: Edwin Mellen Press, 2010.

Van, Thomas A. "False Texts and Disappearing Women in the *Wife of Bath's Prologue and Tale*." *Chaucer Review* 29, no. 2 (1994): 179–93.

Van Buren, Anne Hagiopan. "Reality and Literary Romance in the Park of Hesdin." In *Medieval Gardens*, edited by Elisabeth B. MacDougall, 115–34. Washington, D.C.: Dumbarton Oaks Research Library and Collection, 1986.

Vicari, Patricia. "Sparagmos: Orpheus Among the Christians." In *Orpheus: The Metamorphosis of a Myth*, edited by John Warden, 63–83. Toronto: University of Toronto Press, 1982.

Wade, James. *Fairies in Medieval Romance*. New York: Palgrave Macmillan, 2011.

———. "Ungallant Knights." In *Heroes and Anti-Heroes in Medieval Romance*, edited by Neil Cartlidge, 201–18. Woodbridge, Suffolk: D. S. Brewer, 2012.

Ward, Renée. "Challenging the Boundaries of Medieval Romance: Thomas Chestre's *Lybeaus Desconus*." *Florilegium* 21 (2004): 119–34.

Watkins, C. S. "Fascination and Anxiety in Wonder Stories." In *The Unorthodox Imagination in Late Medieval Britain*, edited by Sophie Page, 45–64. Manchester: Manchester University Press, 2010.

———. *History and the Supernatural in Medieval England*. Cambridge: Cambridge University Press, 2007.

Watson, Nicholas. "John the Monk's *Book of the Visions of the Blessed Virgin Mary*: Two Versions of a Newly Discovered Ritual Magic Text." In *Conjuring Spirits: Texts and Traditions of Medieval Ritual Magic*, edited by Claire Fanger, 163–215. University Park: Pennsylvania State University Press, 1998.

———. "The Phantasmal Past: Time, History, and the Recombinative Imagination." *Studies in the Age of Chaucer* 32 (2010): 1–37.

Watt, Diane. *Amoral Gower: Language, Sex, and Politics*. Minneapolis: University of Minnesota Press, 2003.

Weldon, James. "'Naked as She Was Bore': Naked Disenchantment in *Lybeaus Desconus*." *Parergon* 24, no. 1 (2007): 67–99.

Whitaker, Muriel A. "Otherworld Castles in Middle English Arthurian Romance." In *The Medieval Castle: Romance and Reality*, edited by Kathryn Reyerson and Faye Powe, 27–46. Dubuque, Iowa: Kendall Hunt, 1984.

William of Palerne. Re-edited by G. H. V. Bunt. Groningen: Bouma's Boekhuis, 1985.

Williams, Tara. "The Ellesmere Dragons." *Word & Image* 30, no. 4 (2014): 444–54.

———. "Enchanted Historicism." *postmedieval FORUM* (October 2011). http://postmedieval-forum.com/forums/forum-i-responses-to-paul-strohm/williams/.

———. "Fairy Magic, Wonder, and Morality in *Sir Orfeo*." *Philological Quarterly* 91, no. 4 (2012): 537–68.

———. "Magic, Spectacle, and Morality in the Fourteenth Century." *New Medieval Literatures* 12 (2010): 179–208.

Withrington, John, and P. J. C. Field. "The Wife of Bath's Tale." In *Sources and Analogues of the Canterbury Tales*, vol. 2, edited by Robert M. Correale and Mary Hamel, 405–48. Rochester, N.Y.: D. S. Brewer, 2005.

Wood, Chauncey. *Chaucer and the Country of the Stars: Poetic Uses of Astrological Imagery*. Princeton: Princeton University Press, 1970.

Yearley, Lee H. *Mencius and Aquinas: Theories of Virtue and Conceptions of Courage*. Albany: State University of New York Press, 1990.

Zaerr, Linda Marie. "Music and Magic in *Le Bel Inconnu* and *Lybeaus Desconus*." *Medieval Forum* 4 (2004). http://www.sfsu.edu/~medieval/Volume4/Zaerr.html.

Zipes, Jack. "Introduction: Towards a Definition of the Literary Fairy Tale." In *The Oxford Companion to Fairy Tales*, edited by Jack Zipes, xv–xxxii. Oxford: Oxford University Press, 2000.

———. *Why Fairy Tales Stick: The Evolution and Relevance of a Genre*. New York: Routledge, 2006.

Index

Note: Page numbers in *italics* indicate figures.

admiratio, 5
affective piety, 4, 67, 68
agency
    angel automaton and, 64–65
    fair unknowns and, 43
    miracles, marvels, and, 101, 102–3
    in *Sir Gawain and the Green Knight*, 90–96, 144n54
alchemy, 104–6
Allen, Dorena, 19, 20
Allen, Elizabeth, 98, 110
alliterative romances, 93
Andrew, Malcolm, 87
appearance and virtue, 43, 47–49, 52–53, 60, 128
Aquinas, Thomas, 99
Arthurian texts, 37, 140n12. *See also Sir Gawain and the Green Knight*
astrology, 104–6
Augustine
    on blunting effect of familiarity, 96
    The City of God, 87, 100
    definition of marvels and, 99
    on magic, 102
    on miracles, 101
    on pagan virtue, 43
automatons
    angel, 1, 4, 63–65, 66
    appearance of agency of, 64–65
    political purpose of, 64
    responses to and power of, 84
    as spectacle, 67
Awntyrs off Arthur, The, 130

Bailey, Michael D., 129
Battles, Paul, 91
Beckerman, Bernard, 18
Bennett, Jane
    on enchantment, 26, 27, 127
    on "moral," 28
    on wonder, 5, 96
Biernoff, Suzannah, 28
Bisclavret (Marie de France), 42
Blamires, Alcuin, *Chaucer, Ethics, and Gender*, 98
bodies, human, as site of spectacles, 30
bodies of women
    as devotional symbols, 29–30
    monstrous, 61–62
    in romance, 60
    shape-shifted, 93–94
    as signifying spectacles, 30–35
Bodleian Library MS Ashmole 61, 38
Book of John Mandeville, The, 54–55, 101
Book of Vices and Virtues, The, 42, 46, 54
Burns, E. Jane, 60
Bynum, Caroline Walker
    Christian Materiality, 68
    on distinguishing miracle and marvel, 103–4
    on figures of hybridity and metamorphosis, 41
    on reaction to fairy magic, 12–13
    on women's bodies, 29
    on wonder, 4, 5, 25, 26, 105, 127, 148n28

Camille, Michael, 30, 68, 137n49, 138n75
Cannon, Christopher, 123, 124, 125
Canterbury Tales (Chaucer). See also *Franklin's Tale*; *Squire's Tale*; *Wife of Bath's Tale*
    Canon's Yeoman's Tale, 105–6
    classifying marvels in, 103–9
    Friar's Tale, 107
    language in, 7
    magic in, 98–99, 107–9
    Manciple's Tale, 106–7, 151n68
    Man of Law's Tale, 97–98
    marvels in, 8, 97

INDEX

Canterbury Tales (continued)
  miracles in, 106–7, 128
  morality in, 98–99
  overview of, 96
  Prioress's Tale, 106
  Tale of Sir Thopas, 123
Carle of Carlisle, The, 83, 95
Carruthers, Mary, 24, 72
Charny, Geoffroi de, *A Knight's Own Book of Chivalry*, 42–43
Chaucer, Geoffrey. See also *Canterbury Tales*; *Franklin's Tale*; *Squire's Tale*; *Wife of Bath's Tale*
  English literary tradition and, 123, 124
  House of Fame, 107–8
  on Gower, 110
  spectacles of language and, 124–25
Chestre, Thomas, 37, 38, 44. See also *Lybeaus Desconus*; *Octavian*; *Sir Launfal*
Chevalere Assigne, 69
Chism, Christine, 93
chivalry. See also love, courtly, and magic
  ethical framework of, 6
  identity and, 38
  in romance, 28, 39–40, 44
  in *Sir Gawain and the Green Knight*, 80
  in *Sir Orfeo*, 7, 23–24, 27–28, 35
  virtue and, 39
classifying marvels
  in *Canterbury Tales*, 103–9
  in medieval discourse, 99–103
Cleanness, 70
Cohen, Jeffrey Jerome, 62
Concordia (Maidstone), 65
Confessio Amantis (Gower), 130–31
Cooper, Helen
  on fairies, 14, 15
  on green girdle, 144–45n61
  on identity of Lybeaus, 58
  on magic in romances, 3, 39
  "Magic that Does Not Work," 128
Cotton Caligula A.ii manuscript, 44, 45, 57
Cotton Nero A.x manuscript
  as context for Green Knight, 66
  illuminations in, 8, 72–73, 75–76, 78–79
  moral marvels in, 70–74, 77, 80
courtesy, 54
Crane, Susan, 52, 54, 58, 61, 117, 148n40, 150n65

Daston, Lorraine, 26
demonic magic, 2, 103
didactic power of devotional images, 24–25, 67–68
discourse of marvelous, 99–103
divine, as source of virtue, 43–44
doughtiness, 46, 51, 54, 55, 57
dragon lady in *Lybeaus Desconus*
  appearance, virtue, and, 49, 52–53, 128
  Eve compared to, 60–61
  Green Knight compared to, 85
  interpretation of, 61–62
  Lybeaus reaction to, 53–55, 59
  marriage to, 57–58
  overview of, 37, 38
  speech of, 55–57
  transformation of, 52, 56–57, 60, 61, 62
  visual image of, 69
dramatic spectacle, 18

enchantment, 25–26, 27. See also wonder
ethics
  Arthurian, 71–72
  in Chaucer scholarship, 98
  definition of, 6
  morality compared to, 137n47
  in romance, 140n20
  in *Sir Gawain and the Green Knight*, 80
Etymologies (Isidore of Seville), 102, 103
extramission theory, 66, 67–68

Faerie Queene, The (Spenser), 125
fairies
  audience and gallery of, 23–29
  cultural and literary contexts of, 13–15
  figures "taken" by, 12, 19–20
  moral code of, 21–23
  Orfeo and gallery of, 15–23
  otherness of, 14, 27–28
  overview of, 11
  in *Sir Launfal*, 44–45
  in *Sir Orfeo*, 7, 11–12, 23–24, 27–28, 31, 35
  wonder and, 12–15
fairness and virtue, 45–46
fair unknown tradition. See also *Lybeaus Desconus*
  agency and, 43
  loathly lady figure compared to, 113
  marriage in, 57–58

marvelous trials in, 37, 47
marvels, morality, and, 39–42
revelations of identity in, 59
virtue in, 42
Fanger, Claire, 2–3
Felski, Rita, 25–26
female bodies. *See* bodies of women
female sorceresses, 92. *See also* Morgan le Fay
Finlayson, John, 39, 47
Fisher, Philip, 26
Fletcher, Alan J., 16
Floris and Blancheflour, 3, 40, 150n59
Franklin's Tale (Chaucer)
astrological calculations in, 106
expectations of, 148n30
illusory magic in, 151n68
marvels in, 85, 99, 108
mirabilia in, 104
Friedman, John Block, 19, 136n37, 142n67
Furrow, Melissa, 122–23

gallery in *Sir Orfeo*, as moral spectacle
for audience, 23–29
for Orfeo, 15–23
Gawain
Bertilak and lady's tests of, 91–92, 94–95
girdle temptation for, 86–87, 91
Green Knight and, 73–74, 77, 82–83, 88–89
Lybeaus as son of, 57, 58
in *Lybeaus Desconus*, 38
nature and limits of virtue of, 89–90
as representative of Arthur's court, 86, 89
return to court by, 95–96
testing of, 74, 77, 85–86, 87–88, 89
Gayk, Shannon, 24–25
Geoffrey on Monmouth, *History of the Kings of Britain*, 140n12
Gervase of Tilbury, 8, 99, 100, 101
Gilbert, Jane, 71–72
Gower, John
Confessio Amantis, 130–31
"Tale of Constance," 13
"Tale of Florent," 109–10, 111, 112
Graelent, 48
Green, Richard Firth, 12
Greenblatt, Stephen, 26

Greene Knight, The, 82, 83, 91, 93, 95
Green Knight
appearance of, 81–82, 83
beheading of, 69, 73–74, 82–83, 85
depictions of, 128
dragon lady compared to, 85
Gawain and, 73–74, 77, 82–83, 88–89
marvelous nature of, 81, 83–85
moral authority and agency of, 93, 94, 95–96, 144n54
Morgan le Fay and, 3, 90–91, 92–93, 94
reappearance of, 88–89
religious undertones of, 68
replication of marvel of, 87–88
response to, 4
tests presented by, 85–86, 87–88, 89
transformation of, 3
Gregory the Great, 67
Guigemar (Marie de France), 40

Hahn, Thomas, 130
Harry Potter books, 69
Havelok the Dane, 39–40
Heng, Geraldine, 91
Heurodis
compliance of, 20–21
Fairy King threat to, 19, 21
in gallery, 20
kidnapping of, 16
as signifying spectacle, 29–35
Hilmo, Maidie, 74, 77
hybridity, figures of, 41, 53, 60, 85

identity. *See also* fair unknown tradition
chivalry and, 38
in *Lybeaus Desconus*, 7, 56–57, 62, 145n69
marvels and, 47
moral, tests of, 41–42
virtue and, 38–39
images
religious, didactic power of, 24–25, 67–68
from *Sir Gawain and the Green Knight*, 73–74, 75–76, 77, 78–79, 80
image theory and gallery in *Sir Orfeo*, 24
imagination, 133n5, 137n48
Ingham, Patricia Clare, 119
intention and magic, 103

intromission theory, 66, 67–68, 116
Isidore of Seville, 8, 99, 102, 103

Julian of Norwich, 4

Kang, Minsoo, 83–84
Karnes, Michelle, 2, 117, 120, 146n1
Kieckhefer, Richard, 2, 103, 129
King Horn, 39, 40, 141n48, 150n59
Kipling, Gordon, 63, 66, 143n18
Klaassen, Frank, 2–3
Knight, Stephen, 44, 52
knights. *See also* chivalry; Green Knight
    courtesy of, 54
    doughtiness of, 46, 51, 55, 57
    marvels and, 47
    virtue of, 42–43, 45–46
Knight's Own Book of Chivalry, A (Charny), 42–43

Lambeth Palace MS 306, 57, 139n5
language
    in *Canterbury Tales*, 7
    magic, morality, and, 122–25
    magic and, 111–12, 118–22
    spectacles of, 8, 106, 112
Lanzelet, 55, 60–61
Latham, Minor White, 14
Le Bel Inconnu, 38, 47, 51, 59
Lee, Jennifer A., 73
Le Goff, Jacques, 2
Le Morte d'Arthur, 131
Lerer, Seth, 16, 85
Les Deux Amanz (Marie de France), 40
Lewis, C. S., 14
Lightsey, Scott, 63, 64, 66, 104
literary magic, 3
literary marvels. *See also specific literary works*
    intimate encounters with, 81, 85–86
    mystery about source or agency of, 90
    problem of, 122–23
    as singular, 87
    theory of marvelous and, 1–2
    visual aspects of, 69–70
literary texts, debate about moral significance of, 6
loathly lady figure, 109–11. See also *Wife of Bath's Tale*

love
    courtly, and magic, 3–4, 39–41
    theological virtue of, 125
Lybeaus Desconus (Chestre). *See also* dragon lady in *Lybeaus Desconus*
    critical assessments of, 37–38
    Dame d'Amore in, 48–49, 61, 92
    enchanted or transformed figure in, 38, 41, 56–57
    identity in, 7, 45–46, 56–59, 145n69
    importance of action in, 111
    magic/marvels in, 41, 47–52, 58–59, 62
    morality in, 44
    plot of, 38
    shape-shifted figure in, 52, 61, 93
    testing of Gawain compared to testing of, 145n67
    test of courtly love in, 3, 4
    virtue in, 38–39, 42–47

magic. *See also* fairies; transformations
    in Arthurian texts, 140n12
    atypical literary cases of, 129, 131–32
    Augustine on, 102
    in *Canterbury Tales*, 98–99, 107–9
    categories of, 103
    courtly love and, 3–4, 39–41
    functions of, 40
    language and, 111–12, 118–22
    in *Lybeaus Desconus*, 41, 47–52, 58–59, 62
    marvels distinguished from, 2, 102
    marvels involving, 102–3
    modes of, in literary texts, 3
    morality, language, and, 122–25
    morality and, 44–45
    natural and demonic, 2–3, 103, 129
    practiced by humans, 14
    in romance, 39–41, 128–29
    in *Sir Gawain and the Green Knight*, 12, 15, 95–96
    spectacle and, 69
    in *Squire's Tale*, 98, 108, 115–17
    as test of individual virtue, 38, 41–42, 59–60
    use of term, 124
    in *Wife of Bath's Tale*, 98, 108, 113–14, 145n64
magic-spectacle-morality nexus, 11, 129–32

Malory, Thomas, 47, 57–58, 131, 141n31
Marie de France, 3, 40, 41, 42
Marriage of Sir Gawain, The, 109, 110
marvelous
    philosophy and discourse of, 99–103
    theory of, 1–2, 7, 129–30
marvels. *See also* classifying marvels; literary marvels; visual marvels/spectacles
    ambiguous and subversive undertones of, 6
    definition of, 2
    dual potential of, 1
    in *Lybeaus Desconus,* 47–52
    Middle English, 1–2
    miracles distinguished from, 2, 96, 99, 103–4
    morality and, 3, 8–9
    moving mechanical, 63–66
    mysterious nature of, 18–19, 90, 96, 100, 101, 112
    response elicited by, 4–6, 127
    in romance, 39–42
    seeing, 66–70
    significance of, 3–4
    in *Sir Gawain and the Green Knight,* 66, 69–70
    use of term, in *Canterbury Tales,* 104
    visuality, morality, and, 129–30
McAlindon, T., 95
McDonald, Nicola, 47
McNamer, Sarah, 9, 27, 89
Melusine, 58, 60–61, 141n47
memory and image, 24–25
merveille, 99–100
metamorphosis, figures of, 41. *See also* transformations
Miller, Mark, 98
Miller, Sarah Alison, 62
Mills, M., 37, 47
mirabilia, 104–5
miracles
    agency, marvels, and, 101, 102–3
    Augustine on, 101
    in *Canterbury Tales,* 106–7, 128
    in *Man of Law's Tale,* 97–98
    marvels distinguished from, 2, 96, 99, 103–4
    secular marvels as like, 97
    use of term, in *Canterbury Tales,* 104

Mitchell, Bruce, 15–16
Mitchell, J. Allan, 98
Mitchell, W. J. T., 24
Mitchell-Smith, Ilan, 58
monstrous bodies, 61–62
moral. *See also* morality
    definition of, 6
    use of term, 124
moral code, 6
morality
    in *Canterbury Tales,* 98–99
    in Cotton Nero A.x manuscript, 70–74, 77, 80
    engagement with, in narratives, 6–7
    fairy tales and, 14–15
    images and, 24–25
    in *Lybeaus Desconus,* 44
    magic, language, and, 122–25
    marvels and, 3, 8–9
    poetry and, 70
    in romance, 16, 39–42, 44–45
    secular marvels and, 68–69
    shape-shifted figures and, 93–94
    in *Sir Gawain and the Green Knight,* 87–88, 89–90
    in *Squire's Tale,* 120–22
    visuality, marvels, and, 129–30
    in *Wife of Bath's Tale,* 110–11, 112–13, 115
    wonder and, 4–6, 26–27, 127
Morgan le Fay
    agency and, 8, 77
    Bertilak and, 92
    Green Knight and, 3, 90–91, 92–93, 94
mysterious nature
    of fairy magic, 7, 13–14, 15, 16, 20
    of marvels, 18–19, 90, 96, 100, 101, 112

Nakley, Susan, 33
natural magic, 2, 103, 129

Octavian (Chestre), 44, 48, 59
optical theory, 67–68
Orfeo
    in fairyland, 16–17, 21–23
    Heurodis and, 29–35
    kingship of, 34–35, 135n7
    reunion between Heurodis and, 29, 32–33, 34
    reunion between steward and, 33–34

Orpheus legend and *Sir Orfeo*, 12, 19, 29
otherness of fairies, 14, 27–28
Ovid, 4, 41

pagan virtue, 43
Page, Sophie, 2–3
Park, Katharine, 26
Partonope of Blois, 40, 41
Patience, 70–71
Pearl, 71
philosophy and discourse of marvelous, 99–103
Piers Plowman, 64
poetry and moral work, 70

reading
    as moral activity, 6
    overlap between ideas of seeing or visualizing and, 24
Reichardt, Paul F., 70, 72–73
religion
    angel automaton and, 66
    in *Canterbury Tales*, 106–7
    didactic power of images, 24–25, 67–68
    spectacle and, 67
Renoir, Alain, 80–81
response elicited by marvels, 4–6, 127. *See also* wonder
Richard II
    coronation procession of, 1, 4, 8, 63–64, 66
    reign of, 63, 65–66
Richard of St. Victor, 26
Riddy, Felicity, 18, 136n30
romances. *See also Lybeaus Desconus; Sir Orfeo*
    alliterative, 93
    chivalry in, 28, 39–40, 44
    female bodies in, 60
    giants in, 82
    keeping one's word and, 136n39
    magic in, 39–41, 128–29
    marvels and morality in, 8–9, 39–42, 47
    morality in, 16, 39–42, 44–45, 122–25
    revelatory marvels, virtues, and, 37
    tests in, 3–4, 6, 47–52
    virtue in, 42–47
Rosenfeld, Jessica, 98

Salisbury, Eve, 52, 57, 61, 139n6
Saunders, Corinne
    on classification of magic, 14
    on enchantress figure, 92
    on Green Knight, 143–44n37
    on *Lybeaus Desconus*, 48
    on magic, 103
    Magic and the Supernatural in Medieval English Romance, 3, 128
    on *Sir Orfeo* ending, 139n82
Schiff, Randy P., 92
scientific marvels in *Canterbury Tales*, 104–6
Scott, Kathleen L., 72
self-moving objects. *See* automatons
semblance of virtue, 42–44, 55, 121
serpent-women, 60–61. *See also* dragon lady in *Lybeaus Desconus*
shape-shifting tradition. *See also* transformations
    Green Knight and, 93–94
    in *Lybeaus Desconus*, 52, 61, 93
    in *Wife of Bath's Tale*, 37
Simons, Walter, 30
Sir Cleges, 130
Sir Degaré, 13, 47, 57
Sir Gawain and the Green Knight. *See also* Gawain; Green Knight; Morgan le Fay
    agency in, 7, 90–96
    as Arthurian text, 71–72
    bedroom test in, 89, 91, 92
    beheading scene in, 69, 73–74, 82–83, 85
    Bertilak presence in, 90
    Cannon on, 123
    ethics and chivalry in, 80
    green girdle in, 86–87, 91, 92, 95
    illuminations from, 67, *75–76, 78–79*
    importance of action in, 111
    magic in, 12, 15, 95–96
    marvels in, 66, 69–70
    mode of address of, 71
    moral theme in, 87–88, 89–90
    pentangle in, 46
    revelation scene in, 90–91, 94–95
    spectacles in, 8, 80–90
    transformed figure in, 41, 93–94
    trials in, 37, 54
Sir Launfal (Chestre)
    appearance, virtue, and, 49
    Dame Tryamour in, 53

fairies in, 13, 14
magic in, 48
morality in, 44–45
Sir Orfeo. See also Heurodis; Orfeo
   as aesthetic object, 11–12
   chivalry in, 7, 23–24, 27–28, 35
   contexts of, 11
   critical history of, 11–12
   ending of, 135n6
   fairies in, 13
   focus on external of, 15
   gallery as moral spectacle for audience, 23–29
   gallery as moral spectacle for Orfeo, 15–23
   gallery in, 69
   Heurodis as signifying spectacle in, 29–35
   importance of speech in, 111
   magic in, 14, 128
   mirroring effect between two worlds in, 14, 28–29, 35
Sir Perceval of Galles, 57, 141n31, 141n36
spectacles. See also visual marvels/spectacles
   culture of, 67
   dramatic, 18
   human body as site of, 30
   of language, 8, 106, 112, 118–25
   moral, gallery as, for audience, 23–29
   moral, gallery as, for Orfeo, 15–23
   quality of motion and, 83–84
   representations of and reactions to, 67–69
   signifying, Heurodis as, 29–35
   in Sir Gawain and the Green Knight, 8, 80–90
   transformations as, 4
   visual aspects of, 3–4
Spenser, Edmund, The Faerie Queene, 125
Squire of Low Degree, The, 38–39
Squire's Tale (Chaucer)
   horse in, 99, 117–18, 119
   magic in, 98, 108, 115–17
   marvels in, 85
   mirabilia in, 104
   moral concerns in, 120–22
   optical theory and, 68
   ring in, 115–16, 118–22
   spectacle of translation in, 115–22

Stanbury, Sarah, 67, 69, 81, 144n53
Sweeney, Michelle, 6, 133n3, 145n71, 151n4
Sword of the Valiant, The (film), 69, 74

"Tale of Florent" (Gower), 109–10, 111, 112
"Tale of Gareth" (Malory), 47, 57–58, 141n31
theories of vision, 66–67, 82
theories of wonder, 12, 25, 35
theory of marvelous, 1–2, 7, 129–30
Thomas of Erceldoune, 13
transformations. See also Green Knight; shape-shifting tradition
   of Bertilak, 90
   boundary-crossings and, 27
   in Chevalere Assigne, 69
   of dragon lady, 52, 56–57, 60, 61, 62
   by fairies, 19
   in Lybeaus Desconus, 38, 41, 56–57
   magic in, 60
   as spectacles, 4
   in Wife of Bath's Tale, 41, 109–15
translation, spectacle of, in Squire's Tale, 115–22
Treatise on the Astrolabe, 105
Turke and Sir Gawain, The, 83, 95

viewing subjects, responsibility and responsiveness of, 5–6
virtue. See also Lybeaus Desconus
   appearance and, 43, 47–49, 52–53, 60, 128
   chivalry and, 39
   fairness and, 45–46
   in fair unknown tradition, 42
   identity and, 38–39
   of knights, 42–43, 45–46
   in Lybeaus Desconus, 38–39, 42–47
   nature and limits of, 89–90
   pagan, 43
   semblance and reality of, 42–47, 55, 121
   tests of, 3–4, 41–42, 59–60
   theological, of love, 125
visual marvels/spectacles. See also gallery in Sir Orfeo, as moral spectacle
   appearance of Green Knight as, 81–82
   apprehension and interpretation of, 80
   in Canterbury Tales, 8, 106–7
   in Cotton Nero A.x manuscript, 72–73

visual marvels/spectacles (*continued*)
   dragon lady as, 52–63
   exercise of power guided by values and, 23
   morality and, 129–30
   Sir Gawain and the Green Knight and, 8, 83–85
   tests of love and virtue as, 3–4
   unreliability of sight and, 102
   wonder, enchantment, and, 26
   zenith of, 96

Wade, James, 14, 139n5
Waldron, Ronald, 87
Watkins, Carl, 6
Watt, Diane, 110
Weddyng of Syr Gawen and Dame Ragnell, The, 109, 110
Weldon, James, 52, 59, 139n6, 142n56
Wife of Bath's Tale (Chaucer)
   audience for marvels in, 85
   conclusion to, 114–15
   enchanted or transformed figure in, 41, 109–15
   fairies in, 12, 14
   gentilesse speech in, 111–12
   magic in, 98, 108, 113–14, 145n64
   marvelous trial in, 37
   moral concerns in, 110–11, 112–13, 115
   shape-shifted figure in, 93
   on spectacle, 4
Wigalois, 47, 59
William of Palerne, 40–41, 93
witchcraft, 131
women. *See* bodies of women
wonder
   affective and cognitive reactions to, 25–26
   at appearance of Green Knight, 81–82
   fairies and, 12–15, 25
   limits and pitfalls of, 28
   morality and, 4–6, 26–27, 127
   as reaction to magical spectacles, 4–5
   in *Squire's Tale*, 117
   theories of, 12, 25, 35
   use of term, in *Canterbury Tales*, 104
   visual aspects of, 26
Wonders of the East, 101

Yearley, Lee H., 42
Yonec (Marie de France), 40

Zaerr, Linda Marie, 58–59
Zipes, Jack, 14

www.ingramcontent.com/pod-product-compliance
Lightning Source LLC
Chambersburg PA
CBHW021950290426
44108CB00012B/1017